Ethical Issues in Twentieth-Century French Fiction

Killing the Other

Colin Davis
Lady Margaret Hall
Oxford

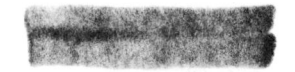

First published in Great Britain 2000 by
MACMILLAN PRESS LTD
Houndmills, Basingstoke, Hampshire RG21 6XS and London
Companies and representatives throughout the world

A catalogue record for this book is available from the British Library.

ISBN 0–333–73371–1

First published in the United States of America 2000 by
ST. MARTIN'S PRESS, INC.,
Scholarly and Reference Division,
175 Fifth Avenue, New York, N.Y. 10010

ISBN 0–312–22396–X

Library of Congress Cataloging-in-Publication Data
Davis, Colin, 1960–
Ethical issues in twentieth-century French fiction : killing the other / Colin Davis.
p. cm.
Includes bibliographical references and index.
ISBN 0–312–22396–X (cloth)
1. French fiction—20th century—History and criticism. 2. Ethics in literature. I. Title.
PQ673.D38   1999
843'.9109—dc21   99-27402
                                                                         CIP

© Colin Davis 2000

All rights reserved. No reproduction, copy or transmission of this publication may be made without written permission.

No paragraph of this publication may be reproduced, copied or transmitted save with written permission or in accordance with the provisions of the Copyright, Designs and Patents Act 1988, or under the terms of any licence permitting limited copying issued by the Copyright Licensing Agency, 90 Tottenham Court Road, London W1P 0LP.

Any person who does any unauthorised act in relation to this publication may be liable to criminal prosecution and civil claims for damages.

The author has asserted his right to be identified as the author of this work in accordance with the Copyright, Designs and Patents Act 1988.

This book is printed on paper suitable for recycling and made from fully managed and sustained forest sources.

10 9 8 7 6 5 4 3 2 1
09 08 07 06 05 04 03 02 01 00

Printed and bound in Great Britain by
Antony Rowe Ltd, Chippenham, Wiltshire

Contents

Acknowledgements vii

Introduction: Ethical Criticism 1

1. Otherness, Altericide 12
2. Hermeneutic and Ethical Encounters: Gadamer and Levinas 31
3. Ethics, Fiction, and the Death of the Other: Sartre and Kant 47
4. Camus, Encounters, Reading 64
5. Didacticism and the Ethics of Failure: Beauvoir 86
6. Humanism and its Others: Sartre, Heidegger, Yourcenar 108
7. Ethical Indifference: Duras 131
8. Readers, Others: Genet 152

Conclusion: Tarrying with the Negative 189

Notes 196

Bibliography 216

Index 225

Acknowledgements

Some of the material in Chapters 3, 4, 5, 7 and 8 originally appeared in *Sartre Studies International*, *Forum for Modern Language Studies*, *Modern Languages Review*, *Comparative Literature Studies* and *French Studies*, respectively. I am grateful to the editors of those journals for permission to reprint. I would also like to thank those who have commented on earlier drafts or otherwise advised and encouraged me during the preparation of this book, in particular Sarah Kay, Emma Wilson, Elizabeth Fallaize, Patrice Bougon, Claire Gorrara, Christina Howells, Ingrid Wassenaar, Nigel Saint and Mireille Rosello.

Introduction: Ethical Criticism

We have not quite got over the belief, or the hope, that poetry, as I.A. Richards proclaimed, might be capable of saving us.[1] Literature has been decried as an elitist irrelevance surpassed by other, more accessible and more democratic cultural media, or as a site where abjection is given the possibility of sharing appalling desires with a gullible audience; but such views have not yet entirely defeated the resilient faith that something good happens to us when we read, that literature reflects and helps to create our moral sensibility, that it teaches us decency and humanity. The following pages present a less sanguine account of the ethics of fiction.

In reading, as in all encounters with other people or other cultures, what is at stake is our ability to experience an occurrence which is not defined in advance, to accept the risk and challenge of an event that does not correspond to any expectations that we might have of it. In terms of the Levinassian ethics which have acquired a central position in recent Continental thinking and which in large part lie behind the analyses of this book, the encounter with otherness is a fundamental ethical moment; the generosity or violence of our response, the degree to which we welcome or reject the proximity of the Other, will determine our standing as moral subjects.

There is no way of being certain in any given case that the kind of encounter with the Other which Levinas's work revolves around has actually occurred. As critics of Levinas have pointed out, my ability to recognize the Other as Other already implies that I must have some prior knowledge of it.[2] The absolute Other, that which is totally alien to my powers of comprehension, would simply pass unnoticed. By characterizing it as *outside* my world, I have already defined it *by reference* to my world and hence as part of it. So the Other which I can encounter is perhaps less other, more a function of myself, than Levinas would like. This book is concerned with encounters with alterity which are thematically inscribed in a variety of theoretical and fictional texts, which are staged in the act of reading, but which may also be missed or rejected, repudiated in acts of incomprehension or violence. I use the term *altericide*, the murder of the Other, to describe the possibility for violence inherent in the fraught relations between selves and others, texts and readers. This book does not take for granted one of the most common premises uniting what has become known as ethical criticism, namely the often unquestioned assumption that the encounter with the Other of literature is both possible and enriching. As I shall suggest in the rest of this Introduction, ethical criticism – for all its diversity – has generally been united and restricted by its adherence to a rather limited set of values and critical protocols.[3]

At the beginning of *The Company We Keep* (1988) Wayne Booth describes how ethical criticism has fallen on hard times: although it is nearly universally practised, it has become theoretically suspect (19). Ethical criticism has been confined to the closet. Booth's claim now seems outdated; his own book is a seminal text in the establishment of ethical criticism as one of the dominant strands of modern critical practice. To some extent, ethics has replaced militant politics as one of the mantras of the literary critic. Moreover, the interest of literary critics in ethics has been matched by the interest of some moral philosophers in literature. Alongside the substantial list of critical and theoretical works concerned with ethics that have been produced by members of literature departments, texts such as Martha Nussbaum's *Love's Knowledge* (1990), Richard Rorty's *Contingency, Irony, and Solidarity* (1989) and Colin McGinn's *Ethics, Evil, and Fiction* (1997) have insisted on the ethical interest of fiction. These latter authors join their literary colleagues in insisting that fiction extends the range of moral experience and ethical reflection:

> Our experience is, without fiction, too confined and too parochial. Literature extends it, making us reflect and feel about what might otherwise be too distant for feeling. (Nussbaum, 47)

> Fiction like that of Dickens, Olive Schreiner, or Richard Wright gives us the details about kinds of suffering being endured by people to whom we had previously not attended. Fiction like that of Choderlos de Laclos, Henry James, or Nabokov gives us the details about what sorts of cruelty we ourselves are capable of, and thereby lets us redescribe ourselves. That is why the novel, the movie and the TV program have, gradually but steadily, replaced the sermon and the treatise as the principal vehicles of moral change and progress. (Rorty, xvi)

Literature is where moral thinking lives and breathes on the page. Philosophers of morality therefore need to pay attention to it. And, if they do, it is likely that the field of moral philosophy will take on a quite different complexion and shape. (McGinn, vi)

One of the common assumptions which draw together many of the proponents of the new ethical criticism is the belief that 'modern theory', and more specifically poststructuralism or deconstruction, has led to a neglect of the moral import of literature. The critics queue up to insist that their interests are more human and humane than those of their over-theoretical precursors. In particular, the assault on the notion of the humanist subject, the alleged relativism and the emphasis on textuality in poststructuralism provide easy targets.[4] The best exponents of the renewal in ethical criticism tend not to go as far as David Hirsch when he claims that modern theories are condemned to a 'moral vacuum' and that they 'seek to blind and deafen readers to all that is human';[5] but nevertheless it is widely alleged that poststructuralism and deconstruction have brought about a neglect of human concerns and more radically an assault on the very possibility of ethics. Despite their intense focus on the detail of texts, poststructuralist critics stand accused of not reading carefully or properly; instead of listening to what the text has to say, they are charged with imposing their dogma on it. This strain of humanistic ethical criticism thus presents itself as a closer, better, more scrupulous practice of reading which attends to the specific wisdom of the text. Ethical criticism should be 'text-guided' (Parker, 28), entailing a practice of reading 'that genuinely "listens to the story"' (Booth, 201). The fact that one of the most positive aspects of poststructuralism was its close attention to textual detail is barely commented upon.

Ethical criticism presents itself as both progress and regress. It is progress because it does not (in its best examples) simply jettison the insights of the New Criticism, poststructuralism or other branches of theoretically informed critical practice; but it is also regress since it entails a return to human, ethical concerns and, in most cases, a restatement of the view of literature as morally significant and potentially morally edifying. Wayne Booth frankly declares his aim of restoring 'the full intellectual legitimacy of our commonsense inclination to talk about stories in ethical terms, treating the characters in them and their makers as more like people than labyrinths, enigmas, or textual puzzles to be deciphered' (Booth, x). For Booth, all literature turns out to be didactic, not necessarily in the sense of setting out to impose rigid views on its readers, but in as far as it contains implicit fixed norms and values which we may accept or resist (Booth, 152). One of the most fundamental beliefs of the ethical critics is that the stories we read play a crucial role in forming the people we are and the values we share:

> [For] most of us our character – in the larger sense of the range of choices and habits of choice available to us – changes, grows, and diminishes largely as a result of our imaginative diet.... [Encounters] with narrative otherness are in large part what we are made of (Booth, 257, 377)

> And by showing the plausibility of the claim that we learn our emotional repertory, in part at least, from the stories we hear, it gives a reason why not only moral philosophy, but also philosophy of mind and philosophy of action, need to turn to literature to complete their own projects. (Nussbaum, 312)

> Stories can sharpen and clarify moral questions, encouraging a dialectic between the reader's own experience and the trials of the characters he or she is reading about. A tremendous amount of moral thinking and feeling is done when reading novels (or watching plays and films, or reading poetry and short stories). In fact, it is not an exaggeration to say that for most people this is the primary way in which they acquire ethical attitudes, especially in contemporary culture. Our ethical knowledge is aesthetically mediated. (McGinn, 174–5)

The privilege of the novel in ethical criticism derives from its focus on character and narrative; it presents individuals in situations of choice and action, and so allows readers to engage with a world or moral outlook which may differ from, and therefore extend, their own. As Wayne Booth puts it, fiction invites me to lead 'a richer and fuller life than I could manage on my own' (Booth, 223). So ethical criticism, however divergent in practice, is united by a number of key assumptions: criticism has strayed too far from the human, ethical dimension of literature; stories are essentially bound up with ethical norms and choices, they reflect values and help form our own; those values can be recovered, and our own may be refined, by paying closer attention to what the text has to say. However, overwhelmingly the values 'discovered' in texts seem to reflect the values which their readers profess at the outset. Aristotelians, neo-pragmatists and anti-relativists prove capable of finding in literature moral positions which are respectively Aristotelian (Nussbaum), neo-pragmatist (Rorty) or anti-relativist (McGinn). Texts which don't fit a critic's preferences can be dismissed as aberrant: Sade is 'absolutely disgusting' (McGinn, 76). Or troublesome authors may after all be enlisted to a sympathetic position by a resourceful reading: Oscar Wilde's *The Picture of Dorian Gray* appears to argue for the separation of aesthetic and moral values, but it actually demonstrates the limits of aestheticism (McGinn, 123–43); D.H. Lawrence displays a range of sympathies and an engagement with others which outshine his darker side (Booth, 456–7); despite all their differences, the achievements of Nabokov and Orwell turn out to be 'pretty much the same' (Rorty, 144). There is, then, a curious levelling going on in ethical criticism: whilst insisting on proper attention to the particularities of the text under consideration, it finds in the works chosen for scrutiny a disconcerting lack of diversity in moral import.

In ethical criticism the defining hermeneutic tension between what the text offers and what the reader wants from it has certainly not been resolved in favour of an unambiguous attentiveness to the text itself. The work of Martha Nussbaum offers the most informative example of this. In the Introduction to the essays collected in *Love's Knowledge* Nussbaum makes a powerful and seductive case for the ethical interest of literature. Literary texts are concerned with 'the passionate love of particulars, with grief, pain and bewilderment', and as such they are 'subversive of morality narrowly construed' (22). But this subversion does not extend to Nussbaum's own ethical stance. Nussbaum characterizes the Aristotelian ethics to which she acknowledges allegiance by four principal features: the non-commensurability of valuable things (so that there is no single measure by which to judge different things held to be of value); the priority of the particular; the ethical value of the emotions; and the ethical relevance of uncontrolled happenings (36–44). She suggests that literary texts, and in particular novels, are especially suitable for investigating these positions, much more so than they are for investigating, for example, Kantian or utilitarian ethical views. According to Nussbaum, utilitarianism, with its organizing question 'How can one maximize utility?', and Kantianism, with its organizing question 'What is my moral duty?', entail a decision not to take account of some of the important areas of human life explored in novels (24). So Nussbaum argues that certain novels are 'indispensable to a philosophical inquiry in the ethical sphere' (23), but only if that inquiry is Aristotelian in tenor.

The suspicion arises (in my mind at least) that Nussbaum's belief that philosophers can learn from fiction is tempered by a predisposition to learn only from those texts that say the sorts of things that she is prepared to hear. Henry James seems exactly to match her requirements. *The Ambassadors*, for example, is 'a major work in moral philosophy' (170); *The Princess Casamassima* expresses political thought which is 'valuable in our actual political lives' (198). Other novelists do not fare so well. After a promising start, Proust is ultimately too solipsistic to achieve the loving openness to others that Nussbaum wants from a novel; and despite her intelligent and sympathetic account of Beckett's novels, they finally provide only a negative lesson, being too deeply religious not to despair at the withdrawal of the absolute, and so distracting from the 'loving acceptance of the world' (311) which Nussbaum regards as the moral lesson of the novel. In the Introduction to *Love's Knowledge* Nussbaum is cautious to insist that her comments on particular literary texts cannot be generalized: 'No claim about novels in general, far less about literature in general, could possibly emerge from this book' (23). By the end of the final essay, such caution has been thrown to the wind. The novel turns out after all to be attached to a particular ethical position, which by chance is identical to Nussbaum's Aristotelianism:

> For the novel as genre is committed, in its very structure and in the structure of its relationship with its reader, to the pursuit of the uncertainties and vulnerabilities, the particularity and the emotional richness, of the human form of life.... If we wish to develop a human ethical philosophy along Aristotelian lines, I suggest that we would do well to study the narrative and the emotional structures of novels, viewing them as forms of Aristotelian ethical thinking.... [Social] democracy and the art of the novel are allies. Their focus is the human being, seen as both needy and resourceful; and their dominant passion is love. (Nussbaum, 390–1)

The reading of particular novels has led to a claim about the novel in general, and that claim is strikingly close to Nussbaum's theoretical starting point in Aristotelian ethics. This illustrates an imperialist tendency to which ethical criticism is far from immune; it is revealed in the habit of taking selected texts as representative of whole genres, or one critical practice as the only correct manner of reading. Nussbaum herself largely avoids normative formulations, but others do not even try:

> [Any] traditionally critical study of English literature is, *and must be*, 'humanist'. Its central concern is with the human or moral significance of literature – 'moral' in every sense of the word, I would claim.... (Goldberg, 4; my emphasis)

> My point is not that these incursions of moral philosophy into literature necessarily pose a territorial threat, though in the short run they might; it is rather that they indicate a new road which literary studies in the end *must* take. (Parker, 4; my emphasis)

> Any theory that does not wish to abandon literature to the margins of culture *needs* to ask how storytelling relates to the everyday world of ethics, politics, and practical experience. It *needs*, in short, to ask how literature contributes to the asking and the answering of the ethical question, 'How should I live?' (Siebers, *Morals and Stories*, 8; my emphasis)

> And one purpose of literary criticism or commentary is (*or ought to be*) to make clear the ethical import of the actions and experiences of fictional characters. (McGinn, 3; my emphasis)

> I would say that it is *simply not possible to discuss literature adequately* without seriously taking on the ethical dimensions of the text. (McGinn, 174; my emphasis)

One critical approach amongst others thus becomes privileged above all. This is most evident in Tobin Siebers's *The Ethics of Criticism*. Stating in his opening sentence that 'literary criticism is inextricably linked to ethics' (1), he goes on to make the exploration of this link into a criterion for good criticism: 'At its best, literary criticism is always ethical' (42). He goes even further than this in his examination of ethical aspects of different forms of criticism when he suggests that the ethical approach may reveal a unity hidden within the bewildering diversity of critical approaches:

Indeed, there is finally a question of whether anyone on the current critical scene conceives of a criticism that is not ethical. Only ethics effectively reveals the coherence implicit in the diversity of critical approaches today. Far from being a battleground of contesting ideologies, modern literary theory comprises a united front when it comes to the importance given to the ethics of criticism. (13)

So ethics becomes the master key for critical practice, the principle of unity within diversity, the privileged focus which all critics should and do share whether they realize it or not. From this perspective it is not difficult to see how the specific aims and practices of, say, feminist or Marxist criticism, queer or post-colonial theory, New Historicism, cultural studies or poststructuralism can all be seen as regional variants on the global discourse of ethical criticism.

A crucial aspect of ethical criticism is its emphasis on the relationship between text and reader, and the ways in which texts form or influence a reader's moral sensibility. Nussbaum describes the relationship between text (or author) and reader as one of friendship, alliance or community (see, for example, Nussbaum, 48, 237–40). Wayne Booth, whom to some extent Nussbaum is following in this respect, develops the metaphor of friendship much further: judged as friends, texts may be intimate, warm, generous or deceptive, their friendship is to be welcomed but cast aside if it turns out to be harmful (Booth, 169–224). What a friend cannot be is totally alien to my world and values, and his or her friendship will not require me to experience something shockingly unexpected. According to Booth, to 'learn to read well' consists in part in getting beyond local deficiencies 'in order to achieve a full meeting with something that is "other", beyond, larger than, or at least different from, what we bring' (439–40). But this 'full meeting' with alterity can never be entirely full, or at least the 'other' which it encounters cannot be entirely other, since, as Booth has already insisted, 'total otherness, whatever that might be, would be unintelligible and in consequence totally uninteresting' (194). The metaphor of friendship radically weakens the conception of the text as Other.[6] Most of us choose friends with values which are similar to, or at least compatible with, our own. The metaphor of texts-as-friends predisposes Booth and others to select texts on the same basis; and this results in a lack of *surprise* both in the texts they tend to select (novels rather than poems, nineteenth-century realist novels rather than modernist and postmodern fiction) and in the kinds of values they find within them (tolerance, forgiveness, sympathy, openness to other people, rejection of cruelty).

The critics within this ethical tradition may (claim to) be changed by the texts they read, but this does not necessarily mean that their readings constitute encounters with alterity. In *Totalité et infini* Levinas argues that the self changes as it accommodates itself to what happens to it:

> Le moi, ce n'est pas un être qui reste toujours le même, mais l'être dont l'exister consiste à s'identifier, à retrouver son identité à travers ce qui lui arrive. Il est l'identité par excellence, l'oeuvre originelle de l'identification.[7]

> (The self is not a being which always remains the same, but the being whose existence consists in identifying itself, in finding its identity again through everything which happens to it. It is identity par excellence, the original work of identification.)

Levinas derives from this view the aphorism according to which 'Le Moi est identique jusque dans ses altérations' (The Self is identical even in its alterations).[8] The question is not whether the self changes, but what parameters are set on change, and whether the self continues to identify and recognize itself through the changes it undergoes. A genuine encounter with the Other, in Levinas's sense, cannot occur if the terms of the encounter are defined in advance, and if fundamental values and assumptions are placed beyond risk. The critics I have been discussing construct the literary encounter as a meeting with a tamed, domesticated Other, a friend rather than a stranger. In order to achieve this, they focus typically on an amiable set of texts: they have more to say about Jane Austen and Henry James than about the Marquis de Sade and Georges Bataille.

The humanist strain of ethical criticism discussed above largely conceives of itself as restoring the ethical dimension of literature which was neglected during the theory wars of the 1970s and 1980s; and poststructuralism generally emerges as the culprit to be indicted for this neglect, despite the intense interest in ethics shown by poststructuralist thinkers and critics in France and elsewhere. What emerges here is the stark contrast of incompatible premises. For the humanist critic, as Goodheart puts it, 'the ethical is a mark of freedom, choice, and agency' (125); on the other hand, writing from a position sympathetic to poststructuralism Keenan insists that 'Ethics and politics – as well as literature – are evaded when we fall back on the conceptual priority of the subject, agency, or identity as the grounds of our action' (3). With such views, from the humanist standpoint poststructuralism simply cannot be ethical, however much it claims the contrary. Yet it would be foolish to deny the ethical sensitivity of some of the best poststructuralist criticism, such as can be found, for example, in Felman and Laub's *Testimony*, Johnson's *A World of Difference*, Newton's *Narrative Ethics*, Caruth's *Unclaimed Experience* or Keenan's *Fables of Responsibility*. Moreover, the insistence on close attention to the text is even more stringent in poststructuralist writing than in humanist criticism:

> By 'reading' I mean our exposure to the singularity of a text, something that cannot be organized in advance, whose complexities cannot be settled or decided by 'theories' or the application of more or less mechanical programmes. Reading, in this sense, is what happens when we cannot apply the rules. (Keenan, 1)

> Cutting athwart the mediatory role of reason, narrative situations create an immediacy and force, framing relations of provocation, call, and response that bind narrator and listener, author and character, or reader and text.... In this sense, prose fiction translates the interactive problematics of ethics into literary forms. Stories, like persons, originate alogically. As ethical performance, in Levinas's sense, they are concussive: they shock and linger as 'traumatisms of astonishment'. (Newton, 13)

The language here is more dramatic than it tends to be in the works of humanist critics, as reading is conceived in terms of what Keenan calls a 'constant, recurrent exposure to risk' (5); even so, a fundamentally similar claim is being made about the critic's responsibility to the text. However, the reference to Levinas, which has become almost as obligatory in poststructuralist ethical discussions as the frequent invocations of the Other (and, as will soon become obvious, both will be much in evidence in this book), serves to distinguish, at least in theory, the poststructuralist claim from its humanist counterpart. Whereas Booth, as we have seen, dismisses total otherness as 'unintelligible and in consequence totally uninteresting' (194), Levinas's work revolves around the possibility of an encounter for which our previous experience leaves us entirely unprepared. We emerge from the encounter not reinforced in our identity or values, but utterly changed; and this opens up the possibility, of course, that we will not necessarily be changed for the better.

If in practice poststructuralist critics are no less likely than others to use the texts they study to reinforce what they already know or believe, in principle at least their readiness to expose themselves to radical strangeness makes available a less timid selection of texts to be studied and encourages a less anxious, defensive approach to works that do not readily fit with their most deeply held views. This book derives from the simple observation that murder, or violence more generally, plays a pivotal role in a surprisingly large number of interesting and important twentieth-century French texts. The encounter between self and Other in these works certainly does not result in edification or the refinement of moral responsibility, at least at a thematic level; and perhaps the conflictual relations within the texts might also be reflected in the encounter which they stage between text and reader. This book examines confrontations with human and textual Others as they are enacted in a range of theoretical and literary works. It does not purport to be a systematic or comprehensive study of altericide, and even less a general survey of the ethical positioning of twentieth-century French fiction. Instead, the following chapters are intended as a series of exploratory essays which attempt to look at the darker side of the ethical concern with alterity; if this does not exhaust the multifarious relations between ethics and fiction in twentieth-century France, it does at least bear upon one of its most important elements. The first chapter begins the exploration by discussing some of the theories of the Other that have emerged in twentieth-century France, and how they illumine, or may be resisted by, altericidal narratives.

1
Otherness, Altericide

Alterities

In his book *Alterities: Criticism, History, Representation* Thomas Docherty implicitly attacks the view of literary texts as friends or allies which informs the ethical criticism discussed in the Introduction. Modern criticism, he argues, is characterized by 'a fear of Otherness'.[1] Reading is a struggle in which the fragile subjecthood of the critic is strengthened by appropriating and mastering the objects of interpretation; in the process, 'ostensibly recalcitrant Others' (1) are annihilated. The 'imperialism of understanding' (82) entails a 'colonization of the space of alterity' (83). The ethics of criticism which Docherty advocates requires a mode of attentive incomprehension rather than the appropriative understanding which domesticates its object in order to shore up the powers of the subject: 'The task for the critic who wishes to restore the materiality of a world outside of consciousness ... is to find a means of thinking alterity, of constructing a critical philosophy which will eschew the solace of identity – always predictable – in the interests of an alterity for which the subject is precisely unprepared' (7).

Docherty's call to accept the challenge to the subject posed by alterity is inspired by French thought which, since the war, has given a central place to the terms *le Même* (the Same) and *l'Autre* (the Other).[2] Increasingly in recent years the question of the Other (often capitalized in order to distinguish it from *autrui*, other people)[3] has been associated with ethics. However, the ramifications for literary criticism of regarding the text as Other have been largely unexplored; in France the ethical concern that has proved so fruitful in English-language criticism has not yet come to the fore. There remain important exceptions. In *La Trahison des clercs* (1927) Julien Benda insisted on the civilizing function of art and accused artists and critics, along with other intellectuals, of betraying their duty to uphold universal, rational, disinterested values.[4] In a rather different vein, Sartre's concern with the ethics of literature remained constant, even if his conception of literary commitment shifted radically from the insistence on the freedom of author and reader in *Qu'est-ce que la littérature?* (1947; reprinted in *Situations, II*, 1948) to the subversion of the reader's security in *Saint Genet, comédien et martyr* (1952) and the demoralization of the reader in *L'Idiot de la famille* (1971–2).[5] Georges Bataille's *La Littérature et le mal* (1957) is another landmark text, and one that perhaps anticipates Docherty's call for a mode of criticism which takes the risk of confronting alterity, or in Bataille's case, Evil. Bataille shows how a series of authors (Emily Brontë, Baudelaire, Michelet, Blake, Sade, Proust, Kafka, Genet) undertake, and permit the reader to share, an intense transgression of moral norms. In Bataille's account, readers emerge radically shaken by this experience; their values are not confirmed or refined, but thoroughly dismantled.

However, in France, the explorations of Sartre and Bataille on the borders of ethics and literature have had little critical follow-up. The letter contributed by Maurice Blanchot to the edition of *Yale French Studies* entitled *Literature and the Ethical Question* (1991) is revealingly non-committal, as Blanchot acknowledges the importance of the question but seems reluctant to say anything about it.[6] The subject is 'inépuisable' (inexhaustible) and 'intraitable' (difficult to deal with). Each term in the title 'La littérature et la question éthique' (Literature and the ethical question) can be put into doubt, even *et* (and): 'Même le mot "littérature" m'est soudain étranger./ Qu'en est-il de la littérature? Et ce "et" entre littérature et éthique?' (5) (Even the word 'literature' suddenly seems strange to me./ What is this about literature? And that 'and' between literature and ethics?) Finally, Blanchot offers a reply of sorts: 'Et j'ajouterai pour balbutier une réponse à votre question sur l'écriture et l'éthique: libre mais servante, face à *autrui*' (7) (And I will add in order to stammer out a reply to your question on writing and ethics: free but a servant, in front of *the other*.)

If Blanchot says little of interest for the study of the relationship between fiction and ethics, it is nevertheless significant that his final suggestion links the ethical question to the relationship with others or the Other. Although French literary criticism has barely addressed this issue, it has dominated French thought throughout the century. The Other is big business. But accounts of the Other are as varied, contradictory and ungraspable as the Other itself. Alterity has been depicted, simultaneously or successively, as a source of desire or hostility, as a threat to the integrity of the subject, as something which encroaches from outside or already occupies the inside; or as something infinitely fragile, requiring careful protection against imperialist or egotistical aggressions. Hostility towards the Other may represent the subject's attempt to reassert its power over a world which escapes it; but the Other may also give the embattled subject the opportunity to achieve an authentic ethical experience if it can respond to the encounter with generosity rather than violence. So the question must be asked: when we talk about the Other, whose Other do we mean? Nearly every important thinker in France since the war has addressed the issue of alterity, but the three figures I take to be of particular importance are Sartre, Lacan and Levinas.

For Sartre more than for Lacan and Levinas, the question of alterity is linked with the presence of other people (hence his tendency to refer to *autrui*). Sartre's account of relations with others is heavily influenced by Hegel's *Phenomenology of Spirit*, and more specifically by the massively influential interpretation of Hegel's text developed in the 1930s in the lectures of Alexandre Kojève.[7] In Kojève's commentary on Hegel, Man is characterized by desire, and more precisely (in anticipation of Lacan), by desire for the Other's desire: I wish to establish myself as the object of the Other's desire in order to claim for myself the value bestowed on that object. Human relations are thus, in Kojève's phrase, 'une lutte à mort en vue de la "reconnaissance".... Et c'est seulement dans et par une telle lutte que la réalité humaine s'engendre, se constitue, se réalise et se révèle à elle-même et aux autres' (a struggle to the death for 'recognition'.... And it is only in and through such a struggle that human reality engenders itself, constitutes itself, realizes and reveals itself to itself and to others).[8] The encounter between human subjects, then, entails a murderous struggle for recognition. In the phrase that Beauvoir would take as the epigraph of her first novel, *L'Invitée*, 'chacun ... poursuit la mort de l'autre' (everyone ... pursues the death of the other).[9] Of course, if one or both antagonists are killed in the course of this *lutte à mort* (struggle to the death), neither can achieve the goal of being recognized as the object of desire. As will be suggested throughout this book, altericide necessarily fails in its aims if it succeeds in bringing about the death of the Other.

Kojève's account of encounter and struggle informs much of Sartre's analysis in *L'Etre et le néant* (1943). In part three of that work Sartre moves on from his analysis of *l'être-pour-soi* (being-for-itself) to what he calls *le pour-autrui* (the for-others). His initial illustration of the discovery of the existence of the Other indicates from the beginning the uneasy nature of the relationship, as Sartre describes how shame is primarily shame before someone else. I feel shame because my being is not solely defined by how I perceive myself; the Other sees me from the outside as an object, and observes a ridiculousness or abjection which otherwise I might overlook. The Other thus dispossesses me and constitutes me as dispossessed since I must recognize that I am an object for the Other as much as I am a subject for myself. The Other limits my freedom, reveals my vulnerability and robs me of my mastery. Rejecting the potential community of Heideggerian *Mitsein*, Sartre argues that '[l]'essence des rapports entre consciences n'est pas le Mitsein, c'est le conflit' (the essence of relations between consciousnesses is not Mitsein, it is conflict).[10]

For Sartre, self and Other are locked in a conflict in which the freedom of the antagonist must be either assimilated (through love, language or masochism; see 413–29) or annihilated (through indifference, desire, hatred or sadism; see 429–63). But each of these options, as Sartre analyses them, is doomed to fail: in love, for example, I want to respect the freedom of the Other, but only in as far as it concords with my own desires; I want the Other to obey me without my having to issue orders. Or in hatred, my attempt to destroy the Other necessarily also entails a recognition of its autonomy and its power over me. The power of the Other is confirmed and strengthened by my attempts to destroy it; even if all other subjects could be suppressed, my own being is contaminated by alterity.

Lacan's Other may be less linked to actual people than Sartre's, but its influence over the subject's behaviour may if anything be even more constraining and tyrannical. Malcolm Bowie describes the Lacanian Other as 'a pliable and sometimes confusing notion. For it designates now one member of the dialectical couple "Subject-Other" and now the limitless field and overriding condition in which both members find themselves – "alterity", "otherness".'[11] The subject has no given identity or original plenitude; it is formed by identifying with, and recognizing as its own, part of the field of alterity in which it finds itself.[12] So the subject exists in, because of and as part of the Other. As the agency which founds and subtends the identity of the subject, the Other is invested with authoritative powers (of speech, law-giving, understanding, or knowledge) and it becomes the elusive partner which the subject seeks to engage in dialogue. This dialogue cannot be an exchange between equals as long as the subject endows the Other with exorbitant authority. The analyst, for example, occupies the role of Other in the analytic situation and is perceived by the analysand as 'le sujet supposé savoir' (the subject supposed to know);[13] and in his seminars, Lacan places himself in the role of Other when speaking to his pupils.[14] The Other, then, offers teaching, understanding, comfort and cure; but given the unequal nature of the attempted dialogue with the Other, the subject has little power of resistance when the relationship turns sour. Slavoj Žižek notes the ambivalence of the Other: 'It can function as a quieting and strengthening reassurance (religious confidence in God's will; the Stalinist's conviction that he is an instrument of historical necessity) or as a terrifying paranoiac agency (as in the case of the Nazi ideology recognizing behind economic crisis, national humiliation, moral degeneration, etc., the same hidden hand of the Jew).'[15] The Schreber case, discussed by Freud and re-examined by Lacan,[16] illustrates how the Other may become a tyrant, a wilful, deranged, harsh and unfathomable judge rather than a dispenser of truth and justice.[17]

In both Sartrean and Lacanian conceptions, there is little prospect of an easy, harmonious coexistence with the Other. For the Sartre of *L'Etre et le néant* it is difficult to see how any ethical perspective could relieve or offset antagonisms which adhere to the very being of *l'être-pour-autrui* (being-for-others). Sartre gives no indication of how a moral community might be established. In a teasing footnote he insists that 'Ces considérations n'excluent pas la possibilité d'une morale de la délivrance et du salut' (These factors do not exclude the possibility of an ethics of deliverance and salvation); but he adds that this is not the moment to discuss the 'conversion radicale' (radical conversion) which would be required (463). And famously, in the final words of *L'Etre et le néant*, as he touches on ethical questions Sartre promises, 'Nous y consacrerons un prochain ouvrage' (692) (We will devote a forthcoming work to this issue). But this 'prochain ouvrage' (forthcoming work) was never completed, Sartre's notebooks being published only posthumously in 1983 as *Cahiers pour une morale*.[18] Lacan's Other is no more ethically accommodating than Sartre's. Rather than the moral conscience of humanist thought, it is, or can readily become, an obscene dictatorial agency formed out of repressed desire. It issues commands which cannot be fulfilled, and the more the subject complies the more tyrannical the Other becomes. Rather than giving me rules to abide by, it makes it impossible for me to live. The ethics of psychoanalysis, to which Lacan dedicated his seminar of 1959–60, is situated in the arena of fluid desires which can be neither abandoned nor fulfilled; it implies what Lacan calls 'l'expérience tragique de la vie' (the tragic experience of life).[19]

The importance of Emmanuel Levinas in this context, and for this book, derives from his much more positive conception of the relationship with alterity as fundamentally ethical. The conflict of Sartre's scenario or the tyranny of Lacan's is certainly possible, but by no means inevitable. Whilst Lacan was giving his seminar on the ethics of psychoanalysis, Levinas was working on *Totalité et infini*, first published in 1961, which brought together the ideas that he had been developing since the Second World War.[20] *Totalité et infini* established him as the leading ethical thinker of the postwar period in France, and formulated the terms and views for which he remains best known. His starting point is an apparently simple observation about the history of Western thought, but it is an observation that he would spend the rest of his career exploring. Western thought, Levinas suggests, has consistently entailed a reduction of the Other to the Same:

> La philosophie occidentale coïncide avec le dévoilement de l'Autre où l'Autre, en se manifestant comme être, perd son altérité. La philosophie est atteinte, depuis son enfance, d'une horreur de l'Autre qui demeure Autre, d'une insurmontable allergie.[21]

> Western philosophy coincides with the unveiling of the Other in which the Other, by manifesting itself as being, loses its alterity. Philosophy is afflicted, from its childhood, with a horror of the Other with remains Other, an insurmountable allergy.

The fundamental move of Western thought, Levinas is suggesting, is to make the Other an object of knowledge, something to be comprehended and thus its strangeness, its constitutive alterity, is destroyed. Levinas's endeavour will be to think of the Other as

Other, not to diminish its strangeness and its irreducibility to my own knowledge or powers. The self and its restricted perspective should not be taken as the key to understanding everything that lies outside it. The encounter with the Other entails '[une] mise en question du Même' (33) (a putting into question of the Same), a radical questioning which is, in Levinas's account, the cornerstone of ethics.

The basic issue of Levinassian ethics is to preserve the Other as Other rather than to let it be reabsorbed into the self or the Same. This conception will be surprising to those who expect ethics to engage with classic questions regarding virtue, duties or rights, or with the formulation of moral principles, rules or codes. Levinas has nothing to say about these questions. He is concerned with what he describes as the fundamentally ethical nature of the encounter with the Other, that is with an alterity which cannot be understood as a mere extension of myself, and which therefore also radically challenges both who I am and what I think. Through this encounter, I discover that I am not alone, that the world is not my possession, nor is it a reflection of my needs and desires. Levinas uses perhaps one of his best known terms, the face (*le visage* in French), to refer to the initial shock of this discovery of alterity. The face is a sort of point of mediation between the real, living presence of another person, and the transcendence of the Other, the fact that he or she is not a simple reflection of myself but rather escapes my world. The face is perhaps also Levinas's response to the Sartrean gaze (*le regard*): whereas the Other's gaze reduces me to an object and robs me of my subjectivity, the face is vulnerable, welcoming, imploring.

The ethical question revolves around the question of how I will respond to this revelation of alterity.[22] Without the presence of the Other, the world is my own sovereign possession, I am at home in it, it belongs to me and responds to my needs. The Other shows me that I am not after all at home, that the very condition of my existence is that the world is shared with the non-me, that it is also inhabited by a radically alien presence which I can neither possess nor understand. It is easy to see that this revelation might be greeted with violence. The Other escapes my powers; but I can reassert my sovereignty by attempting to destroy it. 'Le meurtre', Levinas writes, 'exerce un pouvoir sur ce qui échappe au pouvoir.... Autrui est le seul être que je peux vouloir tuer' (216) (Murder exerts power over what escapes power.... The Other is the only being that I can want to kill). I have no need to kill other beings or objects because I can assimilate them in other ways, by intellectual or physical mastery for example; in the case of food, I assimilate it simply be eating it. But the Other is not so easily mastered. So the encounter with the face of the Other may provoke a violent response, I may attempt to remove alterity by destroying it. Murder is, Levinas insists, simple and banal, 'Cet incident le plus banal de l'histoire humaine' (217) (That most banal incident in human history); it corresponds to the desire of the subject to remain sovereign over a compliant world.

However murder, for Levinas, also inevitably fails to achieve its object. The face of the Other is infinitely vulnerable, it has no physical power over me, but neither can I destroy it by the exercise of my own physical power; this is because the face, in Levinas's sense of the term, is not simply a physical part of the body of another person; it is also a revelation of transcendence, of the bitter knowledge that the world is not entirely my own. Levinas insists that the face cannot be destroyed through acts of violence exercised on the material world: 'Ni la destruction des choses, ni la chasse, ni l'extermination des vivants – ne visent le visage qui n'est pas du monde' (216) (Neither the destruction of things, nor the hunt, nor the extermination of living beings is directed at the face, which does not belong to the world). The attempt to destroy the Other is doomed to failure; killing other people may be simple and banal, but the Other cannot be killed because by definition it does not belong to my world, it escapes any power I might attempt to exert over it. The Other opposes me with a resistance which cannot be measured in quantitative terms; this is what Levinas calls 'la résistance de ce qui n'a pas de résistance – la résistance éthique' (217) (the resistance of what has no resistance – ethical resistance). In a typically Levinassian paradox, whilst being infinitely weak, the Other is also infinitely strong; my acts of violence towards it will always fail because it is beyond my power to touch the face of the Other.

What Levinas is describing here is a primordial encounter between self and Other. He acknowledges that violence, warfare or genocide are potential and indeed real responses to the revelation of alterity; but violence entails a misunderstanding of the true significance of the encounter, which involves a recognition of the irreducible reality of the Other, and hence the obligation to achieve a peaceful, or what Levinas call 'non-allergique' (non-allergic), coexistence with it (218). The various ramifications of Levinas's thought into areas such as language, communication, religion, justice, society and sexuality can all be traced back to the concerted endeavour to preserve and respect the irreducible alterity of the Other. Ethics, in Levinas's sense, is thus not a set of rules or principles; it is rather the strenuous attempt to inhabit the space of alterity, to cohabit with the Other without diminishing its otherness.

In the differing accounts of Sartre, Lacan and Levinas, the Other appears as tyrant and friend, lover and enemy, the source of my paranoia and the object of my violence; it also offers me the possibility of becoming a properly ethical subject. Levinas tells a story in which I meet the Other and, instead of responding with violence, I discover respect and responsibility. However, Levinas's belief that respect rather than violence is what he calls 'le premier événement de la rencontre' (218) (the first event of the encounter) remains an item of faith, one account amongst others, rather than the final word of the discussion.[23] In this book I am concerned with narratives which tell a very different story, a story in which violence of various kinds – including violence towards the reader – is repeatedly enacted by anxious selves against threatening Others. As a first illustration of this violence against the Other, I will examine a story which gives an all-too-persuasive account of the inevitability and futility of killing the Other, a story which Lacan calls 'peut-être le seul mythe dont l'époque moderne ait été capable' (perhaps the only myth of which the modern age has been capable),[24] the story of the murder of the father recounted by Freud in *Totem and Taboo*.

Killing the Other

Freud finally gets around to recounting the story for which *Totem and Taboo* (1913) is best known towards the end of the book. In what Freud would later accept was a 'Just-So Story',[25] he describes a primal horde ruled over by a violent and jealous father who keeps all the females for himself and drives away his sons as they grow up. The sons, however, return from exile:

> One day the brothers who had been driven out came together, killed and devoured their father and so made an end of the patriarchal horde. United, they had the courage to do and succeeded in doing what would have been impossible for them individually. (Some cultural advance, perhaps, command over some new weapon, had given them a sense of superior strength.) Cannibal

savages as they were, it goes without saying that they devoured their victim as well as killing him. The violent primal father had doubtless been the feared and envied model of each one of the company of brothers: and in the act of devouring him they accomplished their identification with him, and each one of them acquired a portion of his strength. The totem meal, which is perhaps man's earliest festival, would thus be a repetition and a commemoration of this memorable and criminal deed, which was the beginning of so many things – of social organization, of moral restrictions and of religion. (203)

The patriarchal horde thus gives way to the fraternal clan. The brothers agree that no male shall again achieve the exclusive authority of the primal father; renouncing a portion of their own exorbitant desires in exchange for a share in what they would otherwise be denied, they establish the systems of codes, rituals and beliefs which mark the origins of civilization.

There is something quaint and crudely literal about the story Freud tells. On the other hand, Freud's rather colourless narrative serves as pretext for an extraordinary display of intellectual virtuosity. If the story is simple, its significance and status turn out to be highly paradoxical. The brothers' violence against their father is motivated as much by love and admiration as by hatred (204); having killed him, they nevertheless continue to obey his orders by renouncing their sexual claim on the women who had been made available by the murder (the incest taboo; 205); in the original totemic system and later religions, the brothers and their descendants repeat and commemorate their triumph over the father, but also honour his memory, confront their guilt at his murder, and contrive to deny their inaugural crime (206, 212, 214); in the subsequent history of humanity, the less the crime is recollected, the more numerous are the substitutes to which it gives rise (217); thus, the cultural legacy, of which according to Freud 'we justly feel so proud', may be founded on 'a hideous crime, revolting to all our feelings' (222).

Freud equivocates over whether his narrative should be read as literally, historically true or as an explanatory fiction. Although he tells the story of the father's murder as if it were an historical event, he ends *Totem and Taboo* by throwing into doubt the factual basis of the story and, more radically, by making explicit the challenge posed by psychoanalysis to received notions of truth and causality: the primal murder may not have taken place, but it is no less a psychical reality; even if the murder is only a fantasy, the causal chain leading from murder to civilized religion and morality is unbroken; fantasies are as real and true as historical facts, perhaps even more so (222–3). Even if it never happened in anything like the way described by Freud, the murder of the primal father loses none of its power to explain the malaise of modern civilizations.

In its more exhilarating moments, Freud's writing is more preoccupied with the complexity of symptoms than their reduction to simple causes, more with theory than facts, more with speculative daring than with the sensible adjudication of competing ideas. For the analyst as for the patient, the 'cause' of a disorder can never be observed or recalled without the mediation of the 'symptom' through which it is filtered and interpreted. So at least in the analytical or hermeneutic situation, the cause is a product of that which it causes, it can be known only as an effect of the symptom which it has apparently brought into being. Ambivalences can be observed, but their sources can only be hypothesised. Just as the reality of the primal scene can never be proven, in *Totem and Taboo* Freud concedes that the 'earliest state of society has never been an object of observation' (202); the parricidal narrative which he elaborates serves as an explanatory grid which by its nature can be neither proved nor disproved. It can only be uncovered in the course of a restless, relentless theorizing which sometimes threatens (or promises) to overwhelm the Freudian text. In reference to the case study of the Wolf Man, Peter Brooks has described Freud's self-questioning as 'one of his most daring gestures as a writer'.[26] Just as the literal truth of the primal scene is less important than the subsequent significance it acquires for the analysand, the father's murder does not need to be a historical reality to have the consequences ascribed to it by Freud. But almost invariably, a more cautious impulse also intervenes in Freud's thought and writing. Freud both questions the factual basis of his narrative and forcefully reasserts it. Freud concludes *Totem and Taboo* with a characteristic combination of authority and caution: 'And that is why, without laying claim to any finality of judgement, I think that in the case before us it may safely be assumed that "in the beginning was the Deed"' (224).[27]

Freud clearly *wants* his story to be simply, literally true. But his hesitations over the historical basis of the narrative do not detract from the brilliant insight of his essay: the father is not murdered because he is an all-powerful tyrant; on the contrary, his power derives from the fact that he has been murdered, or less literally, he is a tyrant in as far as his murder can be desired. Before his murder, the father was merely a bully; his tyranny becomes real (that is, psychically irresistible) only when and *because* he has been killed. As Freud insists, 'The dead father became stronger than the living one had been' (204). Whereas the sons had rebelled against their living father, they obey the dead patriarch to the letter, renouncing their claims on their mothers and resolving that none of them shall ever attain the level of authority held by their father. The inaugural act of civilization is thus not the murder of the father; rather, civilization is founded at the moment when that murder is repeated and commemorated in the totem meal, that is, at the moment when the crime acquires significance for its perpetrators as a desired and forbidden act.

From this it follows that what matters most in Freud's narrative is not that the *father* is murdered, but that the father is *murdered*, that is, the crime is more important than its victim. This reading of *Totem and Taboo* receives powerful support from René Girard in *La Violence et le sacré* (1972). Girard's account of *Totem and Taboo* combines a general hostility towards psychoanalysis with respect for a text in which, Girard claims, Freud approaches (but cannot quite make explicit) a fundamental insight capable of undermining his psychoanalytic premises. Even more strongly than Freud, Girard insists on the factual reality of the murder at the origin of civilization. Where Freud goes wrong is in his obsession with families and fathers, which leads to his depiction of the primal murder in terms of a family squabble. Girard 'corrects' Freud's version of the story[28] by reference to the general thesis of *La Violence et le sacré* concerning the relationship between violence, religion and human communities. The unity of a community, according to Girard, is formed and reformed through the sacrifice of arbitrarily chosen victims onto which is projected all responsibility for the dissension or crisis afflicting that community. The 'victime émissaire' (emissary victim) or scapegoat serves as a focus of hostility; but it is also revered because it is through its (albeit unwilling) agency that the community is preserved. Thus, victims become gods and gods begin as victims. Girard's tribute to *Totem and Taboo* consists in seeing it as prefiguring, but not quite arriving at, his own insight. Correcting the text entails freeing it from the framework of the family romance:

> Achever le mouvement amorcé par Freud, ce n'est pas renoncer au meurtre, qui reste absolument nécessaire puisqu'il est appelé

par une masse énorme de matériaux ethnologiques, c'est renoncer au père, c'est échapper au cadre familial et aux significations de la psychanalyse.... Le père n'explique rien: pour tout expliquer, il faut se débarrasser du père, montrer que l'impression formidable faite sur la communauté par le meurtre collectif ne tient pas à l'identité de la victime mais au fait que cette victime est unificatrice, à l'unanimité retrouvée contre cette victime et autour d'elle. C'est la conjonction du *contre* et de l'*autour* qui explique les 'contradictions' du sacré, la nécessité où l'on est de toujours tuer à nouveau la victime, bien qu'elle soit divine, parce qu'elle est divine. (293)

To complete the movement begun by Freud does not mean to give up the murder, which remains absolutely necessary because it is justified by an enormous mass of ethnological materials; rather it is to give up the father, to escape from the family framework and the meanings imposed by psychoanalysis.... The father explains nothing; in order to explain everything we must get rid of the father and show that the great impression made on the community by the collective murder does not come from the identity of the victim but from the fact that the victim is a unifying force, from the sense of unanimity which is reformed against and around the victim. It is the conjunction of this *against* and *around* which explains the 'contradictions' of the sacred, the necessity that people are in always to kill the victim again, even though it is divine, because it is divine.

Whereas Freud insists that it is the father who is the brothers' victim, Girard describes how communities are formed 'grâce à un meurtre qui est celui de *n'importe qui* et non plus d'un personnage déterminé' (298) (thanks to a murder which is that of *anyone* and not of a particular person). Girard describes this foundational act of collective violence as lying at the source of all religion, mythology and community. In the later books *Des choses cachées depuis la fondation du monde* (1978) and *Le Bouc émissaire* (1982) he goes on to argue that the Christian Gospels are the first documents to reveal and denounce this sacrificial logic; and since the Gospels have been largely misunderstood, it is only with his own work that the possibility of non-sacrificial communities finally becomes possible.

From the point of view of my own discussion, the crucial point of Girard's reading of *Totem and Taboo* is his divergence from Freud concerning the identity of the victim. Freud directs the brothers' murderous desires towards a single object (the father), whereas for Girard the victim is *n'importe qui* (anyone), his or her specific identity being less important than the establishment by the brothers of a community-in-violence. The community is thus founded on an original crime committed against the Other, who becomes an object of fear, respect, desire and hostility.[29] Rather than a master trope, then, parricide is one of the many forms of altericide. What Freud describes in the murder of the father can be read as an urge to eliminate the Other which appears as an inaugural (non-historical) moment in the foundation of both individual subjecthood and larger communities. And the twin paradoxes of altericide appear as leitmotifs throughout *Totem and Taboo*: the more I hate the Other, the more I desire and respect it; and the power of the Other is only increased by the violence which I employ to destroy it. The Other is that figure whom I desire (to kill), and whose murder resolves none of the subject's inadequacy or ambivalence. Indeed, its hold over the murderous subject is only exacerbated by the violence directed towards it.

Whereas for Girard the murder of the scapegoat explains the formation of religions, myths and communities, my book has no such overarching thesis. In the following chapters altericide groups together a set of unresolved tensions directed towards an elusive or evanescent object. Whereas the position of the father may be occupied by a real (or all-too-real) figure, no individual or group such as women, Jews or Arabs can be finally identified as the Other. The Other is a fantasy formation of the subject or collectivity, an imaginary screen onto which desire and hatred can be projected; and alterity is a role that may at given moments be imposed upon individuals or groups (and which they might sometimes accept) by institutional, discursive and conceptual authorities. At the same time, it is important to stress that the effects of violence, exclusion or discrimination are no less real for the fact that they derive from imaginary projections.

From the standpoint of the subject, the Other is a name for that which is perceived as a threat, as embodying a power, knowledge, self-containment, authority or enjoyment which the subject lacks and which it fantasizes it can obtain through the exercise of violence. Žižek attributes this response to 'the late capitalist Narcissistic mode of subjectivity':

[The] 'other' as such – the real, desiring other – is experienced as a traumatic disturbance, as something that violently interrupts the closed equilibrium of my Ego. Whatever the other does – if s/he fondles me, if s/he smokes, if s/he utters a reproach, if s/he looks at me lustfully, even if s/he *doesn't* laugh at my joke heartily enough – it is (potentially, at least) a violent encroachment upon my space.[30]

So it is small wonder, as Žižek suggests in his account of Fritz Lang's film *The Woman in the Window*, that 'in our unconscious, in the real of our desire, we are all murderers'.[31] However, if murder is an attempt to overcome the expropriation of my desire by the Other, it can never achieve its goal. Desire, as 'le désir de l'Autre' (the desire of the Other) (Lacan)[32] or 'désir de l'absolument Autre' (desire of the absolutely Other) (Levinas),[33] can only be made more desperate by the Other's death; its aims are frustrated rather than achieved by the violence which it provokes.

Fictions of Altericide

In the wake of Levinas and to a large extent under his influence, openness to the Other has become an almost indispensable and incontestable factor for any feminist, postcolonial, deconstructionist or postmodern ethics. However, whilst the Other was acquiring its status as an ethical linchpin, French fiction has been staging a series of murders in which the Other is violently suppressed. The parricidal narrative recounted by Freud in the second decade of the century is reflected and refracted, broken up and rewritten, in a long series of texts in which the position of the Other is occupied by the most diverse array of characters: a complete stranger (Camus, *L'Etranger*) or my brother (Genet, *Querelle de Brest*), my enemy (Malraux, *La Condition humaine*), my king (Robbe-Grillet, *Un régicide*) my mother and my mother's lover (Sartre, *Les Mouches*), my husband (Mauriac, *Thérèse Desqueyroux*), my lover (Duras, *Moderato cantabile*) or my lover's lover (Beauvoir, *L'Invitée*). And one of the hypotheses which sustains this book is that these altericides are associated with gestures of authority and violence directed against a further, largely unnamed real or imaginary Other, the reader.

To conclude this chapter I shall indicate how many of the issues to be discussed in the rest of this book are raised in the purest scene of altericide I have come across anywhere in French fiction (rivalled only by the murder of the Arab in Camus's *L'Etranger*), the opening pages of André Malraux's *La Condition humaine* (1933). Malraux's novel begins with a murder.[34] Just as the title of the book suggests that the significance of the work extends beyond its immediate setting in pre-war China, the initial murder has an inaugural, mythical quality which has little to do with its role in the plot. At first, we are told virtually nothing about the location, the identities of murderer or victim, or the motives for the act. The murder takes place away from 'le monde des hommes' (the world of men), in a place 'où le temps n'existait plus' (9) (where time no longer existed); the perpetrator is 'un sacrificateur' (10) (a sacrificer), engaged in a solemn ritual, with his victim lying on a bed as if on an altar. Only after the murder has been committed do we learn that this is Shanghai and that the motive for the crime was to obtain a document with which the Communist insurgents could get hold of much-needed weapons.

The curiously fluctuating status of the victim makes it possible to see him as embodying alterity rather more than he is simply an arms dealer to be assassinated. At first he is merely an object, a foot protruding from a mosquito net which is 'comme un animal endormi' (10) (like a sleeping animal) or, more inanimately still, 'comme une clef' (11) (like a key). As pure object, the Other is merely an obstacle which can easily be destroyed. But the Other is curiously also beyond reach; his vulnerability is a threat:

> Un seul geste, et l'homme serait mort. Le tuer n'était rien: c'était le toucher qui était impossible. . . . Il redevint vivant, vulnérable; et, en même temps, Tchen [the murderer] se sentit bafoué. (11)

> Just one gesture and the man would be dead. Killing him was nothing: it was touching him that was impossible. . . . He became alive once more, vulnerable; and, at the same time, Tchen felt he was being mocked.

The Other may be killed, but not touched; it somehow eludes the violence to which it offers no resistance; its very vulnerability is its strength, the source of its power and of the antagonism to which it gives rise. Moreover, it survives its own death: 'le meurtre ne change donc rien. . . . . . Devrait-il donc le tuer à nouveau?' (14–15) (So murder changes nothing. . . . . . Would he have to kill him again, then?). Malraux's altericidal scene anticipates the reflection on the power and powerlessness of the Other undertaken on a theoretical level by Levinas in his postwar writings, culminating in *Totalité et infini*: others may be killed but the Other is inviolable, it is infinitely weak but also imperious, it is the object of all violence but it cannot be destroyed (215–20). The resistance with which it opposes my display of force reveals my own weakness and exacerbates my hostility. If Tchen, in *La Condition humaine*, sheds 'le sang de l'autre' (13) (the blood of the other), the knife that kills the Other also draws his own blood ('Convulsivement, Tchen enfonça le poignard dans son bras gauche,' 10) (Convulsively, Tchen stuck the dagger into his left arm). When the Other bleeds, so does the self; and the altericidal scene crucially entails the disclosure of the perpetrator's impotence and pain. The act of killing brings with it the bitter knowledge that the Other's suffering is bound up with my own distress.

At the moment of his crime the murderer acts without motive, or at least not for the ostensible motives that the reader is offered: 'Mais, depuis dix minutes, Tchen n'y avait pas pensé une seule fois' (14) (But, for ten minutes, Tchen hadn't thought about that at all). Murder, it seems, is an end in itself.[35] By the time the reader learns where and why the murder takes place, it is perhaps already too late for the explanations that we are given to be fully persuasive: the rights and wrongs of the bitter political struggles which Malraux's novel goes on to document are placed under the shadow of this inaugural scene where one man sacrifices another. The ethics or politics of the novel may seem to be no more than belated rationalizations of the primal antagonism enacted in the opening passage. Moreover, this antagonism towards the Other is echoed in the private, public and colonial conflicts dramatized throughout the novel. France aims to dominate China as the banker Ferral dominates his colleagues; the Other's independent existence as desiring subject or autonomous political entity is denied in each case ('il avait un talent unique pour leur [Ferral's colleagues] nier l'existence', 83) (he had the unique talent of denying their existence). Following a philosophical commonplace that Simone de Beauvoir would analyse and criticize in *Le Deuxième Sexe*, alterity is especially associated with femininity. Ferral counters the threat of the feminine Other by regarding women only as objects to be possessed (217–18), or as a means of achieving more complete self-possession (232). The desire of Kyo, the revolutionary leader, is provoked and enraged by the elusiveness of his sexually liberated wife, May:

Et c'était une femme. Pas une espèce d'homme. Autre chose...
Elle lui échappait complètement. Et à cause de cela peut-être, l'appel enragé d'un contact intense avec elle l'aveuglait, quel qu'il fût, épouvante, cris, coups. (54)[36]

And she was a woman. Not a kind of man. Something else...
She escaped him completely. And perhaps because of that, the crazed urge for an intense contact with her blinded him, whatever it might be, horror, cries, blows.

The political sympathies of *La Condition humaine* are clearly largely on the side of the Communist insurgents. Nevertheless, by placing human relations in general under the shadow of an inaugural altericidal impulse, the novel risks undercutting the grounds upon which one grouping might be preferred over another. The desire to dominate or to suppress the Other explains the historical conflict between the two sides involved in the armed struggle; and it also characterizes relations, especially those between men and women, on both sides of the political divide. Essentially, the novel confronts the problem that Sartre would raise and avoid a decade later in *L'Etre et le néant*: how is an ethics possible if human relations are characterized as fundamentally conflictual? Sartre, as we have seen, famously deferred answering the question. But it is clear that for both Sartre and Malraux the revolution that would change the human condition would not simply be a political one. It would be so radical that the revolutionaries themselves could not survive its success.

The scene of altericide with which *La Condition humaine* begins is also an ethical moment which the rest of the novel explores through a gamut of personal and political ramifications. It sets up an area of ethical investigation deriving from an insight into the murderous nature of human relations, and it subsequently offers no realistic prospect of an end to conflict. The fact that this exploration results in no easily identifiable ethical certainty is surely not an accident. It is a premise of this book that fiction is bound up with ethics so that ethical reflection is one of the most fundamental motors of fiction as well as the inevitable response of the alert reader; but I will also argue (in particular in Chapter 3) that fiction by its nature permits too many and too contradictory interpretations to play any straightforward illustrative or exemplary role. In other words, fiction is ethical in so far as it offers little prospect of resolution in ethical matters.

From a Levinassian perspective, the interest of the fictional texts I shall be discussing lies in the fact that they offer much more conflictual versions of the encounter between self and Other than Levinas himself envisages. As such, they perhaps highlight the utopian aspect of Levinas's thought, suggesting that violence not peace is the primary response to the threat of alterity. Before discussing this further, however, I want in the next chapter to examine texts by Levinas and Gadamer which discuss at a theoretical level a central issue in this study: the nature of the encounter between the work of art and its audience or reader.

2
Hermeneutic and Ethical Encounters: Gadamer and Levinas

The encounter with the Other entails both hermeneutic and ethical responses: my understanding of self and world may be brought into question by a radically alien presence and my values starkly revealed by my reaction to it. This chapter examines some of the theoretical issues associated with this encounter through discussion of the work of Gadamer and Levinas. Levinassian ethics and Gadamerian hermeneutics are both preoccupied with the same fundamental problem, namely the possibility and significance of the encounter with alterity. Levinas's work is characterized by the endeavour to preserve the Other as Other, to avoid its reduction to the familiar and the already known. In the terms which have dominated postwar French thought, the Other eludes totalization and brings into question the primacy of the Same in all its avatars: the Self, the transcendental Ego, Being, essence or Dasein. For Levinas, respect and responsibility for the Other become the ethical principles at the source of nonviolent human relations and a just social organization. Gadamer's thought, though less explicitly concerned with ethics, revolves around a similar respect for the Other. For Gadamer, the task of hermeneutics is to describe and justify the occurrence of a non-appropriative understanding of alterity, as it may be encountered through a literary text, history, other people or nature.

Despite this common concern for the encounter with alterity, Levinas and Gadamer accord a very different status to the work of art. Both thinkers are in dialogue, implicitly and explicitly, with the later Heidegger, particularly with Heidegger's 'The Origin of the Work of Art'.[1] Gadamer follows Heidegger in according pre-eminent status to the encounter with the work of art, since it is through art that truth speaks to those with ears to hear it; for Levinas, on the other hand, such a view is a form of idolatry, giving to art the ability to speak and teach which only living beings can embody. Following the rejection of the written word in Plato's *Phaedrus*,[2] Levinas conceives of literature in particular and art in general as silent or mystifying, unable to explain or defend itself like a living presence.

So despite the shared concern for the encounter with alterity, Levinas and Gadamer, whose lives span almost the whole century (Gadamer was born in 1900, Levinas died in 1995), apparently adopt opposed positions on the availability of that encounter in art. However, in this chapter I shall suggest that they may be closer than they seem, in that both of them may end up missing the encounter which it is precisely their aim to preserve; and finally I shall relate this reading of Levinas and Gadamer to the curious episode in which an angel appears in Gide's novel *Les Faux-Monnayeurs*, an exemplary encounter – or perhaps an exemplary non-encounter – with alterity narrated and offered by a literary text.

Gadamer's Unwelcome Guest

Gadamer's evaluation of art is much more positive than that of Levinas.[3] For Gadamer, it is in the work of art that alterity may be best encountered, and the role of hermeneutics is to describe and make possible a mode of understanding which preserves otherness: 'im Verstehen die Andersheit des Anderen nicht aufzuheben, sondern zu bewahren,' as he puts it (*II*, 5) (in understanding not to overcome the otherness of the Other, but to preserve it). Gadamer insists that hermeneutics entails an openness to alterity, a readiness to encounter views, perspectives or whole worlds which are alien to our own. In accordance with the unapologetic humanism which informs Gadamer's writing, this openness makes possible a beneficial transformation of the self. The dialogue with the Other, be it text or living person, entails a form of self-exceeding: 'Im-Gespräch-Sein heißt aber Über-sich-hinaus-sein, mit dem Anderen denken und auf sich zurückkommen als auf einen anderen' (*II*, 369) (But being-in-conversation means being-beyond-oneself, to think with the Other and to return to oneself as to another). The final phrase 'als auf einen anderen' (as to another) is crucial in the current context; in the encounter between self and Other, the Other must retain its alterity whilst the self if modified, made better, more comprehending and more comprehensive. As Gary Aylesworth has put it, 'On [Gadamer's] model, the philosophical appropriation of texts is not a "becoming self" but a "becoming other" . . . [Our] identity is not fixed in eternity, it is instead the continuity of our becoming-other, in every response, in every application of the pre-understanding that we have of ourselves in new and unpredictable situations.'[4]

Gadamerian hermeneutics depends upon a constitutive lack or incompleteness within both the interpreting self and the object of interpretation. There is no fixed meaning of texts, but only an adventure of meaning, an event which is always different. As Gadamer insists, all acts of understanding are unique, not reproductions of given meanings which can be definitively established: 'Es genügt zu sagen, daß man *anders* versteht, *wenn man überhaupt versteht*' (*I*, 302) (It suffices to say that one understands *differently, if one understands at all*). The adverb *anders* (differently), italicized in Gadamer's text, is important here. Otherness inhabits the very act of interpretation, as both its object and its commanding principle. Disagreement, change, the dynamic, protean renovation of meaning are not annoyances or hindrances to be overcome; they are the very stuff of hermeneutics. The alterity of the object of interpretation, even if it entails an insurmountable instability within its meaning, is the enabling condition of understanding, opening up the perspective of new relationships, new meanings and new selves.[5]

The concern for the nonappropriative understanding of otherness has become one of the central issues of modern thought in general and modern hermeneutics in particular.[6] But this is a relatively new departure. One of the principal aims of hermeneutics has traditionally been to find firm ground for the possibility of understanding by overcoming the apparent strangeness of the object of interpretation. One influential means of achieving this in German hermeneutics has been to posit the essential unity of Spirit in which all humanity participates. The philologist Friedrich Ast, writing at the beginning of the nineteenth century, expresses some of the most abiding presumptions of post-Enlightenment hermeneutics:

> [We could] understand neither antiquity in general nor a work of art nor a text if our spirit were not essentially and originally one with the spirit of antiquity, so that it is able to assume the other, only temporally and relatively alien, spirit into itself. For

it is only temporal and external factors (upbringing, education, situation, etc.) that create a difference of spirit; if one abstracts from the temporal and external, as accidental differences relative to pure spirit, then all spirit is the same.[7]

It is clear here that the hermeneutic endeavour is not so much to preserve otherness as to restore the primacy of sameness. The identity of spirit is essential; differences of language, class or culture are merely accidental. In other words, we can understand the ancient Greeks because they were basically the same as us; the role of philological hermeneutics is to make it possible for us to bracket off accidental attributes such as upbringing or education in order to experience once again the unity of spirit.

Gadamer has been a major, perhaps the major, contributor to the distancing of hermeneutics from these assumptions. He stresses the otherness, rather than the sameness, of the object of understanding; and he insists that interpretation is a productive, dynamic activity rather than the reproduction of given but temporarily occluded meanings. Moreover, the casting off of the accidental associations of the interpreter, which is central to Ast's philological endeavour and to much of the hermeneutic thinking which follows him, is simply impossible from Gadamer's perspective. We are in fact largely constituted by those 'accidental associations' – education, upbringing, class, race, culture, time – so that to cast them off, rather than returning to the unity of spirit, would be to cease to exist at all.

In principle, then, Gadamer theorizes an exciting departure from the hermeneutic tradition; interpretation becomes an unpredictable, self-transforming encounter with otherness, finally liberated from the fetishism of lost objects, the nostalgia for the unity of spirit or the regressive desire for authoritative meanings. However, the question inevitably arises of how, in these circumstances, interpretation is possible at all. E.D. Hirsch, amongst others, has accused Gadamer of consigning hermeneutics to anarchy by undermining the stable ground which underpinned its activities.[8] But hermeneutic nihilism is far from Gadamer's intentions;[9] and in combatting it he shows himself to be not so far removed from the hermeneutic tradition as the above presentation may have implied.

The essential twist in Gadamer's hermeneutics, applying the necessary brake to the freewheeling career of interpretation, is provided by the rehabilitation of prejudice (*Vorurteil*) or pre-understanding

(*Vorverständnis*). In Gadamer's view we cannot cast off our situatedness; moreover, that situatedness, rather than an impediment to understanding, is actually the enabling condition without which understanding could never occur. Like it or not, we belong to a tradition, we are subject to the authority of forces which actively form who we are and what we think. Gadamer can thus rehabilitate prejudices on the grounds that they do not simply constitute a set of subjective aberrations. Rather, they indicate our common rootedness in a shared culture, with shared beliefs and attitudes. Individual prejudices may of course be questioned and if necessary revised; but in Gadamer's understanding of the term, *Vorurteil* is too essential to what we are for it to be possible to eliminate it from the hermeneutic process.

Interpretation, then, entails the encounter between an Other which should be preserved as Other and a self which, if not immovable, is at best irreversibly situated. The openness to alterity which Gadamer advocates is an openness only within certain more or less restricted parameters. Interpretation takes place within the tension between familiarity and strangeness (*I*, 300), or between openness (*Weltoffenheit*) and presuppositions (*Voreingenommenheiten*) (*II*, 223). The readiness to listen to the Other requires, Gadamer says, 'daß man die andere Meinung zu dem Ganzen der eigenen Meinungen in ein Verhältnis setzt oder sich zu ihr' (*I*, 273) (that one places the other opinion in a relation to the totality of one's own opinions or oneself in relation to it). The active party here is *man* (one), the interpreter, who posits a relationship between his or her views and those of the Other. From the perspective of Levinas, the assumption of a relationship already ensures that the Other is less Other than before, because it can be understood as occupying the same ground as me. In Gadamer's account, if the Other is capable of speaking to me, it cannot be saying simply anything; the range of possibilities, or at least the range of what I am prepared or able to hear, is crucially determined by my expectations. Although the Other may disagree with me, or may be offering for understanding an experience different from my own, such differences are underlaid by a deeper consensus; and that consensus is ultimately a projection of my own pre-understandings. However great its openness to alterity, however scrupulously it aims to pay attention to the Other, however daring its readiness to question its own presumptions, hermeneutics begins and ends in the self: 'Damit gewinnt das hermeneutische Unternehmen festen Boden unter den Füßen' (*I*, 273) (In this way the hermeneutic endeavour gains firm ground under its feet).[10] The Holy Grail of hermeneutics – firm grounding for the risk of interpretation – is thus regained.

Gadamer's texts constitute a strange fabric in which two rhetorics coexist in a surprising proximity, often coinciding within the same sentence. One stresses alterity, the new, the different, the lack at the core of meaning, the ever-changing nature of interpretation and the permeability of the self; the other returns to authority, tradition, universality, restriction, stability. The competition of these rhetorics is particularly evident in Gadamer's metaphor of the welcome guest in 'The Universality of the Hermeneutic Problem'. According to Gadamer, we do not only admit into our presence those who can show a pass asserting 'Hier wird nichts Neues gesagt' (Here nothing new is to be said):

> Gerade der Gast ist uns willkommen, der unserer Neugier Neues verheißt. Aber voher erkennen wir den Gast, der zu uns eingelassen wird, als einen, der uns etwas *Neues* zu sagen hat? Bestimmt sich nicht auch unsere Erwartung und unsere Bereitschaft, das *Neue* zu hören, notwendig von dem Alten her, das uns schon eingenommen hat? ... Die hermeneutische Erfahrung is nicht von der Art, daß etwas draußen ist und Einlaß begehrt: Wir sind vielmehr von etwas eingenommen und gerade durch das, was uns einnimmt, aufgeschloßen für Neues, Anderes, Wahres. (*II*, 224–5)

> Precisely the guest is welcome who promises something new to our curiosity. But how do we recognize the guest who is brought into our presence as someone who has something *new* to say? Is not our expectation and our readiness to hear the *new* necessarily determined by the old, which is already familiar to us? ... The hermeneutic experience is not of the sort that something is outside and seeks admittance; rather we are already familiar with something and it is precisely though what we are familiar with that we are open for something new, other, true.

I find something sinister in this image of a guest who must show a pass before being admitted to the presence of the subject of interpretation. Gadamer suggests that we positively welcome the guest who will say something new to us; but why is he or she a guest in the first place? A guest is surely invited and expected, welcomed because we have been expecting her. What does not fall within our expectations would not appear on the guest list and hence would not be admitted. Here, unambiguously, the tension between the old and the new, the familiar and the radically unexpected, is resolved in favour of the old, conceived as logically prior to the new and as the necessary condition of its recognition.

Gadamer's rehabilitation of prejudice, authority and tradition has been subject to a great deal of criticism, notably from Jürgen Habermas.[11] In the context of the present discussion, Peter Haidu, for example, has alleged that Gadamerian hermeneutics, with its reliance upon the unity and continuity of tradition, cannot cope with alterity at all: Gadamer's thought is appropriate for the understanding of works or texts which belong to the same unbroken tradition as the interpreter, but can say nothing about the products of completely alien periods or cultures.[12] Neither can it cope with the hypothesis that even texts from our own culture may be in a situation of radical disjunction in respect of dominant expectations. There is certainly no heady liberation of interpretation from constraint in Gadamer's work. The concerns of E.D. Hirsch that Gadamer relegates interpretation to groundlessness are themselves unfounded. Assumptions of authority constantly ensure that the waywardness, and perhaps also the pleasure, of reading are brought back into line. Some texts, which Gadamer calls 'eminent texts', are more worth interpreting than others, and because they are inherently more worthwhile, they should be read differently, according to more advanced protocols. And hermeneutics does, after all, lead us to the correct reading of texts; commenting on a poem by Mörike, for example, Gadamer has little difficulty in resolving a famous disagreement between Heidegger and Emil Staiger. And he concludes, astonishingly, with an account of the disappearance of the interpreter behind the sovereign text which seems bluntly to contradict his radical account of the essential contribution of the interpreter to meaning: 'Der Interpret... verschwindet, und der Text spricht' (*II*, 360) (The interpreter... disappears, and the text speaks).

Moreover, the belief that an essential unity of humanity underpins the possibility of understanding resurfaces in Gadamer's writing despite his theoretical opposition to the assimilation of otherness to sameness. In 'The Universality of the Hermeneutic Problem', Gadamer refers to 'das Wir-Sein, das wir alle sind' (*II*, 223) (the we-being, which we all are). Who is the *wir* (we) here? The *alle* (all) ('das wir alle sind') suggests that it is everybody, without exceptions.

In this case, the universal participation in being, *das Wir-Sein*, leaves no space for the radical Other. Whereas Hirsch finds Gadamer too dangerously anarchistic, I find him not anarchistic enough. Despite Gadamer's rhetoric of alterity and despite his vigorous repudiation of the charge of appropriating it, the Other in Levinas's sense – that is, the totally unexpected, the radically alien Other – has no place at Gadamer's party. Not only is it not on the guest list, it isn't even in the phone book. However, as we shall see, it is by no means certain that Levinas is any more successful at according to art the ability to give voice to the muted Other.

Levinas and Art

Since the publication of *Totalité et infini* in 1961, Levinas has won wide respect as the foremost ethical thinker in postwar France. He has promoted a simple yet powerful critique of the Western philosophical tradition as the history of the suppression of the Other by the Same; this view leads to his attempt to derive an anti-foundationalist, anti-universalist, non-prescriptive ethics from an originary encounter with alterity. The need to preserve the Other from assimilation by the Same explains the contortions of his thought and prose. It is essential to his philosophical project that he should avoid transforming the Other into an object of knowledge so that its intractability to our categories of thought should be respected. Conceptual thinking, as the etymology of *concept* (*capio*, I capture) and of its German equivalent *Begriff* (*begreifen*, to grasp, take hold of) indicates, is an act of violence which aggressively appropriates its object and reduces it to repeated, familiar patterns. The Other, in Levinas's account, is irreducible to my experience of it; my relationship with it is what Levinas calls a *rapport sans rapport* (relation without relation), a relationship which is also a non-relationship because the participants share no common ground on which to relate.[13]

Where, then, is alterity to be found if any attempt to locate it also circumscribes and thereby annihilates it? One of the privileged means of encountering a source of meaning which exceeds the confines of the Same, for Levinas, is through commentary on the Talmud, to which he dedicated an important part of his work from the early 1960s onwards.[14] The Talmud, in the tradition to which Levinas claims allegiance, is a text with divine authority, though no commentator can achieve definitive understanding of it; it contains multiple, even contradictory meanings because the word of God cannot be translated directly into the human idiom. In *Au-delà du verset*, and particularly in the essay 'De la lecture juive des Ecritures', Levinas comes close to suggesting that the absolute alterity encountered in the Talmud may also be found in all language and all texts. Interpretation, he implies, responds to an excess of meaning inherent in language itself, and this excess constitutes what Levinas calls *inspiration*:

> On peut se demander si l'homme, animal doué de parole, n'est pas, avant tout, animal capable d'inspiration, animal prophétique. On peut se demander si le livre, en tant que livre, n'est pas la modalité sous laquelle le dit s'expose à l'exégèse et où le sens, immobilisé dans les caractères, déchire déjà la texture qui le tient.[15]

> One may wonder whether man, an animal endowed with speech, is not, above all, an animal capable of inspiration, a prophetic animal. One may wonder whether the book, as a book, before becoming a document, is not the modality by which what is said lays itself open to exegesis, calls for it; and where meaning, immobilized in the characters, already tears the texture in which it is held.

For a moment, Levinas entertains the possibility that any text, not just the Talmud, may confront its reader with an excess of meaning which breaks through the expected and the known and which thereby signals the proximity of the Other. This in turn opens up the prospect of a Levinassian ethics of literature based on an understanding of reading as encounter with textualized alterity. But this is only a fleeting implication. Levinas does not fulfil any hope that he might provide the bases for an ethics of reading. Unlike Gadamer, he wrote little and rarely on art, and what he did write betrays a wariness sometimes bordering on outright hostility. This is most blatant in his only sustained attempt to theorize the work of art in an article entitled 'La Réalité et son ombre' (Reality and its Shadow), first published in *Les Temps modernes* in 1948.[16]

Levinas's article begins with an account of the aporia of criticism: the critic is faced with the equally unacceptable options of being parasitic on the work of art, or of suppressing it by substituting his or her interpretations for the work itself. Criticism thus appears as either suspect or pointless. However, Levinas suggests, this view of criticism only holds because we have a high evaluation of the work of art, and Levinas devotes most of the rest of his discussion to dismantling this high evaluation. The full provocation involved in publishing the article in Sartre's *Les Temps modernes* rapidly becomes apparent. Whilst Sartre was proclaiming the ethical relevance of *la littérature engagée* (committed literature), Levinas bluntly asserts on the contrary that art is self-sufficient and radically disengaged from the human world of choice and action: 'On sous-estime l'achèvement, sceau indélébile de la production artistique, par lequel l'oeuvre demeure essentiellement dégagé' (125) (We underestimate the completeness, the indelible seal of artistic production, through which the work remains essentially disengaged). Art is neither dialogue, nor knowledge, nor revelation: 'Il est l'événement même de l'obscurcissement, une tombée de la nuit, un envahissement de l'ombre' (126) (It is the very event of darkening, a nightfall, an invasion of shadow).

Levinas's article develops into a sustained assault on art. In terms that will appear more or less unchanged fourteen years later in *Totalité et infini*,[17] art is described as possession, passivity, magic, sorcery and incantation, it imposes itself on us without our consent and robs us of our subjecthood (128). Worse still, art brings about an internal fissure within reality. It derealizes the world by transforming the objects which it represents into non-objects (131), creating an unreal shadow world which is inhuman and degraded (135); and this shadow world in turn corrodes the consistency of the real world which is divided against itself and made false through art. The distance from Heidegger is at its greatest here. Whereas Heidegger sought the disclosure of truth in the work of art,[18] Levinas sees on the contrary the disclosure of falsehood, a falsehood which in turn saps the reality of the real. Levinas's article portrays art as disengagement, evasion, obscurity and irresponsibility; to enjoy art is to abandon the attempt to understand the world, to give up on science, philosophy or action (145). As Levinas concludes, 'Il y a quelque chose de méchant et d'égoïste et de lâche dans la jouissance artistique. Il y a des époques où l'on peut en avoir honte, comme de festoyer en pleine peste' (146) (There is something wicked and egotistical and cowardly in artistic pleasure. There are periods when one might be ashamed of it, like when one feasts whilst the plague is raging).

It is at this point, at the very end of the article, that criticism is rehabilitated as a valid activity. Criticism integrates the inhuman work of the artist into the human world; it tears the artist from his or her irresponsibility, makes the work speak, restores the full self-possession of the subject (148–9). At last, in the final sentence of the article, Levinas raises the perspective of 'la relation avec autrui' (the relation with others), the cornerstone of his mature philosophy; but he refrains from describing how this may be restored to the silent, self-sufficient, irresponsible world of art. Moreover, the necessity for the critic to *force* the work of art to speak (the vocabulary of the final pages of Levinas's article is violent and coercive)[19] may put into doubt the ethical value of any such endeavour. It is the role of criticism, Levinas asserts, to interpret and thereby to select and restrict,[20] to impose on the text a communicative, human dimension which it would otherwise not have.

The attack on art in 'La Réalité et son ombre' is devastating and uncompromising. It is in part informed by the orthodox judaic rejection of images on the grounds that they falsify the real by imposing a static representation on its essential mobility. Levinas explicitly describes the image as an idol (138), and the reverence for art is thus implicitly a form of idolatry. The best commentators on Levinas's response to art are reluctant to take 'La Réalité et son ombre' as Levinas's definitive position. Certainly there are shifts in Levinas's views; and in particular, as John Llewelyn suggests, a greater willingness in his later writing to regard art as the potential site of an encounter with alterity.[21] Seán Hand also observes a 'softening' in Levinas's position in the later phases of his thinking.[22] But in the 1940s at least, Levinas's views are uncompromising; and those views are never straightforwardly retracted in his later writing. As Robbins puts it in reference to *Totalité et infini*, for Levinas 'poetry is described as and aligned with everything that ethics must struggle against'.[23]

Poetry, which stands for art in general in Levinas's writing, is an ethical scandal; and I suspect, reading the overwhelmingly hostile language of 'La Réalité et son ombre', that Levinas himself did not fully understand the reasons for his opposition to art. That opposition derives, perhaps, from the perception that art allows a glimpse of a form of alterity which endangers Levinas's ethical account of encounters with the Other. In 'La Réalité et son ombre', the work of art threatens the subject through its self-sufficiency and disengagement from my interests and concerns; it is entirely indifferent to me, it occupies a world separate from my own, it does not speak my language or show any readiness to communicate. As such, I would suggest, it is an almost perfect figure of alterity. But this is, as it were, the wrong sort of alterity: not the 'good' alterity of the human Other (the Other in Levinas is pre-eminently human), but an inhuman alterity which invalidates dialogue.[24] However, if this is the case, further problems immediately arise. If the 'good' Other is characterized by its availability to dialogue, surely it is by that very token less alien to my world, less other, than the 'bad' Other which is totally indifferent to me. Surely the absolute Other, in the strict sense described throughout Levinas's work, is either unencounterable, like the work of art, or no longer other in the absolute sense. The absolute Other would have no need of me and nothing to say to me. John Caputo puts the point persuasively:

> If something were, properly speaking, absolutely Other, then it would not be a matter of concern for us and we would simply ignore it, being quite oblivious of it. Now ignoring the Other would greatly distress Levinas, since the Other lays unconditional claim upon us. But that means that the Other is related to us after all, viz., in a very powerful, unconditionally commanding way.... So in fact the absolutely Other is only relatively absolute, almost absolute, not quite absolute.[25]

The problem with the work of art, then, is that it is other in too radical a sense, and hence *distressing* to Levinas in the manner described by Caputo; only the critic can relieve this distress by forcing art into an encounter which it would otherwise refuse. In other words, following a violent schema which elsewhere Levinas forcefully condemns, the critic must circumscribe alterity, give it a familiar, human dimension, and thereby effect the reduction of Other to Same.

The importance of 'La Réalité et son ombre' lies not so much in its theory of art, which strikes me as without interest, as in the anxiety which emerges from it and which has consequences for Levinas's mature thought. The art work gives Levinas a perception of an alterity which is too radical, which permits of no dialogue and no ethical encounter. Perhaps the fact that Levinas never returned in a sustained way to the problem of art indicates that it represents an unresolved tension capable of putting his later thought into question. Levinas's ethics depend upon an encounter with alterity; but if the Other can be encountered, perhaps it is no longer Other in a proper sense, it already to some degree belongs to the same world as me. The radical, 'bad' alterity of art does not permit of any encounter. Having perceived this in the silence of the art work, Levinas avoids a sustained confrontation with art in the rest of his career.

Throughout its history, much of the energy of hermeneutics has been directed towards transforming the potentially vicious hermeneutic circle, which seems to restrict understanding to what the interpreter already knows, into a relatively benign spiral. In effect, hermeneutics has struggled against its own essential insight that interpretation is crucially determined by the pre-understandings of the interpreter. In *Being and Time* Heidegger attempted to turn this to his own advantage by seeing in the hermeneutic circle part of the fore-structure of Being itself;[26] but this entailed conceding that the circle could under no circumstances be escaped, even by the vigilant dialectic of question and answer that Gadamer would later elaborate in *Truth and Method*. The 'hermeneutics of suspicion',[27] entailing the acceptance that interpreters make meanings rather than finding them in inchoate form in the texts they read, would culminate in some versions of deconstruction, and more particularly in Stanley Fish's provocative insistence that readers do not construe works of literature, they construct them.[28] What is at stake here is the extent to which the encounter with art, or with alterity more generally, is an encounter at all. Do we genuinely discover something that we did not already know, or is the encounter merely a re-enactment of deeply embedded predispositions?[29] It is curious that the principal theorists of the ethics and hermeneutics of alterity – Levinas and Gadamer – both end up restricting or denying the place of the Other in art, thereby making more precarious the encounter of which they aim to establish the possibility and effects. Even for such thinkers, the prospects for a genuinely transformative encounter seem at best fragile, easily forfeited through a lack of attention to the muted Other.

Gide's Angel

The murders of the Other described in the literary texts examined in later chapters of this book reflect these theoretical non-encounters, staging the repudiation of alterity with more explicit, anxious violence than the philosophical texts discussed here. To anticipate this discussion, I shall conclude this chapter by looking at a passage from a literary text in which the question of ethical and hermeneutic encounters with alterity is posed. The passage in question comes from Chapter 13 of the third part of Gide's *Les Faux-Monnayeurs*.[30] At a turning point of his life, Bernard is sitting on a park bench when he is accosted by an angel. The angel accompanies him to a church, then disappears. Later it reappears and takes Bernard to a political meeting; the two spend that night wrestling with one another. The following day Bernard goes to see his mentor Edouard having apparently taken important decisions concerning the values which will determine his future. He explains that he cannot live without rules, but that he cannot accept the rules of others; and he concurs with Edouard's formulation of the solution: '– La réponse me paraît simple; c'est de trouver cette règle en soi-même; d'avoir pour but le développement de soi' (339) (The solution seems simple to me; it consists in finding the rule within oneself, in having as goal the development of oneself).

Here, then, is an encounter which is both hermeneutic and ethical, for protagonist and reader alike. Etymologically the angel is a messenger, a deliverer of meaning; and surely few creatures could embody alterity better than an angel, signalling as it does the eruption into the quotidian of unexpected, life-transforming meanings. Through this encounter with the Other Bernard acquires an insight into how he should live his life. However this passage, which clearly alludes to the story of Jacob's struggle with the angel, is no less enigmatic than its biblical intertext; indeed, the biblical passage in question is famously obscure, to the point that Geoffrey Hartman has described it as the struggle for the text itself, the struggle for 'a supreme fiction or authoritative account stripped of all inessentials, of all dissension, of everything we might describe as arbitrary, parochial, even aesthetic'.[31] Unfortunately (perhaps), the text never gives itself without reserve. Neither the biblical angel nor Gide's counterpart reveals the full significance of its appearance; the Other, in the guise of the angel-messenger, delivers less than it promises.

The interlude in *Les Faux-Monnayeurs* is to say the least bizarre in a novel which largely respects realist conventions. On the whole critics seem to me to be remarkably reluctant to comment on the episode. It is as if it were better, more polite perhaps, to ignore the angel's strangeness than to acknowledge the challenge it poses to an understanding of the text. In fact, the critical suppression of surprise is anticipated in the novel by Bernard's own response on first seeing the angel:

Il méditait depuis quelques instants, lorsqu'il vit s'approcher de lui, glissant et d'un pied si léger qu'on sentait qu'il eût pu poser sur les flots, un ange. Bernard n'avait jamais vu d'anges, mais il n'hésita pas un instant, et lorsque l'ange lui dit: 'Viens', il se leva docilement et le suivit. Il n'était pas plus étonné qu'il ne l'eût été dans un rêve. (332)

He had been thinking for a few moments when he saw approaching him, gliding and with so light a tread than one felt it might walk on water, an angel. Bernard had never seen angels, but he did not hesitate for a moment, and when the angel said to him: 'Come', he obediently stood up and followed him. He was no more amazed than he would have been in a dream.

The first sentence of the passage prepares for the surprise of what Bernard sees by delaying the object, *un ange* (an angel), until the very end. But the surprise is then rapidly contradicted by the bland tone of 'Bernard n'avait jamais vu d'anges' (Bernard had never seen angels). Moreover, Bernard's later response to the encounter justifies a reading of it as a momentary aberration in an otherwise realist text. By the following morning, the literal angel has been transformed into a symbolic demon, as Bernard refers to 'je ne sais quel démon' (I don't know what demon) which led him to the political meeting. And the night of struggle offered by the angel ('C'est contre toi que je lutterai. Ce soir, veux-tu?', 335) (I shall fight against you. Tonight, do you want?) is later deliteralized by Bernard's conventional metaphor of self-questioning: 'J'ai débattu cela toute la nuit' (338) (I struggled with/debated that all night).

If the angel is effaced from the later narrative and interpretation of the night, the ethical significance of the encounter nevertheless seems assured. Bernard rejects the belief systems imposed from outside, as represented by the church and the political meeting, and resolves to establish his own values based on his faith in himself. However, at the very best this is a problematic conclusion to draw from the episode. First, it is to say the least a rather dull conclusion to reach after a potentially mind-expanding encounter with an angel; second, it is curious that an angel, the messenger from a transcendent source of value, should deliver a message which is taken to confirm the immanence of values; and third, the belief in the self as a source of values is anyway massively undermined in Gide's novel, which consistently depicts the self as a forgery, an

46 *Ethical Issues in French Fiction*

imaginary construct, a passing fiction which vanishes as soon as you try to grasp it. In trying to understand his struggle with the angel, Bernard seems to have 'discovered' precisely what the rest of the novel invalidates.

If Bernard's interpretation of his experience can be taken as the text's endeavour to understand its own significance, then it is eluded by its own originary enigma, the sudden irruption of the Other into the familiar world. In the pursuit of meaning, strangeness is wrestled from the text, to be replaced by the security of the already-read and the already-known. Bernard fares no better than Levinas or Gadamer in the encounter with alterity. Levinas denies that the work of art may provide a site for the appearance of the Other; Gadamer disagrees, but will only accept alterity on his own terms. In *Les Faux-Monnayeurs*, Gide for a moment offers us the prospect of an encounter, knowing full well that it will immediately be overwhelmed by the resurgence of the familiar. A true encounter with the alterity of art would require, I suspect, a practice of wild interpretation less methodical, less rule-bound, than we are capable of sustaining, or than anything that could easily be performed or recognized under the rubric of 'literary criticism'.

In the thought of both Levinas and Gadamer we can observe a theoretical openness to alterity in tension with an undercurrent of anxious rejection. The Other is both welcomed and excluded; the stranger teaches oddly familiar lessons, or goes unheard. We thus find here, rehearsed in the guise of theory, the altericidal moment which the fictional texts discussed in the rest of this book enact at a more literal level through the themes of murder and violent domination. The next chapter will address more directly the question of the ethical nature of altericidal fictions by examining the treatment of Kant in Sartre's short story 'Le Mur'.

3
Ethics, Fiction, and the Death of the Other: Sartre and Kant

'tout exemple cloche'[1]
(every example is lame)

Philosophers, especially moral philosophers, repeatedly turn to examples to show their principles in action, or to put them to the test, or to refine them. But examples are also a distrusted resource; narrative (even a minimal narrative such as a philosophical example) may have a semantic waywardness which makes it an uncertain ally in philosophical discussion. What is at stake here is the extent to which stories can be contained within clearly delineated conceptual frames. To put it bluntly, can a narrative be relied upon to mean what it is supposed to mean? The question is important because the tactic of exemplarity plays a crucial role in philosophical discourse. The Greek work *paradeigma*, whether taken in the Platonic sense of model or the Aristotelian sense of individual instance, assumes the burden of mediating between the singular and the normative, the particular and the universal.[2] The example is either a model to be imitated or a particular instance of a more general truth; but either way its role consists in its capacity to ensure the connection between separate domains.

This may be true both for relatively short examples or more developed literary narratives. In her study of didactic fiction, Susan Suleiman demonstrates that the exemplary narrative consists of three elements: the story, and then implicitly or explicitly, the interpretation that we are expected to give it, and the generalization that it illustrates.[3] She regards narratives that permit their readers genuine freedom of interpretation as exceptional; but others have suspected that such exceptions are more frequent than the rule, that the slippage of meaning is too inherent in the process of signification to be effectively excluded from it.[4] This slippage may explain both the fascination and the suspicion with which philosophers approach stories. The aim of this chapter is to discuss some aspects of the link between ethics and fiction by examining Sartre's rewriting in 'Le Mur' of an example discussed by Kant. Whereas Kant sought to rein in the example and restrict its ability to signify, Sartre embraces more readily the waywardness of narrative and gives it space to signify more than and differently from its exemplary function.

Kant with Lacan

It would be hard to think of a philosopher who was less of a story-teller than Kant. Moreover, Kant's reluctance to tell stories is entirely in accord with his ethical theory. He makes no allowance for individual situations or circumstances; he excludes all pathological factors from moral decision-making and appeals instead to universal rational principles applicable in all cases. There are to be no exceptions or attenuating circumstances. If Kantian moral subjects live in a perpetual state of tension, it is not because they do not know the right thing to do; it is rather because they can never be certain that they have done the right thing for the right reason (i.e. not just in accordance with duty, but more importantly for the sake of duty).[5] Kant does not need to offer examples which would support or probe his ethical theory because no particular situation, nor any number of particular situations, would ever give rise to an ethical maxim which could not be discovered by reason alone. Conversely, the fact that in any particular case something might or did take place can have no bearing whatever on the principles of duty which should command the actions of an ethical subject.[6]

Kant does, however, admit that examples may have their pedagogical uses. At the end of his *Critique of Practical Reason* he suggests that carefully chosen examples might help children develop their moral sense and powers of judgement.[7] And, as if his readers were children not yet trained in the harsh discipline of reason, on occasion Kant himself uses examples to illustrate his argument. Famously, he demonstrates the freedom of will through two examples, of which I quote the first:

Suppose that someone says his lust is irresistible when the desired object and opportunity are present. Ask him whether he would not control his passion if, in front of the house where he has this opportunity, a gallows were erected on which he would be hanged immediately after gratifying his lust. We do not have to guess very long what his answer would be.[8]

Kant gives a second example[9] and then draws his conclusion: 'He [i.e. the protagonist of Kant's examples] judges, therefore, that he can do something because he knows that he ought, and he recognizes that he is free – a fact which, without the moral law, would have remained unknown to him.'[10]

As a storyteller, Kant displays an unfashionable desire to control the meaning and reception of his narrative. The story is in a relation of strict subordination to the theoretical formulation it is designed to illustrate; it is designed to illustrate a point which he spells out to us unambiguously. However, by using examples to support his argument, Kant also allows an element of play into his text. The very sparseness of his narrative leaves space for future revisionary readers to explore and contest the apparently incontestable conclusions that he draws from them. One such revisionist is Jacques Lacan, who revisits Kant's anecdotes in 'Kant avec Sade' and *L'Ethique de la psychanalyse*. Lacan's response to Kant is effective by its pure simplicity. Kant, Lacan observes, does not allow the protagonist of his stories to speak for himself; he takes for granted that there can be only one response to the threat of the gallows: 'We do not have to guess very long what his answer would be.' For Lacan, Kant is touchingly naive here: 'Pour Kant il ne fait pas un pli que le gibet sera une inhibition suffisante – pas question qu'un type aille baiser en pensant qu'il va passer au gibet à la sortie' (As far as Kant is concerned, it goes without saying that the gallows will be a sufficient deterrent; there's no question of an individual going to screw a woman when he knows he's to be hanged on the way out).[11] Contrary to Kant, Lacan envisages two situations in which the proximity of the gallows would not serve as disincentive: what he calls 'sublimation de l'objet' (excessive object sublimation), when the object of desire is deemed to be worth any sacrifice, and 'ce que l'on appelle communément perversion' (what is commonly known as perversion), when a man may continue regardless of the gallows 'pour le plaisir de couper la dame en morceaux, par exemple' (for the pleasure of cutting up the lady concerned in small pieces, for example).[12] Lacan assures us that criminal records could provide numerous cases of such behaviour.

So Kant's assumption that there can be no doubt about the lover's response when threatened with the gallows is simply wrong. From a Lacanian perspective, the crucial point that Kant misses is that the desire for the loved object is a matter of *jouissance* not pleasure. Whereas pleasure may be spoilt by the threat of compensatory displeasure, *jouissance* entails an acceptance of pain and even death. Lacan repeats the Kantian move of suggesting that his point will be self-evident to those who have properly understood what the anecdote demonstrates:

> Tout un chacun s'apercevra en effet que, si la loi morale est susceptible de jouer ici quelque rôle, c'est précisément à servir d'appui à cette jouissance, à faire que le péché devienne ce que saint Paul appelle démesurément pécheur. Voilà ce qu'en cette occasion Kant ignore tout simplement.[13]

> Anyone can see that if the moral law is, in effect, capable of playing some role here, it is precisely as a support for the *jouissance* involved; it is so that the sin becomes what Saint Paul calls inordinately sinful. That's what Kant on this occasion simply fails to see.

Kant ends his anecdote too quickly; he assumes so strongly that the man will not spend the night with the object of his desire that the conclusion to the story is not necessary. Lacan, however, adds a conclusion which Kant could not envisage. The example is thus made to exemplify not the intended Kantian point about the freedom of will, but a Lacanian thesis about the relationship between the Moral Law and *jouissance*. Rather than impeding passion, the prospect of the gallows may encourage and sustain it.[14] Law is the condition of desire, not its opposite; and thus, in the argument of 'Kant avec Sade', Sade completes and reveals the truth of Kant.

If Kant's simple anecdote can be reread to suggest such un-Kantian positions, then perhaps Kant would have done better to avoid examples altogether. And yet, Kant does use examples, perhaps more than he should, given that what is at stake in the example is precisely its ability *to exemplify*, to represent without ambiguity the philosopher's point, to serve as a bridge between contingent, particular realities and the universal principles which should command them. It is difficult to imagine a practice of ethical thought that refused all recourse to examples. Since ethics is by its nature concerned with how people do and should live, and how they do and should act and relate to one another, it almost inevitably generates narratives. An ethics without respect for the particular (and so without stories) would thus barely be an ethics at all.[15] But it is equally in the nature of stories to resist hermeneutic exhaustion by any single reader, even if that reader is also its author, and even if the story was specifically designed to illustrate a point which might be readily and unambiguously formulated. As Hillis Miller puts it, anticipating his own detailed discussion of one of Kant's examples, 'the moral law gives rise by an intrinsic necessity to storytelling, even if that storytelling in one way or another puts in question or subverts the moral law. Ethics and narration cannot be kept separate, though their relation is neither symmetrical nor harmonious.'[16]

In ethics, then, the recourse to examples is necessary but problematic. The example probes, and thus puts into question, what it was supposed to exemplify. As Frank Kermode has suggested, it is in the nature of narrative to say too little or too much, to leave gaps or to over-explain.[17] Its capacity to produce meanings is not limited by the explicit propositions which it may have been designed to support. There is, then, an inevitable mismatch between the possible clarity of an ethical proposition and the openness or obscurity of meaning that characterizes even the most minimal narratives.

In this light, narrative fiction appears as both the most suitable and the least hospitable locus for sustained ethical reflection. If this is the case for the short example, it is likely to be even more true of lengthier narratives, with their greater opportunities for obscurity, redundancy, excess and misdirection. In the next section this will be shown in relation to Sartre's 'Le Mur', a story which engages with Kantian ethics but which veers away from establishing an ethical position which might confidently be characterized as 'Kantian', 'anti-Kantian', or even 'Sartrean'.

Kant with Sartre

'Le Mur' represents a rereading and extended engagement with the Kantian problematic of lying.[18] For Kant, lying is always and unconditionally wrong. Following the test of the categorical imperative ('So act that the maxim of your will could always hold at the same time as a principle establishing universal law'),[19] no one, Kant assumes, could possibly want lying to become a principle of universal law.[20] To defend this assumption, in a paper entitled 'On a Supposed Right to Tell Lies from Benevolent Motives' Kant once more gets drawn into the discussion of specific examples. Here, he is responding to comments made by Benjamin Constant. Constant raises the issue of whether or not it is justifiable for a person to lie to a murderer who asked if someone he intended to kill was in that person's house. Constant argues that the duty to tell the truth only holds when the person to whom one is speaking has a right to the truth; that right is forfeited by anyone who intends to do injury to others.

Kant's response is robust and uncompromising. Where an answer cannot be avoided, it is the formal duty of everyone to tell the truth, even if this causes harm to others. If you tell the truth, you are faultless; if you tell a lie, however good your intentions might be, you make yourself responsible for whatever unforeseen consequences might ensue. Kant demonstrates this by imagining an unexpected outcome to the benevolent lie:

> It is possible that whilst you have honestly answered Yes to the murderer's question, whether his intended victim is in the house, the latter may have gone out unobserved, and so not have come in the way of the murderer, and the deed therefore have not been done; whereas, if you lied and said he was not in the house, and he had really gone out (though unknown to you) so that the murderer met him as he went, and executed his purpose on him, then you might with justice be accused as the cause of his death. For, if you had spoken the truth as well as you knew it, perhaps the murderer while seeking for his enemy in the house might have been caught by neighbours coming up and the deed been prevented.[21]

If you lie to avoid a murder being committed, but unwittingly bring it about, you are responsible for it. Kant therefore rejects the benevolent lie and concludes that to be truthful is 'a sacred unconditional command of reason, and not to be limited by any expediency'.[22]

Kant's strictures on examples entail a refusal to give philosophical dignity to those areas which are precisely the cornerstones of Sartrean thought: particularity, situation, contingency. In the Sartrean system there can be no universals or absolutes, so Sartre gives the Kantian question, 'Is it ever right to lie?', his own characteristic

Ethics, Fiction, the Death of the Other 53

twist: 'Under what circumstances is it right to lie?' One situation in which lying seems better than truth telling is suggested in 'Le Mur', which takes the Kantian example of lying to the murderer and rewrites it in a specific historical and political context.[23] The narrator of the story is a republican activist captured by the Fascists during the Spanish Civil War. Here we have a situation which tests Kant's insistence on the unconditional duty to tell the truth. According to Kant, the lie 'always injures another; if not another individual, yet mankind generally, since it vitiates the source of justice.'[24] In 'Le Mur' the sources of justice have been vitiated by the very agencies which are meant to preserve them, the civil courts. The trial of the three republicans at the beginning of the story is peremptory, no witnesses are summoned, no evidence is gathered. The three are sentenced to summary execution, without appeal.

Whereas Kant himself, loyal to his principles, might give an affirmative answer to the question, 'Should you tell Fascists the whereabouts of their enemies?', most readers are likely to dispense Pablo, the narrator of 'Le Mur', from the duty to truthfulness. The opening of Sartre's story describes a scene where the Kantian categorical imperative is suspended, to be replaced by an ethics of situation in which decisions must be made according to prevailing circumstances rather than formal rules. Showing himself to be a good anti-Kantian, Pablo lies:

Le type regarda ses papiers et me dit:
– Où est Ramon Gris?
– Je ne sais pas.
– Vous l'avez caché dans votre maison du 6 au 19.
– Non. (12)

The man looked at his papers and said to me:
– Where is Ramon Gris?
– I don't know.
– You hid him in your house from the 6th to the 19th.
– No.

The following morning Pablo lies again (33), and he admits to the reader that he is lying: 'Naturellement je savais où était Gris: il se cachait chez ses cousins, à quatre kilomètres de la ville' (34) (Naturally I knew where Gris was: he was hiding at his cousins' house, four kilometres from town).

A nice variant on situations envisaged by Kant arises when the narrator of 'Le Mur' is offered his own life if he tells the Fascists where Ramon Gris is to be found. In the *Critique of Practical Reason* Kant indicates that promises or threats might induce the truthful man to tell lies, though our admiration for him will be all the greater if he sticks to truthfulness despite the personal cost;[25] in 'Le Mur', on the other hand, the promise of life or the threat of execution are made to induce the liar to tell the truth. Whereas the Kantian hero wins admiration for telling the truth, the moral fortitude of the Sartrean hero depends upon his ability to tell lies; and Pablo has no intention of being truthful.

Up until this point, the ethical significance of 'Le Mur' seems clear: Sartre's story opposes the Kantian categorical imperative, according to which lying is always wrong, in favour of a situational ethics in which lying may be justified in some cases. However, the story now takes a bizarre twist which turns it away from Sartrean situationalism and, problematically, back towards Kant's moral absolutism. When he is asked for the third time where Ramon Gris is to be found, Pablo does not reply 'Je ne sais pas' (I don't know) as he had done on two previous occasions (12, 33). Instead, he tells a different lie: '– Je sais où il est. Il est caché dans le cimetière. Dans un caveau ou dans la cabane des fossoyeurs' (36) (I know where he is. He's hiding in the cemetery. In a vault or in the gravediggers' hut). Once this has been said, Pablo gets caught up in the mechanisms of Kant's story of the benevolent lie. Intending to deceive, Pablo has in fact inadvertently told the truth. Ramon Gris is discovered and killed, and, as Kevin Sweeney argues in his article on 'Le Mur', Pablo is made aware of his responsibility for the unforeseeable consequences of his own actions.[26]

However, the message of what Sweeney calls Sartre's 'didactic story' is by no means clear.[27] The story disorients by the fact that it seems initially designed to refute the categorical rejection of lying from a Sartrean situationalist standpoint, yet it ends up apparently justifying Kant's rejection of lying to the murderer. If Pablo had told the truth throughout, Ramon Gris would not have been found and Pablo would not have been responsible for his death. Yet this reading is in turn weakened by the fact that the match of Sartre's story to Kant's is only approximate. Unlike the example envisaged by Kant, Pablo's final lie is not benevolent: 'C'était pour leur faire une farce,' he explains (36) (I did it to play a trick on them). On the surface it is more of a Gidean *acte gratuit*; he does it for no better reason than that he can, or on the most generous reading for no positive purpose other than to make the Fascists waste their time. Perhaps, rather than supporting Kant, Sartre is after all continuing to mark his distance from him; whereas Kant rejects benevolent lies and *a fortiori* gratuitous ones, Sartre rejects only the latter. The problem for the reader is that the story is likely to elicit confusion rather than offering clear moral precepts. It gives no unambiguous guidelines over how it should be read. It starts from a Sartrean position but swerves towards Kant; yet the swerve is incomplete, the narrative is not quite Kant's story of benevolent lies even though the outcome in the death of Ramon is the same. The narrative might be interpreted from the standpoint of both a Kantian ethic (Never lie) and of a Sartrean ethic (Sometimes lie); but the laughter with which the story ends ('je riais si fort que les larmes me vinrent aux yeux,' 38) (I laughed so hard that tears came to my eyes) implicitly mocks any reader who might claim to have understood what preceded. The joke is on us, and on the possibility of being an authentically moral subject. For that reason the ethics of 'Le Mur' are both un-Kantian and arguably un-Sartrean; the story permits Kantian and Sartrean readings, but fully and unambiguously endorses neither.

The ambiguities of 'Le Mur' might be seen in part as evidence of what has been called the 'uneasy fascination with Kantian ethics' which surfaces throughout Sartre's writing.[28] Sartre credits Kant with being the first great philosopher to elaborate an ethics of action, yet he carefully distances his own situationalist ethics from Kantian moral absolutism; at the same time, even whilst repudiating his German precursor, he continues to sound remarkably Kantian in key texts and formulations.[29] However, the resistance of 'Le Mur' to both Sartrean and Kantian ethics also has important implications for the relationship between fictional narrative and ethical theory in general. In the previous section it was suggested that Kant's examples opened a breach within his texts which permitted radical reassessments both of the particular example and the theoretical context in which it was embedded. In effect, the example contains within itself the potential to fail in its exemplary role, to mean or to suggest something different from what it was intended to illustrate. If this is true of relatively undeveloped narratives, it should be even more the case for larger-scale fictions such as short stories or novels. Fiction, I would suggest, is ethically engaged precisely to the extent that it is neither illustrative (of ethical theory) nor exemplary (of moral behaviour).

The Death of the Reader

One of the consequences of this is that fiction permits ethical reading whilst also disabling the hermeneutic privilege of any particular reader. It is always possible to find texts which support or seem to support one's own ethical positions; the most humane examples of ethical criticism, such as Martha Nussbaum's *Love's Knowledge* or Wayne Booth's *The Company We Keep*, discover largely sympathetic values that can be gleaned from carefully chosen texts. But it is my argument that this entails missing an encounter with what Barbara Johnson has referred to as 'the true otherness of the purloined letter of literature [which] has perhaps still in no way been accounted for'.[30] One of the issues with which this book deals is whether or not any such encounter is possible; since most of the texts discussed here entail failed, missed or wilfully avoided encounters with alterity, it is possible, perhaps almost inevitable, that the encounter with the text itself is also missed.

And if acts of understanding exercised *on* texts fail to exhaust their possibilities, it is even more the case that acts of understanding exercised *within* texts should be greeted with suspicion. When texts begin to explain their own enigmas, their explanations typically raise as many questions as they answer; and the unsatisfactory nature of their self-readings allows readers hermeneutic leeway at precisely the moment when it seems to be excluded. When texts tell us how to read, overwhelmingly they invite us to read differently. And the ethical significance of this invitation may be quite unlike ethical positions explicitly enunciated within the text. This can be seen by following through the failure of Sartre's narrator in 'Le Mur' adequately to explain his final lie concerning the whereabouts of Ramon Gris.

Pablo, as we have seen, offers a decidedly weak explanation for his lie: 'C'était pour leur faire une farce' (36) (I did it to play a trick on them). There is no evidence that he lies specifically in order to cause harm to Ramon Gris. However, he is unaware (presumably) of the Kantian resonance of the story in which he is trapped. Whereas for him the discovery of Ramon Gris is an unforeseeable misfortune, for the story itself it is inevitable once the Kantian lie has been told. Because Sartre's narrative follows the broad lines of Kant's example, then the death of Ramon is the direct and necessary consequence of Pablo's lie. Moreover, Ramon's death is indispensable since it serves as the focus of the various interpretative and ethical difficulties of the narrative. Whatever Pablo's intentions in lying, after he has lied everything proceeds as if he had acted to avoid his own execution. Ramon Gris is found in the cemetery and killed, and in consequence Pablo's life is spared.

In both Kantian and Sartrean versions of the story, lying results in death. For Kant, the lie is never benign; it causes injury, if not to an individual, then to humanity generally.[31] In the example of lying to the murderer which forms the basis of 'Le Mur', the lie also turns out to be murderous in that it causes the death of an innocent party. Ramon, the object of discord between Pablo and the Fascists, is the absent centre of the narrative around whom the conflict between warring factions crystallizes. He never appears directly, but he incites the Fascists' (murderous) desire, and in particular he arouses strongly ambivalent feelings in the narrator. Pablo asserts that he is indifferent to him, whilst also continuing to admire and perhaps to envy him, and even to identify with him in so far as both are equally valuable or equally valueless: 'Je n'aimais plus Ramon Gris.... Sans doute je l'estimais toujours: c'était un dur.... [S]a vie n'avait pas plus de valeur que la mienne; aucune vie n'avait de valeur' (35) (I no longer liked Ramon Gris.... I probably still respected him: he was a tough guy.... [H]is life had no more value than mine; no life had any value). For both Pablo and the Fascists, Ramon thus functions as a figure of the elusive Other, the true object of desire and hostility, hatred and envy.

The murderous nature of Pablo's lie is disguised in Sartre's story by the revisionary process which makes the death of Ramon Gris a mere accident rather than the result of ill will on the part of the liar. Pablo is thus both responsible and not responsible for Ramon's death: he did not want it to happen, he is guilty merely of playing a pointless trick on his Fascist captors; yet were it not for his disregard for the consequences of gratuitous lying, Ramon would not have been killed. The disavowal of responsibility in 'Le Mur' resembles nothing more closely than the logic of Freud's Irma dream, in which the doctor desperately denies responsibility for his patient's suffering whilst everything serves to remind him of it.[32] Read through the logic of disavowal, the death of the Other in 'Le Mur' turns out to be accidental only in an attenuated sense; the narrative both denies and accepts that killing the Other is the liar's unacknowledged intention and unspoken desire.

So, the story of the liar turns out to be another version of an altericidal narrative. Pablo's lie, in 'Le Mur', belongs to the sequence of altericides which sporadically erupt in Sartre's fiction and thought as a violent outlash against alterity. In fact, killing surfaces in an impressive variety of forms in Sartre's literary texts, from the random killing of 'Erostrate'[33] to matricide (Oreste killing Clytemnestre in *Les Mouches*), regicide (Oreste killing Egisthe), infanticide (Estelle in *Huis Clos*) and political assassination (Hugo killing Hoederer in *Les Mains sales*). Mathieu's murderous frenzy in *La Mort dans l'âme* is a rare moment when killing is expressly presented in the form of pure hatred for the Other, sanctioned by the exceptional circumstances of war:

> Il s'approcha du parapet et se mit à tirer debout. C'était une énorme revanche; chaque coup de feu le vengeait d'un ancien scrupule. Un coup sur Lola que je n'ai pas osé voler, un coup sur Marcelle que j'aurais dû plaquer, un coup sur Odette que je n'ai pas voulu baiser. Celui-ci pour les livres que je n'ai pas osé écrire, celui-là pour les voyages que je me suis refusés, cet autre sur tous les types, en bloc, que j'avais envie de détester et que j'ai essayé de comprendre. Il tirait, les lois volaient dans l'air, tu aimeras ton prochain comme toi-même, pan dans cette gueule de con, tu ne tueras point, pan sur le faux jeton d'en face. Il tirait sur l'homme, sur la Vertu, sur le Monde....[34]

> He approached the parapet and began to fire as he stood. It was an enormous act of revenge; each shot gave him revenge for a former scruple. A shot at Lola whom I didn't dare to rob, a shot at Marcelle whom I should have ditched, a shot at Odette whom I didn't want to screw. This one for the books I didn't dare to write, that one for the journeys I never allowed myself, another at all the people, all of them, that I felt like hating and tried to understand. He fired, laws flew into the air, you shall love the other; as yourself, bang in that bastard's face, you shall not kill, bang at that phoney opposite. He was firing at man, at Virtue, at the World....

Sartre's interest in narratives as vehicles for ethical reflection is at a far remove from Kant's suspicion of examples. For Kant, examples threaten to confuse the diamantine clarity of the categorical imperative; for Sartre, it is this confusion which is precisely their interest. A situational ethics comes into its own where hard and fast principles break down. Accordingly, Sartre is interested in instances where normal rules no longer apply, such as revolution or war. Yet it is striking that in these moments of crisis the response of his protagonists is surprisingly consistent, whatever the differing circumstances and motivations. As if repeatedly enacting the fundamentally conflictual relations between self and Other described in *L'Etre et le néant*, in the disarray of normal morality his characters recognize the opportunity to kill.

In 'Le Mur', however, Ramon Gris is not the only victim of the lie. The assault on the Other entails a more generalized violence of which Ramon is only one of the targets. If he is the person who is actually killed, Pablo's lie is more immediately and explicitly directed against his Fascist captors. Pablo wants them to waste their time, and through this waste to experience their own activities as automated, senseless and worthless. Kant's benevolent liar tells the murderer only that his victim has gone out; in a significant variant on this, Pablo tells the Fascists that Ramon is to be found in a cemetery. He then pictures the victims of his lie as a sort of living dead, opening what are perhaps their own tombs and burial vaults: 'Je les imaginais, soulevant les pierres tombales, ouvrant une à une les portes des caveaux' (36) (I imagined them lifting up the gravestones, opening one by one the doors to the vaults). This is the location where Ramon is subsequently killed. The intended victims of the lie turn out to be its beneficiaries; the wrong Other is killed, whereas the other Others fortuitously regain the power of which the lie was intended to divest them. The altericidal act escapes the control of its agent; and Pablo's lie participates in a fantasy in which the Other is both killed and resurrected, emerging from the tomb to take its revenge even after it has been annihilated.

Through all these confusions, in the very perversity of a text which seems designed to counter Kantian ethics but ends up (nearly) sanctioning them, the suspicion may arise that Pablo's lie has a further victim: the reader. One of the reasons why lying is of such interest in the context of fiction is that, along with related activities such as dissembling, pretending, fantasy, role play or mythomania, it bears an evident relation to storytelling. The fascination exercised on their author by Balzac's mythomaniacs, for example, derives in part from the insight that what they are doing is closely akin to his profession as producer of stories. This connection between lying and storytelling may be a further reason behind Kant's suspicion towards the use of examples: by telling stories, he comes uncomfortably close to telling the lies which his categorical imperative unconditionally forbids. Fiction, like a lie, is strictly untrue, though it may contain its own truth. In Sartre's words, the artist is obliged to 'mentir pour être vrai' (to lie in order to be true);[35] or in Cocteau's, 'Je suis le mensonge qui dit toujours la vérité (I am the lie which always tells the truth).[36] The lie of fiction gives utterance to what normal processes of self-censorship insist on keeping unspoken, such as the hatred that accompanies kinship and love.[37] In the case of 'Le Mur', the lie shows the truth of desire, which is the longing to annihilate the loved and envied Other even when he is my friend and ally; and Pablo's explanation of it, 'C'était pour leur faire une farce' (36) (I did it to play a trick on them), could just as easily be the implied author's comment on the reasons for writing his fiction. As the Fascists are sent to the cemetery on what is intended to be a wild goose chase, the readers are dispatched to the graveyards of meaning in search of an answer which they won't find.

This, of course, implies a very different relationship between author and reader from the generous recognition of one freedom by another that Sartre would describe nearly ten years later in *Qu'est-ce que la littérature?*.[38] This more unnerving, agonistic relationship is adumbrated in 'Le Mur' through the figure of the Belgian doctor who joins the narrator and two other condemned men on the night before their execution is due to take place. The doctor behaves with an appearance of kindness. He offers cigarettes to the prisoners, and comforts Juan when he is distressed. Yet throughout the night he takes notes, and it is suggested that he is present in order to observe the effects on the men of their imminent death. His apparent kindness allows him to make his observations more easily: the comfort he offers Juan gives him the opportunity to take his pulse surreptitiously (19). Moreover, he is known to be allied with the Fascists (18). What gives the doctor's apparently kind yet in fact morbid, disengaged behaviour particular resonance is that it exactly parallels what the implied author is doing as he documents the physical and emotional effects of his characters' impending execution. The Fascist doctor is only one step away from the literary phenomenologist who observes whilst his characters face death; and the doctor's presence in the story provides a flash of reflexivity through which the author represents himself as repugnant and sadistic.

The hostility towards the Other contained and concealed in the uncontrollability of the lie is replicated in the relationship of the text to its reader. In his classic essay 'La Mort de l'auteur' Barthes describes the death of the Author as coterminous with the birth of the Reader.[39] Far from celebrating this birth as a liberation, altericidal narratives characteristically convert it into the occasion of an existential or textual struggle for self-possession. If the Other/Reader exists, the self/text is diminished. The twentieth-century murder narrative, in line with the dominant trends of modernist and postmodern fiction, is quintessentially a narrative in which meaning is put at stake and withheld: not so much a whodunit but, in Geoffrey Hartman's very successful joke, 'a whodonut, a story with a hole in it'.[40] As the protagonist of Mauriac's *Thérèse Desqueyroux* watches her husband unwittingly take a dangerous overdose of his medicine, the narrator cautiously refuses to enter into her thoughts, unwilling to come too close to understanding the crime.[41] The murder of the Arab at the centre of Camus's *L'Etranger* remains unexplained in the text. Anne and Chauvin in Duras's *Moderato Cantabile* seek in vain to understand the novel's inaugural murder, and in the end can only symbolically repeat it as a fundamental but incomprehensible act; likewise, Duras's *L'Amante anglaise* revolves around an investigation into a murder which is never explained, the victim's unlocatable head serving as the gruesome missing piece in an uncompleted jigsaw puzzle.

The example, at its least threatening, is like a riddle with a concealed but ultimately available solution. The adroit philosopher or critic will tease out the message it was designed to deliver. As such, it is like the crime in a detective story which is committed in order to be solved. However, as Hillis Miller has argued, 'the example always disrupts and alters the conceptual argument it is adduced to support'.[42] And the authors of modernist and postmodern murder narratives have understood this to the point that they knowingly impede the reader's effort to make the text exemplify or signify anything at all. Nowhere is this more evident than in Robbe-Grillet's *Un régicide* (first drafted in 1949, published in 1978). The assassination of the king around which the novel revolves takes place three times. The first murder turns out to be imaginary; in the second murder scene the king fails to appear; after the third murder scene he seems still to be alive, but later it transpires that he has died after all. The sequence of events surrounding the king's murder is as unclear as the fate of the photograph of him kept by his intended murderer. After the murder, Boris tears up the photograph that is hanging on his wall;[43] on the following page he tears it up once again; later, however, it is still intact, still hanging in its place on the wall.[44]

Texts such as *Un régicide* deny access to solutions and resist acts of reading which would finally explain their mysteries. This can be contrasted with the classic logic and deduction detective story as analysed by Žižek in *Looking Awry*.[45] In Žižek's account, the logic and deduction detective, whose best-known example is Sherlock Holmes, serves as a guarantor that normality is ultimately secure; the traumatic shock of the murder with which the novel begins, the senselessness of the sequence of events to which the crime belongs, are overcome as meaningful narratives are elaborated around bewildering occurrences: 'The very presence of the detective guarantees in advance the transformation of the lawless sequence into a lawful sequence; in other words the reestablishment of "normality"' (58). The pleasure for the reader in all this lies in the discovery of the guilty individual. Initially, there are (typically) a whole host of suspects; almost anyone could have committed the crime. Guilt is free-floating, disturbingly universal. By the end, however, the perpetrator has been found, guilt is localized, and all other suspects are exonerated. Žižek describes how the resolution of the mystery relieves us of our own unconscious guilt: 'the detective's act consists in annihilating the libidinal possibility, the "inner" truth that each one in the group might have been the murderer (i.e., that we *are* murderers in the unconscious of our desire, insofar as the actual murderer realizes the desire of the group constituted by the corpse) on the level of "reality" (where the culprit singled out *is* the murderer and thus the guarantee of *our* innocence)' (59). In the logic and deduction novel, then, we have our cake and eat it: the unconscious desire for murder is realized, but not by us; we retain our innocence. This solution, according to Žižek, is existentially false: 'our desire is realized and we do not even have to pay the price for it' (59). The Real of desire is avoided because we are reassured that it was never our desire all along. The ambiguous texts I have been discussing, with their unresolved mysteries and open endings, offer no such restoration of normality and relief from guilt. Instead, they suggest that guilt has not been, and cannot be, removed by the expulsion from the community of a convenient scapegoat. Just as Sartre's Pablo may be responsible for Ramon's death, and may even have willed it at the level of unconscious desire, so readers' acts may have equally disastrous consequences and their unconscious desires may be equally murderous. The lack of resolution in the narrative flips over into an act of accusation against the reader.

The openness to multiple readings typical of modern fiction in general, and of altericidal narratives in particular, can be and has sometimes been conceived as a liberation. But it might also be understood as an act of aggression through which the text keeps its secrets for itself. Readers are disempowered as much as they are empowered; the solutions they might propose are always possible but never authorized. Too many possibilities of reading may come discomfortingly close to no possibility of reading at all. If we can't be right, we must be wrong. Readers are potentially excluded by the very openness which might have seemed to give them new privileges. The interest of altericide as a literary topic, then, is that it presents as existential theme what might also be understood as textual process. The lie of Sartre's narrator in 'Le Mur' represents a way of sharing the pain of his powerlessness and mortality; this goes together with an assault through fiction on the reader whose transcendent gaze, and the accompanying power to comprehend, judge and survive, is wrested away.

The ethical encounter with fiction does not consist in the possibility of deriving from the text an established ethical vision which the text would serve to exemplify. Ethics may be at stake in reading to the extent that the encounter with the text entails the same unease, tensions, hostility and struggle as the encounter with alterity. Whether it is the reader or the text which occupies the role of the Other depends entirely on where one is speaking from; the reader experiences the text as Other just as the text construes its reader as Other. And fiction becomes a site where we may glimpse, encounter or fail to encounter the Other as friend, lover, ally, enemy, murderer, victim and finally as ourselves.

4
Camus, Encounters, Reading

The remaining chapters of this book are concerned with the ways in which a variety of literary texts describe and stage encounters – or failed encounters – with alterity. This may entail tacit aggressions and gestures of mastery directed at the elusive, fragile and invulnerable Other, and at the text's implied reader, who actualizes the Other's alienating gaze in the process of reading. This and the following chapters discuss how such tacit aggressions may betray a more hostile relation to alterity than attitudes foregrounded within the texts, or authors' recorded views, would lead us to expect. Altericide frequently seems to be humanism's reverse side, and perhaps its occluded foundation.

Camus is a particularly interesting case in point. His popular image, supported by a string of biographies and partisan studies, still presents him as the proponent of revolt and solidarity, as the anguished witness and lucid conscience of a tortured age. His rift with Sartre appears as a liberal humanist's rejection of his contemporary's Stalinist leanings. For others, however, he is a humourless and sometimes glib moralist, or the macho white man who could never quite rid himself of colonialist attitudes.[1] He is also, as I shall argue, the author of texts which fail to achieve the ethical generosity they are sometimes thought to exemplify and which remain, in their darker impulses, fundamentally altericidal.

The issue of altericide serves to connect the thematic concerns of Camus's writing and the fraught relations which are established between text and reader. It has become uncontroversial to describe the Arab murdered on the beach in *L'Etranger* as a figure of the Other;[2] and in one of the most challenging recent readings of *La Chute*, Shoshana Felman describes how the text bears witness to

64

'the Other's death' and portrays history as 'the space of the annihilation of the Other'.[3] In the reading of *L'Etranger* and *La Chute* which I shall offer here, those texts do not simply diagnose the altericidal temptation; in their various textual practices, their evasiveness or arrogations of interpretative authority (and even in the theory of revolt and solidarity elaborated in *L'Homme révolté*), they embody and reproduce the urge to eliminate the Other, represented here by the reader who threatens the solipsistic text's full possession of its own meaning.

Encounters

Meursault's encounter with the Arab on the beach constitutes the enigma which is structurally and thematically at the centre of *L'Etranger* and which has exercised the hermeneutic capabilities of all Camus's critics and readers. Why does Meursault kill the Arab, and moreover why does he fire four more bullets into the already lifeless body?[4] At the risk of simplifying a complex range of responses, I would suggest that the explanations offered fall into three broad categories: chance, malice aforethought and unconscious hostility.

1 Chance. According to this explanation, we should take Meursault at his word: there was no ulterior motive, conscious or unconscious, behind the murder, only a random sequence of events and the oppressive heat of the sun. As even sophisticated readers have argued, there is no reason to disbelieve Meursault's own account of events.[5]

2 Malice aforethought. More suspicious readers see the sequence of events leading to the murder as anything but random. Having taken Raymond's revolver, Meursault returns to the very spot of his earlier encounter with the Arab and callously executes him. As Fitch, for example, has implied, this explanation of Meursault's actions effectively concords with the interpretation offered by the prosecution lawyer at the trial;[6] and it portrays Meursault as a manipulative, dishonest narrator who attempts to mislead the reader by presenting intentional acts as meaningless accidents.

3 Unconscious motivation. In this account, Meursault may not be consciously misleading the reader, though this does not mean that his actions are as unmotivated as he implies. The murder may be explained in the light of deeply concealed psychological

factors, or by reference to racial tensions between Arabs and *pieds-noirs* in contemporary Algeria; and in a variant of this reading, the unconscious motivation may be attributed to Meursault or to Camus himself, since Camus as author collaborates in the murder, allowing the portrayal of the unnamed, faceless Arab as a menacing figure who endangers the white colonialist community.[7]

It would be hazardous to make a confident, definitive choice between these explanations, given that none of the options of acceptance, suspicion or unprovable speculation seems likely to win a final victory over other possibilities.[8] My own account corresponds most closely to the third of the options outlined above. I shall suggest that the sequence of events which culminates in the murder is characterized by a highly volatile but never explicated interplay of community and exclusion; this interplay is present throughout the text and, crucially, it is reproduced in a substantially unaltered form in *La Chute*. The murder of the Arab represents the most overtly violent, literal attempt to commit altericide in a set of texts which repeatedly dramatize the suppression and reappearance of the Other.[9]

The Arab makes his first appearance in *L'Etranger* when Raymond recounts a violent encounter with him:

> L'autre, il m'a dit: 'Descends du tram si tu es un homme.' Je lui ai dit: 'Allez, reste tranquille.' Il m'a dit que je n'étais pas un homme. Alors je suis descendu et je lui ai dit: 'Assez, ça vaut mieux, ou je vais te mûrir.' Il m'a répondu: 'De quoi?' Alors je lui en a donné un. Il est tombé. Moi, j'allais le relever. Mais il m'a donné des coups de pied de par terre. Alors je lui ai donné un coup de genou et deux taquets. Il avait la figure en sang. Je lui ai demandé s'il avait son compte. Il m'a dit: 'Oui.' (1145–6)

> The other said to me, 'Get out of the tram if you are a man.' I said to him, 'Calm down.' He said to me that I wasn't a man. So I got out and said to him, 'Look, that's enough now, or else I'll give you a thrashing.' He said, 'You and who else?' So I gave him one. He fell over. I was going to pick him up. But he gave me a kick from down on the ground. So I gave him a kneeing and a couple of thumps. His face was covered in blood. I asked him if he had had enough. He said, 'Yes.'

Raymond's story is a narrative within a narrative, concerning 'un type qui lui cherchait des histoires' (1145) (a man who was looking for trouble; literally, looking for stories); it is thus also a story about stories, a *mise en abyme* of the violence against the Other which lies at the core of *L'Etranger*. The fight narrated here anticipates Meursault's own encounter with the Arab when the latter will get more than the fair deal ('son compte') (enough) which Raymond thinks he receives here. From his first appearance in the text, the Arab ('L'autre') (The other) appears as a threat to the virility of the subject ('Il m'a dit que je n'étais pas un homme') (He said to me that I wasn't a man). With his insulting use of *tutoiement*, he invites his antagonist to enter into a violent encounter which Raymond accepts. The repeated use of *donné* (given) may even convey the impression that there is generosity in this virile exchange: 'je lui en ai donné un ... il m'a donné des coups de pied ... je lui ai donné un coup de genou et deux taquets' (I gave him one ... he gave me a kick ... I gave him a kneeing and a couple of thumps).

This story of antagonism is recounted in part to establish a bond between its narrator and its audience, Raymond and Meursault respectively. Raymond's virility is reaffirmed by his defeat of the Arab, and Raymond in turn affirms the virility of Meursault ('il m'a déclaré ... que moi, j'étais un homme', 1146) (he told me ... that I was a man)[10] before asking him a favour which will cement their relationship ('je pouvais l'aider et ... ensuite il serait mon copain', 1146) (I could help him and ... then he would be my friend). The alliance of Meursault and Raymond is thus inaugurated by the story told by Raymond; Meursault accepts the token of friendship and subsequently makes the story his own as he replicates Raymond's violence towards the Arab.

On the day of the murder, when the Arab is first glimpsed he is with a group which is perceived as hostile to and exclusive of the group Meursault now forms with Raymond and Marie: 'Ils nous regardaient en silence, mais à leur manière, ni plus ni moins que si nous étions des pierres ou des arbres morts' (1161) (They looked at us in silence, but in their own way, neither more nor less than if we were stones or dead trees). One group is reduced to the status of inanimate object ('des pierres ou des arbres morts') (stones or dead trees) by the other. Subsequently, however, even Meursault's position within his own group appears precarious. When he meets Masson, Raymond's friend, there is a suggestion that he feels excluded by their longstanding friendship: 'Pour commencer, Raymond et Masson ont parlé de choses et de gens que je ne connaissais pas. J'ai compris qu'il y avait longtemps qu'ils se connaissaient et qu'ils avaient même vécu ensemble à un moment' (1164) (At first, Raymond and Masson talked about things and people I didn't know. I understood that they had known each other for a long time and that they had even lived together at one stage). Shortly afterwards, in the initial fight on the beach, Meursault is further excluded when he is given no role to play ('S'il y a de la bagarre, toi, Masson, tu prendras le deuxième. Moi, je me charge de mon type. Toi, Meursault, s'il en arrive un autre, il est pour toi', 1164) (If there's a fight, you, Masson, you take the second one. I'll deal with my man. You, Meursault, if anyone else comes, he's yours). Only later, when Masson is no longer present and the two Arabs are once again encountered, does Meursault's use of the first person plural indicate the restitution of companionship: 'Nous avons marché longtemps sur la plage.... Là, nous avons trouvé nos deux Arabes' (1165) (We walked for a long time on the beach.... There we found our two Arabs). Raymond's antagonism towards the brother of his mistress is now shared by Meursault, who will later kill Raymond's Arab ('mon type', 1164) (my man) in his place and with his revolver.

The sequence of events which leads to the Arab's murder is driven forwards by a set of alliances which is successively formed, weakened and reformed, and which relies for its cohesion on symmetrical and hostile alliances amongst a rival grouping. It is important to note that similar oscillations between companionship and exclusion are at work throughout *L'Etranger*. Meursault observes that the concierge at his mother's old people's home thinks of himself as markedly different from the other inhabitants: 'J'avais déjà été frappé par la façon qu'il avait de dire: "ils", "les autres", et plus rarement "les vieux", en parlant des pensionnaires dont certains n'étaient pas plus âgés que lui. Mais naturellement, ce n'était pas la même chose. Lui était concierge, et, dans une certaine mesure, il avait des droits sur eux' (1130) (I had already been struck by the way he said 'they', 'the others', and more rarely 'the old', when he was talking about the residents, some of whom were no older than he was. But of course it wasn't the same. He was a concierge, and to a certain extent he had rights over them). Later, Meursault himself adopts the concierge's use of *ils* (they), as his mother's friends appear as a unified, vaguely hostile group:

> Ils étaient en tout une dizaine, et ils glissaient en silence dans cette lumière aveuglante. Ils se sont assis sans qu'aucune chaise ne grinçat.... Presque toutes les femmes portaient un tablier et

le cordon qui les serrait à la taille faisait encore ressortir leur ventre bombé.... Les hommes étaient presque tous très maigres et portaient des cannes.... Lorsqu'ils se sont assis, la plupart m'ont regardé et ont hoché la tête avec gêne, les lèvres toutes mangées par leur bouche sans dents, sans que je puisse savoir s'ils me saluaient ou s'il s'agissait d'un tic.... [Ils] étaient tous assis en face de moi à dodeliner de la tête, autour du concierge. J'ai eu un moment l'impression ridicule qu'ils étaient là pour me juger. (1131-2)

There were about ten of them in all, and they slid silently in the blinding light. They sat down without a single chair creaking.... Almost all the women wore smocks, and the cord tied around their waists made their rounded stomachs stick out even more.... The men were almost all very thin and were carrying sticks.... When they sat down, most of them looked at me and shook their heads in embarrassment, their lips eaten away by their toothless mouths, so that I couldn't tell if they were greeting me or if it was just a twitch.... [They] were all seated facing me, their heads nodding gently, around the concierge. For a moment I had the ridiculous feeling that they were there to judge me.

Moments later, fractures appear within this homogeneous group, as one of the women begins to cry and is seemingly ignored by her companions: 'Les autres avaient l'air de ne pas l'entendre. Ils étaient affaissés, mornes et silencieux' (1132) (The others looked as if they couldn't hear her. They were collapsed, doleful and silent). Later still, Meursault is admitted to the group, as *ils* (they) is replaced by *nous* (we): 'Nous sommes restés un long moment ainsi.... Nous avons tous pris du café, servi par le concierge' (1132) (We remained like this for a long time.... We all took coffee, served by the concierge). Finally, although the *ils* (they) resurfaces, its significance is transformed from opposition to intimacy: 'Ils se sont levés.... En sortant, à mon grand étonnement, ils m'ont tous serré la main – comme si cette nuit où nous n'avions pas échangé un mot avait accru notre intimité' (1133) (They stood up.... As they left, to my great amazement, they all shook my hand – as if that night during which we had not exchanged a word had established our friendship).

Throughout *L'Etranger* Meursault's response to those around him is governed by a shifting, unstable sense of belonging or exclusion.

He seeks to be like others, no different from anyone else: 'J'avais le désir de lui affirmer que j'étais comme tout le monde, absolument comme tout le monde' (1173) (I wanted to tell him that I was like everyone else, absolutely like everyone else). He finds the examining magistrate 'sympathique' (1171) (friendly), desires the 'sympathie' (friendship) of his own lawyer (1173), wins the 'sympathie' (friendship) of the prison warden (1181); at his trial he is questioned 'avec une nuance de cordialité' (1187) (with a hint of cordiality), he wants to speak 'cordialement' (cordially) to the prosecution lawyer (1196), and later his own lawyer speaks to him with 'cordialité' (1200) (cordiality). Before his trial begins, Meursault has 'l'impression ridicule de "faire partie de la famille"' (1176) (the ridiculous feeling of 'belonging to the family'). On the other hand, at his trial Meursault finds uniform, hostile groups ranged against him: all the jurors look the same (1185) as do (with one exception) the journalists (1186). The court is like a club: 'J'ai remarqué à ce moment que tout le monde se rencontrait, s'interpellait et conversait, comme dans un club où l'on est heureux de se retrouver entre gens du même monde' (1185) (At that moment everyone was meeting or calling to others and conversing, like in a club where you are glad to find yourself once more amongst people who belong to the same world). This makes Meursault feel excluded, as he records 'la bizarre impression que j'avais d'être de trop, un peu comme un intrus' (1185) (the bizarre feeling I had that I was surplus to requirements, a bit like an intruder). His exclusion reaches its most extreme point when the defence lawyer speaks of Meursault's crime in the first person, dispossessing his client of his crime and his own life: 'Moi, j'ai pensé que c'était m'écarter encore de l'affaire, me réduire à zéro et, en un certain sens, se substituer à moi' (1198–9) (As for me, I thought it was to exclude me even more from the matter, to reduce me to zero, and in a certain sense to substitute himself for me).

Even if racism is one of the outlets of altericide, hostility towards the Other in L'Etranger is not specifically or exclusively racist.[11] Some critics have seen significance in the fact that it is precisely an *Arab* that Meursault kills, interpreting the murder in either psychological or racist terms.[12] On the other hand, those who wish to defend Meursault (or Camus) against the charge of racism, be it conscious or unconscious, have pointed to the episode in jail when the Arab prisoners show him how to lay out his mattress (1177).[13] On that occasion, Meursault is accepted by, and accepts, the Arabs despite their initial (understandable) silence when he tells them that he is in prison for killing a man of their own race. This shift from hostility towards one group of Arabs to fellow feeling with another raises an important question: what is the identity of the Other which altericidal desire seeks to annihilate? The alterity of the Arab in *L'Etranger* does not reside in his racial difference from Meursault; it has more to do with his apparently mocking *indifference* to him ('il avait l'air de rire', 1168) (he looked as if he was laughing), revealed most hurtfully in the gaze which reduces him to the status of object (1161). So, the alterity of the Arab is not an aspect of his identity; he appears as Other only when viewed from the standpoint of an endangered subject as it encounters something that lies absolutely beyond its powers. Annihilation is an option chosen when other forms of coercion and control have no prospect of success. Alterity, then, is not a constant or defining feature; rather it is a position in an economy of violence which characterizes how the Arab is perceived at a given moment, a moment which unfortunately for him is his last. And just as the Arab, for a moment, occupies the role of Other for Meursault, so Meursault plays the role of Other for society, indifferent as he is to some of its fundamental imperatives. And Meursault's altericidal impulse towards the Arab obeys basically the same mechanisms as society's need to rid itself of Meursault. In this respect at least, Meursault is not as different from society in general as he might appear; but this point of convergence, rather than holding out any prospect of peace, ensures that violence towards the Other remains a primary element in individual and social relations.

In this version of alterity, the Other which provokes the embattled subject to violence may be characterized as much by familiarity and proximity as by strangeness and difference. Raymond's violence is directed towards his mistress ('Je la tapais, mais tendrement pour ainsi dire', 1147) (I used to beat her, but tenderly so to speak) and her brother; Salamano beats his dog which resembles him physically ('Ils ont l'air de la même race et pourtant ils se détestent', 1144) (They looks as if they belong to the same species and yet they hate each other) and which serves to replace his dead wife (1158); and as Meursault himself insists, 'Tous les êtres sains avaient plus ou moins souhaité la mort de ceux qu'ils aimaient' (1172) (All healthy beings had more or less desired the death of those they loved). So the position of Other as object of violence may be occupied by someone, or even a dog, who is closest and most similar to the altericidal subject. As Raymond Gay-Crosier has suggested, the Arab may be just as much the *étranger* (outsider, stranger) as Meursault;[14] and the Other which Meursault destroys may thus be infinitely distant from him, but also dangerously, frighteningly close.

In *L'Etranger* the murder of the Other surfaces as an act which aims to curtail or stabilize the dizzying interplay of companionship and exclusion, alliance and hostility, which insistently re-emerges throughout the text. The Other, as that which endangers solidarity and the stability of the system, is eliminated in the always frustrated hope that violence will re-establish a fantasized paradise of sameness. These fundamental structures found in *L'Etranger* survive substantially intact in the later text *La Chute*, despite the many differences between the works; and more surprisingly, perhaps, hostility towards the Other can also be seen in the theory of solidarity elaborated in *L'Homme révolté*.

In both *Le Mythe de Sisyphe* and *L'Homme révolté* Camus makes it clear that the Absurd should be regarded as a starting point for reflection, not as an intellectual dead end.[15] In the Absurd, Man is solitary and his suffering is entirely his own; he finds himself cut off from the world and from others. *L'Homme révolté*, Camus's major attempt to think beyond this view, attempts to transcend the solitude of the individual subject through revolt. This is implied in Camus's alteration to the Cartesian cogito: 'Je me révolte, donc nous sommes' (36) (I revolt, therefore we are). The community established through revolt saves the individual from being 'un étranger ployant sous le poids d'une collectivité ennemie' (256) (an outsider bending under the weight of a hostile collectivity). In other words, the murderous antagonisms of *L'Etranger* – between Meursault and the Arab, or Meursault and society – are overcome.

However, in order to take this step forward, Camus also takes a step backward which leaves his thinking no further advanced than the altericidal relations of *L'Etranger*. What Camus calls *le raisonnement absurde* (the reasoning of the Absurd) entails the recognition that 'la première chose qui ne se puisse nier, c'est la vie d'autrui' (18) (the first thing that cannot be denied is the life of the other). In the Absurd, the Other exists as a source and a sign of my failure fully to comprehend the world; the Other is a stranger to me, radically opaque and claiming respect rather than understanding. The court in *L'Etranger* falls short of an ethics of the Absurd precisely because it seeks to annihilate what it cannot understand. But, most disturbingly, Camus's ethics of collective revolt also entails a murder of the Other, at least at the level of theory. As the *je* (I) is triumphantly subsumed into the *nous* (we) in Camus's 'Je me révolte, donc nous sommes' (I revolt, therefore we are), no space is left for the Other which is neither *je* (I) nor *nous* (we), and which subsists as a source of radical obscurity. Revolt is an endeavour to make everyone intelligible to everyone else, it entails reference to 'une valeur commune, reconnue par tous en chacun' (39) (a common value, recognized by all in everyone). As Camus's language overwhelmingly indicates, it is an aspiration for unity and order, the desire for some ultimate (even if distant) totalization in which all areas of darkness will disappear. It aims to establish 'une complicité transparente des hommes entre eux, une texture commune, la solidarité de la chaîne, une communication d'être à être qui rend les hommes ressemblants et ligués' (337) (a transparent complicity of men amongst themselves, a common texture, the solidarity of a chain, a communication from being to being which makes men akin and in league). This chain links men together (Camus is cheerfully unconcerned about the masculinist nature of his rhetoric), but also constrains them to a fundamental, deep-rooted identity, bringing to light 'l'identité de l'homme avec l'homme' (338) (the identity of man with man) and 'une nature commune des hommes' (352–3) (a common nature of men).

Levinas argues that it is possible to kill others, but not the Other; in a curious reversal of this position, the theory of revolt entails the utmost respect for the lives of others, but an uncompromising destruction of the Other. Camus has been portrayed as a thinker who lucidly grasped the connection between totalizing philosophies and totalitarian politics, but there is also a totalizing, essentializing movement in his own thought. An anxious and tense passage suggests how not one single person can be allowed to remain outside the community of men, for fear that the slightest spot of obscurity will destroy the whole chain of solidarity:

[Le révolté] peut dire que quelques-uns, ou même presque tous, sont avec lui. Mais, qu'il manque un seul être au monde irremplaçable de la fraternité, et le voilà dépeuplé. Si nous ne sommes pas, je ne suis pas, ainsi s'explique l'infinie tristesse de Kaliayev et le silence de Saint-Just. (338)

[The rebel] may say that some, or even nearly all, are on his side. But if even one sole being is missing from the irreplaceable world of fraternity, then it depopulated. If we do not exist, then I do not exist, that explains the infinite sadness of Kaliayev and the silence of Saint-Just.

L'Homme révolté represents an advance on the *raisonnement absurde* in that the isolation of the subject is overcome; yet it also represents a step back in that its theoretical impulse effectively makes respectable the same hostility towards the Other which is portrayed in its most nakedly violent form in the murder of the Arab on the beach in *L'Etranger*. That Camus was not entirely unaware of the darker side of the theory of solidarity, or (less biographically) that his writing remains to some extent unduped by its rationalizations of altericide, is perhaps indicated by the fact that *La Peste*, the novel which holds out most prospect of establishing a human community based on collective action, contains clear signs of internal dissonance to its own foregrounded message: the near-absence of women and Arabs in the novel, the unresolved ambiguities hanging over the actions of Rieux and his companions, the embarrassing glibness of some of the conceptually most important exchanges between Rieux and Tarrou which invite mockery rather than ready acceptance, the indications that not all of the occupants of Oran share the ideals of the protagonists, the haunting presence of concentration camp imagery.[16]

Such signs of strain against the foregrounded themes of solidarity and communal achievement are nevertheless kept relatively muted in *La Peste*; in *La Chute*, on the other hand, they dominate the text to such an extent that the novel can be read as Camus's corrosive, ironic commentary on his own boy scout morality. Solidarity, which in *L'Homme révolté* had been related to 'une communication d'être à être qui rend les hommes ressemblants et ligués' (337) (a communication from being to being which makes men akin and in league), appears in a less flattering light in *La Chute*. Clamence realizes that he helps those whom he most despises: 'Avec courtoisie, avec une solidarité pleine d'émotion, je crachais tous les jours à la figure de tous les aveugles' (1519) (With courtesy, with a solidarity full of emotion, I spat every day in the face of every blind person). Even the structure of the sentence mimics the reversal of perspectives which operates in the text in general: the language of respect and community in the first half ('Avec courtoisie, avec une solidarité pleine d'émotion') (With courtesy, with a solidarity full of emotion) is abruptly contradicted after the second comma ('je crachais')

(I spat), and thus revealed to be a deceptive surface masking a more fundamental contempt. Clamence borders on making explicit what is only implicit within *La Peste* and *L'Homme révolté*: the rhetoric of human solidarity puts a triumphalist, morally enabling and nearly complacent gloss on desires which might also be read as altericidal.

The scene lying (literally) at the centre of *La Chute*, when Clamence fails to assist the woman on the bridge who presumably commits suicide, is presented as a sort of primal scene which provokes the 'découverte essentielle' (38) (essential discovery) about Clamence's true character. However the indifference towards, and even desire for, the destruction of the Other generates the entire unfolding of Clamence's narrative. It can be seen, for example, in the encounter with the motorcyclist which precedes the scene on the bridge in the text and probably also chronologically.[17] A motorcycle stalls in front of Clamence's car at a set of traffic lights. When the green light appears, Clamence asks the rider, 'avec [son] habituelle politesse' (1502) (with [his] usual politeness), to pull aside so that he can advance, whereupon the tensions between apparent civility and actual hostility are made manifest: 'Il me répondit donc, selon les règles de la courtoisie parisienne, d'aller me rhabiller' (1502) (So he replied to me, following the rules of Parisian courtesy, that I could go and get stuffed). Clamence insists on his own continuing politeness, but the episode seems to be heading towards a violent confrontation. He gets out of his car 'dans l'intention de frotter les oreilles de ce mal embouché' (1502) (in the intention of giving this foulmouth a clip around the ears). However, he is intercepted by another man who emerges from the gathering crowd and strikes him. As the motorcyclist drives off, Clamence is disoriented by the blow and by the sound of horns from cars behind his own: 'Alors, encore un peu égaré, au lieu de secouer l'imbécile qui m'avait interpellé, je retournai docilement vers ma voiture et je démarrai, pendant qu'à mon passage l'imbécile me saluait d'un "pauvre type" dont je me souviens encore' (1502) (So, still a little disoriented, instead of dealing with the idiot who had addressed me, I quietly went back to my car and drove away, whilst the idiot hailed me with a 'poor guy' which I still recall).

This episode parallels the encounter on the beach between Meursault and the Arab, except that Clamence fails where Meursault succeeds. The disorienting power of *La Chute*, and its deconstructive potential in respect of Camus's earlier texts, lie in Clamence's ability to tease out the violent impulses at play within apparently insignificant encounters. Where Meursault acts, Clamence theorizes. As the narrator of *La Chute* explains, the encounter with the Other puts into question the identity of the subject; violence is a way of reasserting dominance and self-control which can be endangered by the slightest, most trivial and senseless incidents. Clamence has analysed and deconstructed the encounter until he has revealed his guiding motivation in the desire to dominate:

> Je m'étais en somme dégonflé publiquement.... Après coup, je m'apercevais clairement ce que j'eusse dû faire. Je me voyais descendre d'Artagnan d'un bon crochet, remonter dans ma voiture, poursuivre le sagouin qui m'avait frappé, le rattraper, coincer sa machine contre un trottoir, le tirer à l'écart et lui distribuer la raclée qu'il avait largement méritée.... J'avais rêvé, cela était clair maintenant, d'être un homme complet, qui se serait fait respecter dans sa personne comme dans son métier. Moitié Cerdan,[18] moitié de Gaulle, si vous voulez. Bref, je voulais dominer en toutes choses.... Mais après avoir été frappé en public sans réagir, il ne m'était plus possible de caresser cette belle image de moi-même.... [Je] brûlais de prendre ma revanche, de frapper et de vaincre. Comme si mon véritable désir n'était pas d'être la créature la plus intelligente ou la plus généreuse de la terre, mais seulement de battre qui je voudrais, d'être le plus fort enfin, et de la façon la plus élémentaire. La vérité est que tout homme intelligent, vous le savez bien, rêve d'être un gangster et de régner sur la société par la seule violence. (1503–4)

> All in all, I had lost face in public.... After the event, I could see clearly what I should have done. I could see myself felling d'Artagnan with a blow, getting back in my car, pursuing the swine who had struck me, catching him, wedging his motorcycle against the pavement, pulling him aside and giving him the beating that he had thoroughly deserved.... I had dreamed, it was clear now, of being a complete man, who would be respected in his person as in his vocation. Half Cerdan, half de Gaulle, if you like. In short, I wanted to dominate in all things.... But after I had been struck in public without reacting, it was no longer possible for me to cherish this fine image of myself.... I was burning to take my revenge, to strike and to conquer. As if my true desire was not to be the most intelligent and generous person on earth, but only to beat whoever I wanted, to be the

strongest in short, and in the most elementary way. The truth is that every intelligent man, as you well know, dreams of being a gangster and ruling over society by violence alone.

The antagonism between self and Other is both complicated and reinforced by the situation of narration. In narrating the story, Clamence undermines any positive image we may have of him, and thereby completes the *dégonflement* (deflation) of his endangered ego ('Je m'étais en somme dégonflé publiquement') (All in all, I had lost face/been deflated in public); at the same time the narrative act aims to re-establish the sense of community with his listener which is shattered as the episode turns from civility to violence. His storytelling follows the same mechanisms as when Raymond tells Meursault about his fight with the Arab in *L'Etranger*: the story concerns violence towards the Other, but its purpose is to form a bond with the reader-listener. This, indeed, may be the narrative principle which informs the narrators' storytelling in *L'Etranger* and *La Chute* in general. Most importantly, the narrative act is *also* an act of domination: Clamence reserves for himself the right to reveal the *truth* of the episode ('mon véritable désir', 'La vérité') (my true desire, the truth) as he endeavours to coerce his listener into acquiescence.

La Chute attempts to mediate between contradictory impulses as it simultaneously seeks fellowship with and dominance over the Other. Clamence aims to be sole master and only subject of his own discourse, the ultimate referent of language and memory: 'Moi, moi, moi, voilà le refrain de ma chère vie, et qui s'entendait dans tout ce que je disais.... Je vivais donc sans autre continuité que celle, au jour le jour, du moi-moi-moi.... Je ne me suis jamais souvenu que de moi-même' (1500–1) (Me, me, me, that is the refrain of my dear life, and it could be heard in everything I said.... So I lived without any continuity other than, from day to day, that of me-me-me.... I never remembered anything except myself). At the same time, Clamence also seeks a universal complicity (1513) or fraternity (1548) based on a stock of experiences common to all: 'Je prends les traits communs, les expériences que nous avons ensemble souffertes, les faiblesses que nous partageons, le bon ton, l'homme du jour enfin, tel qu'il sévit en moi et chez les autres' (1547) (I take the common features, the experiences which we have all suffered together, the weaknesses we share, good taste, the man of the day in short, such as he rages in me and in others).

The tension between this simultaneous urge for uniqueness and resemblance is resolved through the paradox of the judge penitent who decries himself in order to judge others, achieving dominance through self-accusation (1546–8). The narrative aims to form a bond through which the subjectivity of the listener is overwhelmed and invaded by the presence of the narrator.

Camus's critics have been puzzled as much over the relationship between his major works as by the detailed interpretation of individual texts. In the light of what I have been suggesting so far, despite differences of narrative mode and in the attitudes which are foregrounded, there is a striking continuity between *L'Etranger* and *La Chute*. The anxieties and energies of each text derive from a fundamental ethical moment, an encounter with the Other, which brings to the surface a volatile mixture of fellowship and hostility, identification and difference, community and exclusion. And consistently, Camus's texts respond to this ethical moment with altericide, either through the literal murder committed by Meursault, the fantasized aggressions of Clamence, or the theoretical annihilation of the Other which lurks behind the moral postures of *L'Homme révolté*. Throughout Camus's writing the Other appears as a dangerous friend, a desired enemy, too close to or distant from the self for comfort. Despite Camus's best moral intentions, his texts dramatize, enact and are even constituted by a repeated, insistent rejection of the non-self.

At the midpoint of *La Chute*, Clamence recounts the incident on the bridge when he sees an unknown woman on a bridge over the Seine in Paris. A moment later he hears the sound of a body hitting the water. Why does this episode occupy such an important place in Clamence's memory and in Camus's text? Did the woman jump, did she fall or was she pushed? Clamence claims to have been some distance away when he heard the woman's cries, but he has already warned us not to trust him: 'Ne vous y fiez pas' (1500) (Do not trust). Perhaps he succumbed to the moment's temptation and pushed the unsuspecting, defenceless, infinitely vulnerable Other to her death. And who was the woman? Seen only from behind, she is as anonymous as Meursault's Arab. Yet Clamence, like Meursault, feels robbed by her of something most intimately his own: his ease with himself, and more fundamentally, his secure sense of his own unquestioned place in a world which yields to his sovereign will. Perhaps the Other momentarily represented by the woman, as by the Arab in *L'Etranger*, is also a figure of the reader, whose murder is staged at the centre of the text in order to deny her the possibility of stealing its secrets.

Reading

In a brilliant and moving essay,[19] Shoshana Felman describes the scene on the bridge in *La Chute* as 'a missed encounter with reality' (167), an event which is not experienced by Clamence and which he cannot describe. *La Chute*, in Felman's account, critically rethinks the stakes of witnessing nine years after *La Peste*:

> In *The Plague*, the scene of witnessing is thus the scene of the historical recording – and of the historical documenting – of an event. In *The Fall*, the scene of witnessing is, paradoxically enough, the scene of the non-recording and of the non-documenting of an event.... In *The Plague*, the event is witnessed in so far as it is fully and directly *experienced*. In *The Fall*, the event is witnessed in so far as it is *not experienced*, in so far as it is literally *missed*. (168)

Felman relates *La Chute* to its political and historical context and to the general problem of post-Holocaust testimonial literature. The Holocaust corrodes the testimony of its survivors by destroying their ability to bear witness; *La Chute* enacts this crisis in witnessing with the utmost lucidity:

> In bearing witness to the witness's inability to witness – to the narrating subject's inability to cross the bridge towards the Other's death or life – *The Fall* inscribes the Holocaust as the impossible historical narrative of an event without a witness, an event eliminating its own witness. Narrative has thus become the very writing of the impossibility of writing history. (200–1)

In drawing a sharp distinction between the full and direct experience of history in *La Peste* and the missing of the encounter in *La Chute*, Felman (as in her chapter on *La Peste*) rather underplays the problems of narration within the earlier text.[20] Moreover, the comparison of *La Chute* to *La Peste*, and not to *L'Etranger*, allows Felman to establish a rather simple chronological scheme which relates the crisis of witnessing to the Holocaust; yet this crisis is already palpable in *L'Etranger* (published before the most barbaric episodes of the Holocaust had occurred), the narrative of a man who is barely witness to his own life, who consistently fails to see the significance of his own acts, and who remains absent to himself in his disjointed, unreliable account of his own story. In the present context, however, a more interesting problem with Felman's reading derives from her equivocations about the status of the Other. What is witnessed in *La Chute* is 'the Other's death' (171); the text poses the question of what it means 'to *inhabit history* as crime, as the space of the annihilation of the Other' (189); it makes of the narrator and all those who witness atrocity with silence into 'historical participants, *accomplices* in the execution of the Other' (192). So the Other is the text's victim; but in Felman's account the Other is also the addressee of the narrative. Camus's text '[deflects] the position of the Other toward ourselves' (202); we as readers are put in the position of the silent interlocutor, given the opportunity to witness and bear witness where Clamence and his contemporaries had failed to respond. *La Chute* is a narrative which dramatizes the failure of testimony; but by transforming the Other from the executed victim to the surviving witness-reader, Felman also transforms this *failure* into the author's success: 'Camus succeeds in giving to the very silence of a generation – and to [the?] very voicelessness of history – the power of a *call*: the possibility, the chance of our *response-ability*' (203).

Felman's reading of *La Chute* is informed by an intriguing discrepancy: the text *narrates* a failed encounter, but it *constitutes* a successful one; the text (or Camus) succeeds where Clamence fails. The possibility of the encounter which plays such an important part in Felman's understanding of *La Chute* is also essential to her conception of reading and critical practice in general. In the postface (printed as the first chapter) of *What does a Woman Want?*, Felman calls for 'ways of reading as concrete events (unique encounters with another's story)'.[21] The literary text is conceived as a privileged site, containing 'a never quite predictable potential of *surprise*'.[22] So literature maintains, and is perhaps the only cultural manifestation to maintain,[23] the possibility of real encounters, unexpected and unique, with the radical, unknown Other. And this remains the case even if what the text *describes* is the impossibility of any such encounter.

However, it is far from certain that Felman's belief in the possibility of authentic encounters is either shared or justified by Camus's novel. The encounter which she discovers (in a text describing the failure of encounters) may itself turn out to be a missed encounter, a cherished hope rather than a genuine discovery made through reading the text. This possibility is strengthened by Felman's apparent blindness to some of the consequences of her designation of the Other as both the addressee and the victim of the text. More than he is respected in his otherness, the interlocutor is badgered and manipulated by Clamence. The narrator's endeavour in *La Chute* consists in the presentation of himself as a reflection of his interlocutor, and the construction of his interlocutor as the reflection of himself:

> Non, je navigue souplement, je multiplie les nuances, les digressions aussi, j'adapte enfin mon discours à l'auditeur, j'amène ce dernier à renchérir.... Quand le portrait est terminé, comme ce soir, je le montre, plein de désolation: 'Voilà, hélas! ce que je suis.' Le réquisitoire est achevé. Mais du même coup, le portrait que je tends à mes contemporains devient un miroir. (1547)

> No, I steer a supple course, I multiply nuances, digressions as well, in short I adapt my language to my listener, I lead the latter to go further..... When the portrait is finished, as it is this evening, I show it, full of sorrow: 'That is what I am, alas!' The indictment is complete. But at the same time the portrait I offer my contemporaries becomes a mirror.

Clamence's narrative is motored, then, not by a generous recognition of otherness, but by the imperative to wrest the initiative from the reader-Other. He addresses his audience directly ('pensez un peu à ce que serait votre enseigne', 1499) (think a bit about what your sign might be), carefully times key revelations ('l'aventure... dont je ne peux différer plus longtemps le récit', 1510) (the adventure... which I can no longer put off narrating), maintains suspense ('je vous dirai demain en quoi consiste ce beau métier', 1536) (I will tell you tomorrow what this fine vocation consists in), and he anticipates and plays upon his audience's responses:

> Qu'est-ce qu'un juge-pénitent? Ah! je vous ai intrigué avec cette histoire. Je n'y mettais aucun malice, croyez-le, et je peux m'expliquer plus clairement.... Mais il me faut d'abord vous exposer un certain nombre de faits qui vous aideront à mieux comprendre mon récit. (1484)

What is a judge-penitent? Oh! I have intrigued you with all this. There was no malice involved, believe me, and I can explain myself more clearly.... But first of all I must tell you a certain number of facts which will help you to understand my story better.

Most importantly, Clamence maintains command over the meaning of his story. Just as he accuses himself in order not to be accused, he interprets his own text so as to prescribe the interpretative routes which his reader may follow. So the text comes to us exhaustively pre-interpreted, with Clamence arrogating the position of ultimate, authoritative self-analyst. Although we can tell from Clamence's words that his interlocutor does speak, what he says is not reproduced in the text: rather than an encounter with the Other, this suggests a muting of alterity, the denial that it has anything to say or any response to give other than what the text has laid out in advance. Felman sees *La Chute* as *witnessing* the annihilation of the Other, whereas I regard it as collaborating with, or *performing*, that annihilation in its textual practice.

By different strategies, but to a similar end, *L'Etranger* also strives to deny the reader any coherent interpretative position not anticipated by the text itself. *La Chute* is offered complete with its own compelling self-interpretation, whereas *L'Etranger* is understated and evasive. Camus's preface to an American edition of his novel, sometimes taken as directing the reader to a correct understanding of his text, does little to help matters. Camus rearranges fragments of Meursault's narrative[24] and, describing the novel as 'l'histoire d'un homme qui... accepte de mourir pour la vérité' (1928) (the story of a man who... accepts to die for the truth), he proposes a highly dubious account of the work; and it is unclear whether the key description of Meursault as 'le seul Christ que nous méritions' (1929) (the only Christ we deserve) should be read as a comment on Meursault (he is a Christ figure) or as a comment on us (he is the only Christ that *we deserve*). Camus's simplifying or misleading comments of his own novel serve to highlight the resistance to interpretation of the text itself. Throughout *L'Etranger* Meursault's evasiveness denies the reader an interpretative handhold which would allow some progression towards understanding. His characteristic stance is to imply that something is going on beneath the surface of what he chooses to say, though we are given no clear clue as to what it may be. Take, for example, the following passage:

Un peu plus tard, pour faire quelque chose, j'ai pris un vieux journal et je l'ai lu. J'y ai découpé une réclame des sels Kruschen et je l'ai collée dans un vieux cahier où je mets les choses qui m'amusent dans les journaux. Je me suis aussi lavé les mains et pour finir je me suis mis au balcon. (1139–40)

A little later, in order to do something, I took an old paper and read it. I cut out an advertisement for Kruschen salts and I stuck it in an old book in which I put things from the papers that amuse me. I also washed my hands and finally I went out onto the balcony.

This may be simply an illustration of the banal, insignificant activities which help Meursault to get through a dull Sunday. But the studied inconsequentiality of the passage also raises the suspicion that more may be going on here than is made explicit: why is Meursault so interested in the advertisement for health salts? Should this newspaper clipping be related in some way to the one he later finds under his mattress in prison (1182)? And does he just wash his hands because he has got newsprint or glue on them, or does the incident imply some more mysterious, perhaps even neurotic, fastidiousness? Only a few pages later, it is worth remembering, Meursault dwells once again on the pleasures and problems of hand washing:

Avant de quitter le bureau pour aller déjeuner, je me suis lavé les mains. A midi, j'aime bien ce moment. Le soir, j'y trouve moins de plaisir parce que la serviette roulante qu'on utilise est tout à fait humide: elle a servi toute la journée. J'en ai fait la remarque un jour à mon patron. Il m'a répondu qu'il trouvait cela regrettable, mais que c'était tout de même un détail sans importance. (1143)

Before leaving the office to get lunch, I washed my hands. At midday, I like this moment. In the evening I find it less pleasurable because the towel that is used is completely damp: it has been in use all day. I once told this to my boss. He replied that he was sorry about that, but that it was after all a detail without importance.

Whether or not this is 'un détail sans importance' (a detail without importance) is precisely what is at issue here. Meursault's trial, itself a dramatization of the difficulties of interpreting the novel,[25] hinges on the question of which details are significant and which are trivial: is there a connection between drinking white coffee over your mother's coffin and murdering an Arab, is it relevant that Meursault returns to precisely the same spot on the beach where he had seen the Arab earlier? By leaving the reader no clue as to which connections are legitimate and which are misguided, *L'Etranger* gives with one hand and takes away with the other: the interpretative creativity which it allows is counterbalanced by the collapse of adequate understanding. This does not mean that the novel cannot be interpreted; on the contrary, as Adele King wryly comments, 'Is it possible to find any incident, sentence, even detail that has not been subjected to some critical analysis?'[26] But critics, conventionally and almost compulsively, accompany their readings with acknowledgements that the text escapes them. King suggests that 'every word seems fraught with meaning';[27] Showalter accepts that there are 'arbitrary assumptions and ideological biases' in his reading;[28] and Fitch refers to the 'ambiguity which, in the final analysis, the text itself does not allow one to resolve in any wholly satisfactory manner'.[29] The amount of interpretative activity which *L'Etranger* (and perhaps any text) generates seems to be in inverse proportion to the prospect of achieving critical consensus.

L'Etranger evades critical mastery whereas *La Chute* offers adequate understanding to those who will accept its narrator's interpretative authority; but each text aims to deny the reader a satisfactory position of his or her own, to reject the critical gaze of the Other which might find unexpected secrets in the text. Perhaps the best option the novels leave us with is to read the mechanisms of non-reading through which they coerce, manipulate or frustrate a reader's curiosity.

In this exclusion of the reader as Other, as a gaze which might see what the text does not wish to reveal, there is a remarkable convergence between the theme of altericide as dramatized in the texts and the murder of the reader as performed in the texts' strategies of domination and bafflement. The Other is perceived as a source of primal violence which robs the subject (or text) of its self-creating, self-sufficient freedom, reducing it to the status of an object: Clamence is classified as a 'pauvre type' (1502) (poor guy), Meursault and his companions are gazed upon 'ni plus ni moins comme [s'ils étaient] des pierres ou des arbres morts' (1161) (neither more nor less than if [they] were stones or dead trees). Camus's texts gesture towards an ethics of generosity based on the identity of subjects in a unified community; yet communities operate as much by exclusion as by inclusion, and the other face of generosity towards one's own kind is hostility towards the outsider. Society and human relations in Camus's writing are a delicate fabric of identification and violence. The victory of one football team over another, reduced to the triumphant cry 'On les a eus' (*L'Etranger*, 1141) (We beat them) represents this senseless but persistent antagonism of one group to another. The identities of the *on* (we/one) and the *les* (them) are unexplained and perhaps even unimportant; what matters is that one group has scored its victory over another. Human organization, according to Clamence, is no different from that of carnivorous fish who strip the flesh off the bones of unwary swimmers: 'c'est à qui nettoiera l'autre' (1479) (it comes down to who will clean the bones of the other). And since this endemic hostility seeps into every level of Camus's texts, defining the darker side of solidarity, Clamence's account of pervasive, often implicit aggression perhaps also foreshadows the fate awaiting the unwary reader. As Clamence, if he had turned to writing, might have said, 'L'écriture, c'est à qui nettoiera l'Autre' (Writing comes down to who will clean the bones of the Other).

5
Didacticism and the Ethics of Failure: Beauvoir

The Didactic Novel

It has long been known that the fictional and non-fictional writings of Simone de Beauvoir are preoccupied with death and more specifically with murder.[1] Her first published work, the novel *L'Invitée* (1943), ends with the murder which the epigraph from Hegel ('Chaque conscience poursuit la mort de l'autre')[2] (Each consciousness pursues the death of the other) had predicted from the very beginning. In *Tous les hommes sont mortels* (1946), Fosca kills his own son who is attempting to assassinate him.[3] *Une mort très douce* (1964) and *La Cérémonie des adieux* (1981) chart the physical decline and death of Beauvoir's mother and Sartre respectively. Moreover a number of critics (notably Jardine, Moi and Hughes) have related these deaths to a matricidal impulse through which the phallic mother (represented on occasion by Sartre) is dismembered and annihilated.[4] Patricide, filicide, matricide: these are the various figures of a more generalized altericide, a murder of the Other, in which the very act of writing becomes embroiled. Beauvoir herself indicated that writing *L'Invitée* was an equivalent or substitute for the act of murder with which the novel culminates.[5] In the words of Toril Moi, writing serves as 'a weapon against the power of the Other'.[6]

In this sequence of deaths and murders, Beauvoir's second novel, *Le Sang des autres* (1945), occupies a place of particular importance.[7] Written during the Second World War, in the course of what Beauvoir called the 'période morale' (moral period) of her literary career,[8] it attempts to place the struggle of antagonistic consciousnesses dramatized in *L'Invitée* within a framework which is more concretely historical and more tangibly ethical. Murder, in this text, is to cease being the petulant lashing out of a pained ego, enraged on discovering that others do not respect the sovereignty of its desire; instead, violence appears as a calculated political act, undertaken in full lucidity and justified – perhaps – in the context of the fight against the occupying German forces.

The ethical framework within and through which the question of violence is contained in *Le Sang des autres* is indicated from the outset by the epigraph of the novel. Hegel's 'Chaque conscience poursuit la mort de l'autre' (Each consciousness pursues the death of the other), with which *L'Invitée* began, is superseded by a quotation from Dostoyevsky's *The Brothers Karamazov*: 'Chacun est responsable de tout devant tous' (10) (Everyone is responsible for everything before everyone). On two occasions in the course of *Le Sang des autres*, the epigraph is echoed by the central male character, Jean Blomart (see 159, 242). Lifted from its Christian context,[9] it appears as the moral underpinning for an existentialist ethics. Through the conversion of all the major characters in the novel to clandestine Resistance activity at the time of the German Occupation, the violence of the embattled ego is transformed into morally justified terrorist action.

Written during the Second World War and firmly rooted in the political struggles of the 1930s and 1940s, *Le Sang des autres* has been read as a Resistance novel with didactic intent. Blanchot described the novel as a *roman à thèse* in the 1940s, and Beauvoir readily (too readily?) accepted his judgement.[10] Subsequent critics have followed this line of reading. In her study of Resistance fiction, Margaret Atack examines Beauvoir's text in the light of what she calls a 'structure of unity': antagonisms between individuals (principally the conflicts between the non-communist Blomart and the communist activist Paul, or between Blomart and his lover Hélène or his bourgeois parents, but also conflicts between other characters such as the unhappy husband and wife Marcel and Denise) are finally resolved as the characters are all subsumed into a unified Resistance group with a clearly defined primary antagonist, the Germans.[11] The final unity of the Resistance group seems to indicate a movement in the novel towards resolution and disambiguation. *Le Sang des autres* thus exemplifies what Susan Rubin Suleiman describes as the defining features of the *roman à thèse*:

[The] story told by a *roman à thèse* is essentially teleological – it is determined by a specific end, which exists 'before' and 'above' the story. The story calls for an unambiguous interpretation, which in turn implies a rule of action applicable (at least virtually) to the real life of the reader.... The only necessary condition is that the interpretation and the rule of action be unambiguous – in other words, that the story lend itself as little as possible to a 'plural' reading.[12]

Suleiman is fully aware that the 'single meaning and total closure' for which the *roman à thèse* aims[13] are out of step with much modern writing as well as the still current critical preference for ambiguities, slippages or explosions of meaning. Accordingly, *Le Sang des autres* has been criticized for its didacticism. Terry Keefe refers to the 'over-schematized or didactic treatment of certain themes', and asserts that 'criticisms that the ending itself is contrived and "closed" are difficult to dismiss';[14] and Alex Hughes refers to the '(excessively?) ethico-didactic character' of the novel.[15] Neither of these critics believes that *Le Sang des autres* is a text without ambiguity; nevertheless, they seem to share the assumption that the novel proposes a summarizable message, even if parts of the text fail to support it. The didactic intention appears to be essential to the text whereas any residual ambiguities or dissonance are somehow inessential to its design.

This is most evident in Alex Hughes's account of the novel. She asks what 'in summary' are the ethical arguments of the novel, and responds that 'In essence, there are three of them',[16] which I summarize in turn:
1 Our entanglement with the Other imposes a debt which we must accept and assume.
2 Our assumption of responsibility for the Other should not encroach upon his/her freedom, but should on the contrary entail an active commitment to the freedom of the Other.
3 Any action is morally justifiable if it combats oppression and helps establish the conditions by which others may achieve freedom.

Having thus laid out the arguments of the text, Hughes then goes on to question how convincing they might be. She gives powerful reasons to think that the novel may be more ambiguous than the above summary implies: Blomart's defence of the freedom of the Other fits uneasily with the fact that he violates the freedom of those who will be shot as a result of his decisions; and his assumption of responsibility may seem exaggerated, even pathological, rather than admirably moral.[17] Moreover, the text also offers 'hard-hitting counterarguments' (29): Hélène calls into question the defence of responsibility and solidarity; Blomart's mother refuses to endorse his actions; and other characters voice pacifist or even collaborationist arguments, implying the possibility that Resistance activity may result only in 'crimes inutiles' (248) (pointless crimes). Despite these elements, however, Hughes concludes that 'the didactic dimension of *Le Sang des autres* is unmistakable and primordial' (30). In terms which Hughes will adopt later in her study, the didacticism of the text constitutes its conscious element; any critical, self-subversive or dissenting elements are attributed to the unconscious of the text. However, this reading depends upon a prior decision concerning what is 'essential' and 'conscious' which I find highly questionable. Elements attributed by Hughes to the unconscious of the text (the motifs of bloodiness, the mother/child division, and food-as-problem; see 55–6) are heavily and explicitly present in the text and as 'conscious' as the moral aspects of the work; and the counter-arguments to ethical positions proposed by the novel are only 'inessential' if we are already confident of what those positions are.

In her study of Beauvoir's novels Elizabeth Fallaize maintains a more subtly equivocal stance; she observes the tension between didacticism and ambiguity in *Le Sang des autres* and explains it by distinguishing between Beauvoir's intention and her textual practice. Fallaize argues that the narrative structure and argument of the novel are organized 'with a much more didactic intention' than *L'Invitée*.[18] At the same time Fallaize finds in the novel a number of dissonant elements which make of it a dialogic text; and she thus concludes that its commitment to praxis and history is 'a highly ambiguous one' and 'subverted from the outset'.[19] This reading is sensitive to the historical context in which the novel was written whilst also respecting the modern critical preference for subversion and ambiguity. This preference has not, however, been shared by all Beauvoir's readers. Margaret Burrell seems to regret that the novel is not more didactic. Having set out to examine how Beauvoir 'manipulates her characters in order to present her particular moral thesis',[20] she finds that such a thesis is obscured by the constant twists and turns of the characters: 'the issues of individual and collective responsibility, and the exercise of free will, remain unresolved in the exposition of their vacillating moral stances.'[21]

The vacillating stances of Beauvoir's characters are reflected in those of her commentators: *Le Sang des autres* appears as didactic in intent yet ambiguous in achievement, or didactic yet unconvincing because of dissonant elements; and its didacticism or lack thereof can be evaluated in turn positively or negatively. In this chapter I shall suggest that the hesitations of the text and of its readers, the instability of positions, choices and evaluations, do not obscure the point of the novel; they *are* the point of the novel. And this is implied, in fact, by the very epigraph which can be taken to signal the moral seriousness of the text, Dostoyevsky's 'Chacun est responsable de tout devant tous' (Everyone is responsible for everything before everyone). This epigraph summarizes what appears to be Blomart's final ethical position; yet it is also insistently suggested in the novel that, as much as a statement of existentialist ethics, it might signal a paranoid disorder.[22] In the second allusion to the epigraph within the main text, for example, Blomart voices a self-punishing solipsistic fantasy through which he views himself as the direct cause of the war engulfing Europe:

> Les femmes et les nouveaux-nés crèvent dans les fossés. Sur ce sol qui n'est déjà plus le nôtre un immense réseau de fer s'est abattu, enserrant par millions les hommes de France. A cause de moi. Chacun est responsable de tout. (242)

> Women and new-born babies are dying in ditches. On this earth which is no longer our own, a huge network of iron has swooped down, hemming in the men of France in millions. Because of me. Everyone is responsible for everything.

In the light of such passages, it appears possible that the moral framework of the novel may after all be bound up with the same drama of wounded egos and interpersonal conflict which Beauvoir had begun to chart in *L'Invitée*. In the rest of the chapter I shall argue that this conflict, along with the violence, vacillations and self-delusions of the characters, is in fact at the centre of the novel's powerful engagement with the risks of decision-making. In the next section, a context for understanding this will be provided by Beauvoir's attempts to elaborate an existentialist ethics which presupposes and takes account of the war of consciousnesses.

An Ethics of Failure

At the end of *L'Invitée* Françoise opens a gas tap which will cause the death of her rival Xavière:

> En face de sa solitude, hors de l'espace, hors du temps, il y avait cette présence ennemie qui depuis si longtemps l'écrasait de son ombre aveugle; elle était là, n'existant que pour soi, tout entière réfléchie en elle-même, réduisant au néant tout ce qu'elle excluait; elle enfermait le monde entier dans sa propre solitude triomphante, elle s'épanouissait sans limites, infinie, unique: tout ce qu'elle était, elle le tirait d'elle-même, elle se refusait à toute emprise, elle était l'absolue séparation. Et cependant il suffisait d'abaisser ce levier pour l'anéantir. Anéantir une conscience. Comment puis-je? pensa Françoise. Mais comment se pouvait-il qu'une conscience existât qui ne fût pas la sienne? Alors, c'était elle qui n'existait pas. Elle répéta: 'Elle ou moi.' Elle abaissa le levier.[23]

> In face of her solitude, outside space, outside time, there was this hostile presence which for so long had crushed her with its blind shadow; it was there, existing only for itself, entirely reflected in itself, reducing to nothing everything that it excluded; it enclosed the entire world in its own triumphant solitude, it opened up without limits, infinite, unique: everything that it was it drew from itself, it refused all outside influence, it was absolute separation. And yet it was enough to lower this lever to annihilate it. To annihilate a consciousness. How can I? thought Françoise. But how could it be that there existed a consciousness which was not her own? In that case, it was she who did not exist. She repeated, 'Her or me'. She lowered the lever.

Published in 1943, as the Final Solution was being implemented, the gassing of Xavière has historical resonance of which Beauvoir may not have been aware. However, what is dramatized here at the level of (as Moi calls it) 'existentialist melodrama',[24] is a fundamental situation of conflict between self and Other that was being played out on a broader historical scale in the Second World War and the systematic annihilation of the Jews. Whereas the self is experienced as permeable and insecure, the Other appears as self-sufficient and firmly grounded; and this perception of the Other both reveals and exacerbates the insecurity of the self. Thus the

Other becomes a 'présence ennemie' (hostile presence), a threat and a danger to my own autonomy by its very existence. The only way out of the struggle is to destroy the Other in a violent assertion of the supremacy of the self.[25]

Both the language and the implications of this passage from Beauvoir's first novel call to mind Sartre's *L'Etre et le néant* (1943), a work dedicated to Beauvoir ('Au Castor') and published in the same year as *L'Invitée*.[26] However, the question of an existentialist ethics which Sartre so conspicuously avoided in *L'Etre et le néant* (see Chapter 1) was confronted directly by Beauvoir in two books published in the 1940s, *Pyrrhus et Cinéas* (1944) and *Pour une morale de l'ambiguïté* (1947).[27] In these books Beauvoir endeavours to open up an ethical perspective from within the conflict of consciousnesses analysed in *L'Invitée* and *L'Etre et le néant*. Rejecting all recourse to universality, absolute ends, external moral authorities or immutable moral codes, Beauvoir takes freedom and responsibility as the two essential terms of her ethics. In *Pyrrhus et Cinéas* she refers to and glosses the Dostoyevsky quotation used as the epigraph to *Le Sang des autres*:

> Je suis là, confondu pour [autrui] avec la scandaleuse existence de tout ce qui n'est pas lui, je suis la facticité de sa situation. Autrui est libre, à partir de là: à partir de là seulement; totalement libre: mais libre en face de ceci et cela, en face de moi. La fatalité qui pèse sur autrui, c'est toujours nous: la fatalité, c'est le visage figé qui tourne vers chacun la liberté de tous les autres. C'est en ce sens que Dostoïevski disait que 'chacun est responsable de tout, devant tous'. Immobile ou agissant, nous pesons toujours sur la terre; tout refus est choix, tout silence a une voix. Notre passivité même est voulue; pour ne pas choisir, il faut encore choisir de ne pas choisir; il est impossible d'échapper. (331)

> There I am, bound up for [the other] with the scandalous existence of everything that is not him, I am the facticity of his situation. The other is free, on the basis of that; only on the basis of that; totally free, but free in face of this or that, in face of me. The fatality which weighs down on the other, it is always us: fatality is the frozen face which turns to everyone the freedom of all others. It is in this sense that Dostoyevsky said that 'everyone is responsible for everything, before all'. Motionless or active, we always weigh down on the earth; all refusal is

choice, all silence speaks. Our very passivity is intended; in order not to choose, you must still choose not to choose; there is no escape.

Beauvoir describes here precisely the discovery that Blomart makes in *Le Sang des autres*: like it or not, my actions or refusals to act, my words or my silences impinge on the lives of others. Freedom only exists in concrete historical situations which are shared with others and in which, therefore, my decisions inevitably have consequences on other subjects. However, this imbrication of the self with the world of others does not lead to the possibility of consensus in political and ethical matters. Because subjects are separate and free, they will always make conflicting choices and judgements. Beauvoir maintains as an ethical imperative the necessity of respecting the freedom of others; but the darker side of her ethics emerges in the realization that unconditional respect for the freedom of all others is impossible. Serving one cause means opposing another, defending the oppressed means combatting the oppressor:

> Je ne suis instrument pour les uns qu'en devenant obstacle pour les autres.... Si je sers le prolétariat, je combats le capitalisme; le soldat ne défend son pays qu'en tuant ses adversaires. Et la classe, le pays ne se définissent comme unité que par l'unité de leur opposition à l'autre. (282-3)

> I can only be an instrument for some if I become an obstacle for others.... If I work for the proletariat, I fight capitalism; a soldier can defend his country only by killing his enemies. And class or country are only defined as unities by the unity of their opposition to the other.

Beauvoir is arguing against what she sees as the Kantian or Hegelian prospect of ultimate resolution in ethical matters. This is illustrated in *Pour une morale de l'ambiguïté* by what she calls 'les antinomies de l'action' (the antinomies of action). The Kantian antinomies present contradictory maxims (for example, aesthetic judgements are said to be based on firm criteria, and at the same time to be not susceptible to rational dispute); these maxims are then elegantly resolved as they are shown to be only apparently contradictory (aesthetic judgements are not susceptible to rational dispute because the criteria upon which they are based are unknowable).[28] The resolution of the antinomies may appear to be theoretical only, with few practical consequences. Beauvoir's antinomies, on the other hand, remain unresolved and present in a stark from the real dilemmas of judgement and action: to combat oppression, you must treat the oppressor as a means to an end (thereby transgressing one of the principles of Kantian ethics)[29] and thus oppress him or her; to achieve one end, it is necessary to neglect or even to oppose other, perhaps no less desirable, goals; and even the victims of oppression for whom we are fighting are transformed in the struggle into means to an end, and therefore further oppressed (139–43). As Beauvoir summarizes her discussion, 'aucune action ne peut se faire pour l'homme sans se faire aussitôt contre les hommes. Cette vérité évidente, universellement connue, est cependant si amère que le premier souci d'une doctrine de l'action est ordinairement de masquer cette part d'échec que comporte toute entreprise' (143–4) (no action can be undertaken for man without also being undertaken against men. This self-evident truth, known universally, is nevertheless so bitter that the first concern of a doctrine of action is normally to mask the degree of failure entailed in any undertaking).

If Sartre failed to establish an existentialist ethics, Beauvoir radicalizes his non-completion of the *Cahiers pour une morale* by making failure itself the unsurpassable horizon of moral action. The word *échec* (failure) recurs in numerous key passages of *Pyrrhus et Cinéas* and *Pour une morale de l'ambiguïté*. The error of Kant and Hegel, according to Beauvoir, lies in their desire to remove failure from ethics, either through the search for infallible maxims, or by denying the irreducible singularity of individual subjects. Beauvoir, on the other hand, focuses on the risk or wager involved in all choice (215); for her, failure is at the heart of any ethical project. *Pyrrhus et Cinéas*, written and published during the Occupation, is in part a defence of violence as a legitimate political tool; but violence also entails an ethical failure, even as it is presented as an ethical necessity:

> On ne peut donc accepter d'un coeur léger le recours à la force: il est la marque d'un échec que rien ne saurait compenser. Si les morales universelles de Kant, de Hegel s'achèvent en optimisme, c'est que, niant l'individualité, elles nient aussi l'échec. Mais l'individu est, l'échec est.... Nous sommes condamnés à l'échec parce que nous sommes condamnés à la violence; nous sommes condamnés à la violence parce que l'homme est divisé et opposé

à lui-même, parce que les hommes sont séparés et opposés entre eux: par violence on fera de l'enfant un homme, d'une horde une société.... Mais cependant aucune réussite n'effacera jamais le scandale absolu de chaque échec singulier. (363)

So one cannot accept this recourse to violence with a light heart: it is the mark of a failure for which nothing can compensate. If the universal ethics of Kant, of Hegel, conclude in optimism, this is because, denying individuality, they also deny failure. But the individual exists, failure exists.... We are condemned to failure because we are condemned to violence; we are condemned to violence because man is divided and opposed to himself, because men are separate and opposed to one another: by violence, the child will be made into a man, a horde into a society.... However, no success will ever efface the absolute scandal of each individual failure.

Existentialism, according to Beauvoir, requires a permanent, exhausting tension (220). Violence is authorized, but never definitively justified; it is permissible in circumstances which cannot be described in advance, and it always entails an element of defeat. Ends are corrupted by means, means are always impure, failure inhabits all success. The ethical turn of existentialism does not, then, overcome or resolve the antagonism between self and Other; on the contrary, it must continue to contend with the complex interaction of competing subjects, incompatible goals and unacceptable means. Beauvoir's ethics require that the moral subject is never moral enough,[30] that it lives and acts with a perpetual unease: '[L'homme] agit dans le risque, dans l'échec. Il doit assumer le risque.... Mais l'échec ne peut s'assumer' (365) ([Man] acts in risk, in failure. He must accept the risk.... But failure can not be accepted). Here there is no Sartrean *qui perd gagne* (loser wins) whereby ethical failure is transformed into success. Failure is failure, and as such the necessary condition of moral action; or, as Beauvoir bluntly puts it, 'sans échec, pas de morale' (14) (without failure, no ethics).

Violence

If, then, *Pyrrhus et Cinéas* is a defence of violence, it is at best a hesitant one. Violence may turn out retrospectively to have been justified; but by definition its perpetrators cannot know what a retrospective judgement would be at the moment of action. Existentialist morality entails risk and the real possibility of being disastrously wrong. In a passage from *Pour une morale de l'ambiguïté* Beauvoir discusses the question of Resistance violence during the Occupation. The aim of Resistance actions was not, she suggests, to weaken the German forces materially, but to produce 'un état de violence' (a state of violence) which would make collaboration impossible; the justification of this entails a difficult and precarious calculation involving ends and means: 'en un sens, c'était payer trop cher la suppression de trois officiers ennemis que de la payer par l'incendie de tout un village français; mais ces incendies, les massacres d'otages, faisaient eux-mêmes partie du plan, ils créaient un abîme entre occupants et occupés' (217)[31] (in one sense it was too high a price to pay if the killing of three enemy officers led to the burning of an entire French village; but these burnings, the massacres of hostages, were themselves part of the plan, they created a gulf between occupied and occupiers).

Precisely the same calculation is made in *Le Sang des autres* by Jean Blomart as he takes steps to establish a Resistance group. Warned by Parmentier that Resistance actions will result in reprisals, Blomart responds that this is precisely what he wants:

– Ce sont ces représailles que j'escompte, dit-il. Pour que la politique de collaboration soit impossible, pour que la France ne s'endorme pas dans la paix, il faut que le sang français coule.
– Ainsi, vous laisseriez fusiller sans remords des innocents? dit Parmentier.
– J'ai appris de cette guerre que le sang qu'on épargne est aussi inexpiable que le sang qu'on fait verser, dit Blomart.... Pensez à toutes ces vies que notre résistance sauvera peut-être.
Ils se turent longtemps.
– Mais si notre effort avorte, dit Parmentier, nous nous retrouverons chargés de crimes inutiles. (248)

– I am counting on these reprisals, he said. So that a policy of collaboration will be impossible, so that France doesn't fall asleep in peace, French blood must flow.
– So you would let innocent people be shot without remorse? said Permentier.
– I have learned that in this war the blood that one spares is as impossible to expiate as the blood that one sheds, said

Blomart.... Think of all the lives that our resistance will perhaps save.
They were silent for a long time.
– But if our efforts come to nothing, said Parmentier, we will find ourselves responsible for pointless crimes.

The dialogic nature of *Le Sang des autres* emerges very clearly here, as the text provides ample grounds for rejecting Blomart's plans: innocent people will be murdered, Blomart cannot be certain that his strategy will work, and if it does not the crimes of the Resistants will turn out to have been 'inutiles' (pointless). In the course of the novel Blomart has learned that there can be no guarantees in the domain of morality, and that action depends upon the ability to discard the desire for secure moral justification:

Il devait agir sans garantie. Compter les vies humaines, comparer le poids d'une larme au poids d'une goutte de sang, c'était une entreprise impossible, mais il n'avait plus à compter, et toute monnaie était bonne même celle-ci: le sang des autres. On ne paierait jamais trop cher. (249)

He had to act without guarantees. Counting human lives, comparing the weight of a tear to the weight of a drop of blood, was an impossible undertaking, but he no longer had to count, and all currency was good even this one: the blood of others. The price would never be too high.

At the end of *Le Sang des autres* a number of disparate characters have joined or support the Resistance group: Blomart, who earlier in the novel had rejected all political violence; the previously apolitical Hélène; the communist Paul; the troubled artist Marcel and his unhappy wife Denise; even Blomart's father, the representative of bourgeois capitalist conservatism, lends support. This movement towards unification has been taken as indicating at the level of structure the didactic intent of the novel, and moreover as an inscription in the text of the dominant Gaullist myth of Resistance as commanding broad public support.[32] In effect, the dialogic element of the novel is suppressed in favour of an unequivocal commitment to Resistance violence. I would suggest, however, that part of the power of the conclusion of the novel, and of the unease to which it gives rise, derives from the fact that resolution or moral serenity have not (yet) been achieved. The title of André Malraux's *L'Espoir* (1937), written and published before the end of the Spanish Civil War, turned out to be cruelly ironic, as the hope that it expresses for a Republican victory proved to be unjustified. Similarly, *Le Sang des autres* ends with the war still being fought, and thus with its conclusion still uncertain. Hélène is dead, and after a night's agonizing Blomart authorizes another mission which may cause more blood to be shed pointlessly. The moral risks taken by Blomart and his companions may yet turn out to serve no positive purpose.

A further, perhaps more damaging factor brings into question the justification of violence in *Le Sang des autres*. Beauvoir's second novel attempts to place violence within a moral framework which had been absent from the depiction of murder in *L'Invitée*; but Elizabeth Fallaize implies that the second novel may not be fundamentally different from the first: 'The sacrifice of the main female character on the altar of the political and moral education of the male hero means that the woman – the "Other" – is again destroyed in this text, as Xavière is destroyed in [*L'Invitée*], this time in the interests of commitment.'[33] Different interests, same result. Are Blomart's altericidal instincts ultimately any more 'moral' than those of Françoise in *L'Invitée*? Most readers and commentators are struck by his excessive sense of responsibility for the suffering of others; perhaps through that excess it is possible to see that dread of the death of the Other is only a short step from desire for it.[34] As Blomart awaits the death of Hélène, he utters the phrase: '*je t'ai tuée pour rien*' (250, 281) (I killed you for nothing); although not literally true, his words may express a fundamental truth at the level of desire.

This reading of Blomart's altericidal inclinations entirely concords with his endeavour throughout *Le Sang des autres* to exclude the threat of the Other from the fragile citadel of his own consciousness. One of the respects in which Hélène is a radically more positive character than him is that she is perpetually open to the desire of the Other (in active and passive senses) in a way that he is not. Blomart, on the contrary, is terrified of permeability to alterity, of influencing and being influenced by others. Whereas for Hélène the self is permanently in question ('Moi. Qui? Quelqu'un qui dit moi,' 69) (Me. Who? Someone who says me), Blomart wards off insecurity by adopting an air of immovable solidity ('Mais comme il avait l'air sûr de lui!' 66) (But how he seemed sure of himself).

He aspires to be 'rien qu'un homme, un homme vrai et sans tache, ne dépendant que de soi-même' (32) (nothing but a man, a true and stainless man, depending only on himself). In his relationship with Madeleine, as he admits, he gives little of himself (89), aiming instead to achieve a flawless self-containment: 'Je ne me sentais responsable que de moi-même, et c'est une responsabilité que j'assumais dans la paix; j'étais ce que je désirais être, ma vie ne se distinguait pas du dessein concerté que j'en formais' (90). (I felt responsible only for myself, and it was a responsibility that I accepted calmly; I was what I wanted to be, my life was entirely identified with the plan that I devised for it). To Hélène at least, he seems to be 'sans désir, sans besoin; il ne dépendait de personne, ni de rien, fût-ce de son propre corps' (116) (without desire, without need; he didn't depend on anyone or anything, even his own body); he appears to be 'vraiment lui-même' (truly himself), existing 'dans son absolue vérité' (117) (in his absolute truth), self-sufficient and self-created (137).

Even Blomart's syndicalist fantasies of solidarity and fraternity are commanded by a strict preservation of subjective autonomy: 'Depuis des années j'avais lutté patiemment pour en arriver là: à l'affirmation de cette solidarité sereine où chacun puisait chez les autres la force d'imposer sa propre volonté, sans empiéter sur la liberté de personne et tout en demeurant responsable de soi' (76) (For years I had struggled patiently to reach this point: the affirmation of that serene solidarity in which each drew from the others the power to impose his own will, without infringing the freedom of anyone, and whilst remaining responsible for oneself). It is important to distinguish carefully here between this desire for solidarity with *les autres* (others) and a readiness to embrace alterity; in Blomart's utopian vision, *les autres* turn out not to be Other at all, but merely representatives of a single unified humanity:

> Bientôt la guerre, la violence, l'arbitraire, deviendraient impossibles; la politique même serait inutile, car il n'y aurait plus de séparation entre les hommes, mais une seule humanité. C'était là l'espoir suprême qu'ils saluaient au fond de l'avenir: la réconciliation de tous les hommes dans la libre reconnaissance de leur liberté. (87)

> Soon war, violence, arbitrariness, would become impossible; even politics would be pointless, since there would no longer be

separation between men, but one single humanity. That was the supreme hope that they hailed in the distant future: the reconciliation of all men in the free recognition of their freedom.

This vision does not, then, entail the recognition and acceptance of alterity, but rather its total elimination. Women are evidently excluded from the unified world of *les hommes* (men), as is indicated by Madeleine's rather cool response to Blomart's speech: 'Je te voyais là-bas qui t'agitais' (88) (I saw you over there getting agitated). Moreover, a critical distance towards Blomart's words is also implied by the italicized passage which precedes it, suggesting a quite different view of alterity as inexpungible from human relations: '*chacun soi seulement pour soi, existant à côté des autres à jamais séparé d'eux: un autre*' (87) (everyone himself only for himself, existing alongside others forever separated from them: an other).

Despite his description of Hélène as 'une sale petite égoïste' (97) (a dirty little egoist), the novel clearly portrays Blomart as the character most powerfully motivated by the drama of the would-be solipsistic ego; aiming to establish itself as self-created and self-legislating, the ego is at the same time terrified of a loss of autonomy through the encounter with alterity. *Le Sang des autres* narrates Blomart's successive failures to maintain this transcendental detachment; and he responds to his loss of control with literal or imaginary violence. Most notably, his sense of responsibility for the death of Hélène is preceded by his desire to kill her when she causes him, against his will, to be removed from the front line after the outbreak of the war: 'j'aurais voulu serrer mes mains autour de son cou jusqu'à ce qu'il n'y ait plus *rien* entre mes mains.... J'avais pensé à la battre, à l'étrangler' (235-6) (I felt like squeezing my hands around her neck until there was no longer *anything* between my hands.... I thought of beating her, strangling her).

The recourse to violence, here only imaginary, becomes real when Blomart forms a Resistance group. But the parallel between the public and the private is instructive: the Occupation is another context in which Blomart loses control and resorts to violence in order to reassert mastery. This is one example of the important emphasis throughout *Le Sang des autres* on the direct connections between public and private domains, and on the way the nexus of choice and consequence operates in both. Blomart discovers that his initial refusal to get involved in the life of Hélène is itself a form of involvement; inaction is a choice with real consequences. Precisely the same principle is illustrated at a political level later in the novel when Blomart and his companions choose not to intervene in the Spanish Civil War or in the German *Anschluss* with Austria; their failure to act, while maintaining their illusion of control, positively contributes to events which they had wanted to avoid.

This consistent parallel between public and private is illustrated in the language of enmity and struggle. As the war approaches and Blomart prepares to fight the enemies of France, he discovers that Hélène has also become 'presque une ennemie' (207) (almost an enemy). Later, as she attempts to persuade Blomart to accept a posting away from the front line, she refuses to see the war in terms of altruistic struggle:

> – Il ne s'agit pas de nous, dit Jean.
> – Si, dit Hélène. Ses mains se crispèrent sur le tapis de la table: C'est toujours pour soi qu'on lutte.
> – Hélène! il ne devrait pas être question de lutte entre nous.
> – Moi, je ferais n'importe quoi pour toi, dit-elle avec haine. Je volerais, j'assassinerais, je trahirais...
> – Mais tu n'est pas capable d'accepter le risque de ma mort!
> – Non, dit Hélène. Non. Tu n'obtiendras pas ça de moi. Tu vois bien que nous sommes en lutte. (227–8)

> – It's not a question of us, said Jean.
> – Yes it is, said Hélène. Her hands tightened on the table cloth: It's always for oneself that one fights.
> – Hélène! It shouldn't be a question of fighting between us.
> – I would do anything for you, she said with hatred. I would steal, I would kill, I would betray...
> – But you are not capable of accepting the risk of my death!
> – No, said Hélène. No. You won't get that from me. You can see that we really are fighting.

Later, Blomart tells Hélène, 'Tu m'as traité en ennemi' (237) (You treated me like an enemy). Against the background of the onset of the Second World War, this language acquires added significance. Shortly after the encounter when Blomart and Hélène realize that 'nous sommes en lutte' (we are fighting), the word *lutte* (fight, struggle) takes its place as a positively valorized term in an ethic of humanist Resistance:

102 *Ethical Issues in French Fiction*

> Mais il savait que tout arrive par les hommes et que chacun est tout un homme. L'un après l'autre, il alla trouver ses camarades. Nous ne sommes pas seuls si nous nous unissons, disait-il. Nous ne sommes pas vaincus si nous luttons. Tant que nous serons là il y aura des hommes. Il parlait, et ses camarades allaient trouver d'autres camarades et parlaient. Et déjà parce qu'ils parlaient, ils étaient unis, ils étaient en lutte, les hommes n'étaient pas vaincus. (246)

> But he knew that everything happens through men and that everyone is a complete man. One after the other, he went and found his comrades. We are not alone if we unite, he would say. We are not defeated if we fight. As long as we are there, there will still be men. He spoke, and his comrades went and found other comrades and spoke. And already as they spoke they were united, they were fighting, men were not defeated.

Hélène and Blomart are *en lutte* (fighting) with one another just as the Resistants and the Germans are. The political mirrors the private; and this mirroring may weaken any attempt to establish a reliable moral distinction between the struggles of individuals and those between political or national groups. The war appears as a larger version of the battle for dominance between subjects; the rivalry of nations may only extend the rivalry of consciousnesses onto a different scale. And if this is the case, the shadow which accompanies the ethical 'didacticism' of *Le Sang des autres*, the risk which must be taken as the price of effective action, is that the Resistance activity of Blomart and his companions may be no more moral or justified than the murder of Xavière in *L'Invitée*.

We return, then, to the basic tension of Beauvoir's ethics: violence may seem necessary, but we can never know that it is right. Moreover, even the most morally high-minded actions may be motivated by the altericidal impulses of an endangered ego. This would explain the curious pleasure that Blomart experiences at the prospect of killing enemy soldiers;[35] in the context of war, a normally submerged desire to destroy the Other is unleashed, made compulsory even, so that it can be indulged without guilt:

> Les belles vacances![36] Voilà qu'il était seul, comme dans les prairies de son enfance où les pommes craquaient sans remords sous

Didacticism and the Ethics of Failure 103

la dent et tout était permis: il pouvait sans danger s'étirer, se vautrer, prendre, briser; ses gestes ne menaçaient plus personne; il n'y avait plus personne en face de lui; les hommes n'étaient que des instruments, ou des obstacles, ou un décor, et toutes les voix s'étaient tues, les voix chuchotantes, les voix menaçantes, les voix de l'inquiétude et du remords.... Tranquillement, comme on craque une pomme, il lançait les grenades, il déchargeait son fusil. Les canons tiraient sur les chars et sur les camions blindés; lui, son travail c'était de tirer sur les hommes.... 'C'est moi', pensa-t-il un jour avec stupeur, couché à la lisière d'un bois, avec un fusil mitrailleur entre les mains; et il eut envie de rire; là-bas, au milieu du champ labouré, des hommes tombaient sous les balles et son coeur était léger. 'C'est moi qui les tue.' Même cela était permis. Parce qu'il savait ce qu'il voulait. (240–1)

What fine holidays! He was alone, as in the fields of his childhood in which apples crunched without remorse as you bit them and everything was allowed: without danger, he could stretch out, wallow, take, break; his actions no longer threatened anyone; there was no longer anyone facing him; men were only instruments, or obstacles, or a stage set, and all the voices had gone silent, the whispering voices, the threatening voices, the voices of anguish or remorse. Calmly, as when one crunches an apple, he threw grenades, he fired his rifle. Cannons fired on tanks and armoured trucks; his job was to fire on men.... 'It's me,' he thought one day in astonishment, lying at the edge of a wood with a machine gun in his hands; and he wanted to laugh; over there, in the middle of a ploughed field, men fell under the bullets and his heart was light. 'It's me who is killing them.' Even that was allowed. Because he knew what he wanted.

The war provides the suspension of normal constraints which makes forbidden actions possible. Freed from his qualms about responsibility, Blomart can now regard the Other as pure matter ('tout était également matière,' 240) (everything was matter to an equal extent), an instrument to be used or an obstacle to be destroyed. War, it is implied, may be no more than the extraordinary circumstance which temporarily authorizes free expression of a conflict at the core of human relations.

Reading and the Struggle for Meaning

When Blomart is asked to comment on Denise's novel, he criticizes it for being too directive, for example in relation to her characters: '– Vous dites ce qu'il faut penser d'eux' (183) (You say what it is people should think of them). Commentators have observed that Blomart's criticisms are applicable to *Le Sang des autres* itself, and this would be one of the elements that made of it a didactic novel. The imposition on the reader of the author's conclusions is, according to Susan Rubin Suleiman, a distinguishing feature of didactic fiction. Perhaps the most important trait of *romans à thèse*, she suggests, is that they 'formulate, in an insistent, consistent, and unambiguous manner, the thesis (or theses) they seek to illustrate'; ambiguity is eliminated, and the 'correct interpretation' must be inscribed in such a way that there is no mistaking it; Suleiman insists that the *roman à thèse* 'appeals to the need for certainty, stability, and unity that is one of the elements of the human psyche; it affirms absolute truths, absolute values.'[37]

If Suleiman is correct, then *Le Sang des autres* cannot be a *roman à thèse* in any straightforward sense.[38] The 'certainty', 'stability', 'unity', 'absolute truths' and 'absolute values' of which Suleiman speaks are precisely what Beauvoir's novel eschews at every stage. It is, for example, of crucial importance that Blomart's mother dissents from Resistance violence by appealing to Blomart's own fundamental ethical maxim, respect for the freedom of the Other: 'Mais ces hommes-là [victims of reprisals] ne voulaient pas mourir, on ne les a pas consultés. Sa voix s'étrangla: On n'a pas le droit, c'est un assassinat' (293) (But those men did not want to die, they weren't consulted. Her voice became strangled: You don't have the right, it's murder). The novel's most dominant and apparently self-assured voice, that of Blomart, is insistently divested of its authority by his inconsistencies, his pathological terror of alterity, his disabling sense of guilt and his infantile desire for moral purity. Moreover, to see what Atack calls the 'structure of unity' of the novel as leading to the resolution of conflicts through an unambiguous embracing of Resistance violence entails a fundamental misunderstanding of the ethics of the novel. To ascribe certainty or lack of ambiguity to Blomart's final decision to continue the path of violence misses the point: namely, that ethics is the domain of risk not knowledge. Therefore, the possibility of interpreting his decision as wrong (as his mother does), or of finding it historically futile (as might have been the case if the war had ended differently) is essential to the tension of the final pages of the text. If there is didacticism in *Les Sang des autres*, it is tense, anguished, and constitutively unsure about its own message.

This has important consequences for the place of the reader in Beauvoir's novel. In the *roman à thèse*, according to Suleiman, the role of readers is strongly 'programmed'.[39] Rather than being invited to form their own views, readers are subjected to a higher authority which presents them with a knowledge in which they will be confirmed (if they already share it) or of which they are to be persuaded (if they initially dissent). This entails an 'infantilization'[40] of readers which, in existentialist terms, would be tantamount to a gross violation of freedom; yet in *Le Sang des autres* such violation is conceived as an essential moment in the process of art, even if freedom is violated in order to be restored. This is expressly formulated when Marcel explains his return to art:

> Je voulais que mon tableau existe tout seul, sans avoir besoin de personne. Pour de vrai, ce sont les autres qui le font exister. Mais c'est passionnant au contraire. Parce que c'est moi qui les force à le faire exister. Il eut un sourire mystérieux et un peu cruel: Comprends-tu? ils sont libres, et moi je viens et je viole leur liberté; je la viole en la laissant libre. (287)

> I wanted my picture to exist all alone, without needing anyone. In fact, it is others who make it exist. But that turns out to be exciting. Because it is me who forces them to make it exist. He smiled in a mysterious and slightly cruel way: Do you understand? They are free, and I come along and violate their freedom; I violate it whilst leaving it free.

What is most striking here is that this conception of art has direct parallels with Blomart's anxious engagement with the world of others. Like Marcel's paintings, Blomart aims to be 'tout seul, sans avoir besoin de personne' (all alone, without needing anyone); but he also learns to recognize his own imbrication in the lives of others. And this leads to his later, unresolved attempts to hold together the conflict between an impulse towards violence (the Other as enemy, invading my freedom) and the imperative of justice (the Other as ally, whose freedom must be respected). The situation becomes ethically convoluted when it is only through violence that justice can be achieved, yet justice is destroyed through violence. Marcel's hope of perpetrating through art a violence which leaves freedom intact ('je viole leur liberté; je la viole en la laissant libre') (I violate their freedom; I violate it whilst leaving it free) does not represent a realized goal so much as the fantasy of an impossible synthesis between competing forces. Their resolution would entail an ethical clarity and an easy conscience which neither Blomart nor the text in which he appears are able to attain.

The hesitations and moral quandaries that are the themes of *Le Sang des autres* are consistently represented at a textual level by the confusions and ambiguities with which the reader is confronted. The reader may be infantilized or patronized, told what to think and how to respond; but these aspects of the text are also shown to be unpersuasively authoritarian, the main mouthpiece of authority (Blomart) being revealed as pompous, self-important, inconsistent and misogynist, avoiding at all costs a self-endangering and self-transforming encounter with the Other. The novel's didactic element, its search to attain moral clarity, is in tension with a residue of self-questioning ambiguity. The resulting instability within the text is reproduced in the shifting position of the narrative voice. One of the most common (though not obligatory) features of the *roman à thèse*, according to Suleiman, is a narrator 'who "speaks with the voice of Truth" and can therefore lay claim to absolute authority'.[41] Such a narrator is entirely absent from Beauvoir's novel. Instead, the text (in the chapters centring on Blomart) displays a disorienting instability in its switches between first- and third-person narrators; and the novel as a whole oscillates between the viewpoints of Blomart and Hélène, and between different time scales.[42] We are successively and simultaneously told what to think, warned that we were wrong to think it, and enjoined to form our own views. In other words, Beauvoir's novel displays the same ambivalences towards the Other (the role here occupied by the reader) as do Marcel and Blomart. The reader's freedom of response is respected and maintained through the ambiguities of the narrative, as it is manipulated, cajoled and violated through the converging moral evolution of the various Resistants; the reader is addressed by the text on equal terms, treated as an ally, but also as a potentially hostile gaze, which might refuse to follow where the text wishes to lead. The ethical tension of the text (When can violence serve the purposes of justice?) is thus mirrored in the struggle for meaning, as the text offers and withholds hermeneutic security, relaying to the reader the anxiety of a choice which must and cannot be made.

The traces of this struggle for meaning can be seen in the critical responses to *Le Sang des autres* with which this chapter began. Beauvoir's novel has been portrayed as having a moral and philosophical message to impart, but failing to be persuasive because that message is not imparted with sufficient clarity; it subscribes to the Gaullist version of Resistance activity, though it may also subvert it;[43] its 'main intentions' are 'ethical and philosophical',[44] yet it fails to fulfil those intentions in a persuasive or unambiguous manner; it is 'unsettling in its complexity',[45] yet also excessively didactic; its philosophical aspects have the potential 'to alienate and irritate the reader',[46] whilst (or perhaps because) its ideas turn out to be 'strangely elusive'.[47] For some readers, the novel seems to arouse hostility both for being didactic and for preserving ambiguities which detract from its alleged didactic message.

Suleiman has suggested that the *roman à thèse* is 'a form of terrorism' in that it seeks to impose a single authoritarian reading.[48] I would suggest that *Le Sang des autres* is a terroristic text in a rather different sense, precisely in the way that the protagonists of the novel themselves become terrorists. They do not expect or get universal assent to their actions; they provoke as much opposition as agreement. But what they ensure is that no one is dispensed from making decisions and taking sides. Their violence exemplifies and exposes the failure and risk at the core of any ambitious ethical project. Failure permeates the novel at all levels, in the ethical failure represented by the necessity of violence, in the repeated failures of characters to find happiness or moral purity, and in the failure of even the most attentive readers to resolve the text's tensions between assertion and ambiguity. *Le Sang des autres* portrays the struggle of competing consciousnesses as the unsurpassable horizon of ethical decision-making and aesthetic practice. The acknowledgement of conflict lies behind Beauvoir's bold acceptance of failure as fundamental to ethics, and it informs the tense, violent, respectful, compliant and resisting moments which constitute reading relations.

6
Humanism and its Others: Sartre, Heidegger, Yourcenar

The Limits of Man

On 28 October 1945 Sartre held a public lecture in which, drawing support from the thought of Heidegger, he famously announced that 'l'existentialisme est un humanisme' (existentialism is a humanism).[1] A year later Heidegger addressed what became known as his *Lettre sur l'humanisme* to Jean Beaufret and the French philosophical world in general; in that letter Heidegger repudiated both existentialism and humanism as being rooted in precisely the patterns of thought which his own work aimed to destroy. However, Heidegger does not reject the term *humanism* outright, even if he appears unsure about continuing to use it; he argues that a proper understanding of the human (that is, his own understanding of it) may constitute what could be called a humanism, albeit a humanism 'd'une étrange sorte' (119) (of a strange kind). As one commentator puts it, Heidegger's use of the word *humanism* 'has nothing other than the name in common with the term as used in the Western intellectual tradition.'[2]

It came as a surprise – and a disappointment – to some that thinkers of the calibre of Sartre and Heidegger should appropriate a term which the main thrust of their work seemed to repudiate.[3] Julien Benda's diatribe against contemporary intellectual trends in *La Trahison des clercs* (1927) powerfully associated humanism with conservative intellectual elitism. Benda distinguishes between two forms of humanitarianism, one which focuses on the abstract quality of what it means to be human, and one which entails love for actual human beings; he defends the first at the expense of the second:

Le premier de ces movements (qu'on nommerait plus justement l'humanisme) est l'attachement à un concept; il est une pure passion de l'intelligence, n'impliquant aucun amour terrestre; on conçoit fort bien un être s'abîmant dans le concept de ce qui est humain, et n'ayant pas le moindre désir de seulement voir un homme; il est la forme que revêt l'amour de l'humanité chez les grands patriciens de l'esprit, chez un Erasme, un Malebranche, un Spinoza, un Goethe, tous gens peu impatients, semble-t-il, de se jeter dans les bras de leur prochain.[4]

The first of these movements (which might more properly be called humanism) is the attachment to a concept; it is a pure passion of the intelligence, implying no earthly love; it is easy enough to conceive of a being immersed in the concept of what is human, and not having the slightest desire even to see anyone else/a man; this is the form that the love of humanity takes for the great patricians of the mind, for someone like Erasmus, Malebranche, Spinoza, Goethe, all people who are scarcely impatient, it seems, to throw themselves into the arms of their neighbour.

This humanism is the only one which makes it possible, according to Benda, to love all men; but it does not imply or require love for anyone in particular.[5] In his pre-war novel *La Nausée*, Sartre had poured ridicule on such abstract humanism; and in their major philosophical works both Sartre and Heidegger tend to avoid referring to Man as such, with all the attendant risks of falling into essentialism, preferring instead to talk respectively in terms of consciousness or *Dasein*.

In the 1940s, however, it was as difficult not to be a humanist as it would be unfashionable in the late 1960s (after Foucault had famously announced the imminent end of Man) to be one.[6] The particular tonality of mid-century French humanism derived from partial readings of the so-called three Hs (Hegel, Husserl and Heidegger). In a series of extraordinarily influential lectures delivered in the 1930s, Alexandre Kojève promoted a reading of Hegel in which Man[7] (rather than Spirit) was the centre of attention. Husserl and Heidegger had been subjected to equally anthropomorphic interpretations. The transcendental dimension of Husserl's thought was neglected in favour of his more concrete phenomenology; and Heidegger was read less for his analysis of Being than for the aspects of his work which constituted a philosophical anthropology focussed on human beings.[8] This latter reading was encouraged by Corbin's controversial mistranslation of Heidegger's *Dasein* by *réalité-humaine* (human-reality),[9] a translation accepted and adopted by many thinkers of the period including Sartre. The three Hs, then, were enlisted as allies in a philosophical enquiry into the nature and limits of Man. As Derrida puts it in an overview of postwar French humanism, 'la lecture anthropologique de Hegel, de Husserl et de Heidegger était un contresens, le plus grave peut-être' (the anthropological reading of Hegel, Husserl and Heidegger was a nonsense, the most serious of all perhaps); but he adds, 'C'est cette lecture qui fournissait ses meilleures ressources conceptuelles à la pensée française d'après-guerre' (It is this reading which provided postwar French thought with its best conceptual resources).[10]

Heidegger was rapidly becoming one of the most prestigious philosophical reference points of the day, being the only one of the three Hs still alive and able to intervene in the reception of his work;[11] and both he and Sartre had good reasons to present their work in a humanist light. Sartre had been politicized by his experiences during the war, and was concerned to dissociate himself from the morally anarchic individualism of some of his pre-war writing; Heidegger, still in disgrace in Germany because of his association with Nazism in the 1930s, was becoming increasingly influential as a thinker in France, and he was keen to present a view of his work as morally untainted.[12] Humanism thus provided a convenient label for both Sartre and Heidegger, even if they maintained the right to define the term pretty much as they wished.

In terms of contemporary debate, then, Sartrean existentialism could hardly be anything other than a humanism. Man is placed at the centre, indeed he is established as the sole value, in a discourse of which the key words are action, choice, self-creation, responsibility. But who is Man? Or, more pertinently in the context of this chapter, who isn't Man, who or what is excluded under the general category of Man? My hypothesis here is that humanism may effectively be defined by what it omits or suppresses as much as by what it includes and celebrates. At a theoretical level, this will be sketched initially through the accounts of humanism offered by Sartre and Heidegger; then I shall look more directly at patterns of exclusion as they can be found in an apparently exemplary work of humanist fiction from the postwar period, Marguerite Yourcenar's *Mémoires d'Hadrien*.

Towards the end of *L'Existentialisme est un humanisme* Sartre acknowledges that in his pre-war novel *La Nausée* he had allowed his protagonist ruthlessly to mock humanism;[13] yet now he is reclaiming the battered term for his own philosophy. Following one of the standard moves in the recuperation of humanism (one which will be reproduced a year later in Heidegger's *Lettre sur l'humanisme*), Sartre defends his own position by distinguishing between different senses of the word: 'En réalité, le mot humanisme a deux sens très différents' (90) (In reality, the word humanism has two very different meanings). The first form of humanism celebrates Man's highest achievements; the value of the species is founded solely on the actions of its finest representatives: 'Par humanisme on peut entendre une théorie qui prend l'homme comme fin et comme valeur supérieure' (90) (By humanism you might mean a theory which takes man as an end and as a higher value). Sartre dismisses this cult of human excellence as absurd and potentially fascist. Instead, he endorses a second sense of humanism which avoids essentialism and implies no fixed, external judgement on mankind: 'l'homme est constamment hors de lui-même, c'est en se projetant et en se perdant hors de lui qu'il fait exister l'homme' (92) (man is constantly outside himself, it is by projecting himself and losing himself outside himself that he makes man exist). In this 'humanisme existentialiste' (93) (existentialist humanism) Man is his own legislator in an entirely human world, seeking liberation and self-realization outside himself; the human is thus not an essence, but something to be created and constantly recreated.

There is for Sartre nothing beyond the contingent world of human subjectivity; and rather than giving rise to pessimism and moral anarchy, this is the foundation of Man's moral worth. Our actions, projects and decisions create an image of Man as we want him to be: 'Ainsi, notre responsabilité est beaucoup plus grande que nous ne pourrions le supposer, car elle engage l'humanité entière.... Ainsi je suis responsable pour moi-même et pour tous, et je crée une certaine image de l'homme que je choisis; en me choisissant, je choisis l'homme' (26, 27) (Thus our responsibility is much greater than we might suppose, since it engages all humanity.... Thus I am responsible for myself and for everyone, and I create a certain image of man which I choose; in choosing myself, I choose man). Sartre's formulations here are surprisingly Kantian, echoing Kant's 'Fundamental Law of Pure Practical Reason', the categorical imperative: 'So act that the maxim of your will could always hold at the same time as a principle establishing universal law.'[14] Even so, the similarities are only superficial. Kant's categorical imperative is founded on the universality of reason: 'the rule is objectively and universally valid only when it holds without any contingent subjective conditions which differentiate one rational being from another';[15] and the moral law is 'a law for all rational beings in so far as they have a will'.[16] Without causality other than reason itself and thus comprising a freely accepted obligation for all rational subjects, the moral law should be objective and universal. Sartre's references to choices determining 'l'humanité entière' (all humanity) have no such aspirations for universality or definitive validity. Each choice engages the whole of humanity, but the whole is never finally totalized; rather than achieving a fixed essence, Man is created and recreated through an open-ended series of complex and contradictory manifestations.

Sartre's foundation of humanism on a definition of Man as self-exceeding ('l'homme est constamment hors de lui-même', 92) (man is constantly outside himself) constitutes anything other than a gesture of exclusion. The human world is the only one that we can experience, and nothing that can be experienced is rejected as non-human. Something is nevertheless lost in this generous all-inclusiveness. In the existentialist cogito, the Other is discovered at the same time as the self (66); yet the Other is subsumed in a redefined universality consisting of subjects who are all comprehensible to one another, in principle at least:

> Tout projet, même celui du Chinois, de l'Indien ou du nègre, peut être compris par un Européen. Il peut être compris, cela veut dire que l'Européen de 1945 peut se jeter à partir d'une situation qu'il conçoit vers ses limites de la même manière, et qu'il peut refaire en lui le projet du Chinois, de l'Indien ou de l'Africain. Il y a universalité de tout projet en ce sens que tout projet est compréhensible pour tout homme.... Il y a toujours une manière de comprendre l'idiot, l'enfant, le primitif ou l'étranger, pourvu qu'on ait les renseignements suffisants. (69–70)

> Any project, even that of a Chinese man, an Indian or a Negro, can be understood by a European. It can be understood, which means that, taking as his starting point a situation of which he can conceive, the European of 1945 can cast himself to his lim-

its in the same way, and that he can remake in himself the project of the Chinese man, the Indian or the African. Any project has universality in the sense that any project is comprehensible for any man.... There is always a way of understanding the idiot, the child, the primitive, the foreigner, provided that you have sufficient information.

Only women and Jews seem to be omitted from the otherwise comprehensive litany of Others (the Chinaman, the Indian, the African, the idiot, the child, the primitive, the stranger) which are implicitly contrasted with the true subject of experience, the adult white European male. These Others, however, can harbour no irreducible kernel of strangeness, since they all participate in the universality of Man.

Sartre's lecture illustrates one of the fundamental dilemmas which have exercised French humanist thought since the Enlightenment: how to avoid the Scylla of racism (foreigners are *different* from us) without falling prey to the Charybdis of taking one's own position as the universal measure of mankind (foreigners are *the same* as us).[17] Sartre denies that humanity has a fixed essence or nature, but maintains the prospect of a redefined universality through the insistence that all human projects are theoretically intelligible to all humans.

In his *Lettre sur l'humanisme*, which is in part a riposte to Sartre's assimilation of his thought to existentialism and humanism, Heidegger sets out to respond to the question (put to him by Beaufret): 'Comment redonner un sens au mot "humanisme"?' (33) (How might one restore some meaning to the word 'humanism').[18] Whatever the answer to this may be, in Heidegger's view Sartre has certainly not found it. Sartre's reversal of the traditional priority of essence over existence (so that 'l'existence précède l'essence' *L'Existentialisme est un humanisme*, 17, quoted in *Lettre sur l'humanisme*, 69) (existence precedes essence) remains dependent upon the scheme it overturns. Sartre's existentialist humanism merely replicates the misdirection of thought characteristic of metaphysics: 'Tout humanisme se fonde sur une métaphysique ou s'en fait lui-même le fondement' (51) (All humanism is founded on metaphysics or makes itself the foundation of it). Metaphysics, which in Heidegger's use of the term seems to encompass nearly all thought from Plato to the present day, endeavours to determine the essence of Man without regard to his relationship to Being. Its whole conceptual framework, including terms such as existence, essence, ethics, ontology, is implicated in the forgetting of Being which Heidegger seeks to overcome.

One of the steps in Heidegger's uncovering of the problem entails an analysis of the historical formation of philosophical terms. Heidegger finds the origins of metaphysical humanism in Republican Rome and the translation of the Greek *paideia* by the Latin *humanitas*. The key issue in this conception of humanity is to distinguish between the human and the inhuman, Man and the Barbarian: 'L'homo humanus s'oppose à l'homo barbarus' (47) (Homo humanus is opposed to homo barbarus).[19] The error of metaphysics, and more specifically of all variants of humanism since the Romans, is to define the human by designating man as an *animal rationale*, an animal capable of thought. By posing the question of Man's essence in terms of inherent qualities, metaphysics fails to think the question of Being itself, of Being (*das Sein, l'être*) as distinct from beings (*das Seiende, l'étant*). Once this question is posed correctly, Heidegger believes that our view of Man will be radically transformed, and the anthropological reading of his thought can be repudiated: Man is characterized by his relationship to Being rather than through a nature, essence or social organization; he is the shepherd of Being who watches over its Truth (77). Man's true dignity is finally realized, and he is revealed as more than and different from an *animal rationale*. Heidegger proclaims that his definition of the human is 'plus originel, et par le fait plus essentiel dans l'essence [*im Wesen wesentlicher*]' (109) (More original, and by this fact more essential in its essence).

In some respects this account of Man represents a radical transformation of the metaphysical scheme, though in others not so much seems to have changed. Heidegger is anxious that his endeavour to question humanism and its values should not taken as an endorsement of the values of barbarism:

> Parce que cette pensée est contre 'l'humanisme', on craint une défense de l'in-humain et une glorification de la brutalité barbare [*eine Verherrlichung der barbarischen Brutalität*]. Car quoi de plus 'logique' que ceci, à savoir qu'il ne reste à quiconque désavoue l'humanisme d'autre issue que d'avouer la barbarie [*Unmenschlichkeit*]? (121)

> Because this thought is against 'humanism', people fear that it is a defence of the in-human and a glorification of barbarian

brutality. For what could be more 'logical' than this, namely that anyone who rejects humanism has no other option than to embrace barbarism?

In order to avoid the charge of barbarism, Heidegger is keen to emphasize that, if he is not a humanist in a traditional sense, neither is it true to say that he is simply opposed to humanism. In a move that would be adopted by Heidegger's poststructuralist admirers, Heidegger both rejects and retains the term *humanist*:[20]

> L'unique propos est bien plutôt que les plus hautes déterminations humanistes de l'essence de l'homme n'expérimentent pas encore la dignité propre de l'homme. En ce sens, la pensée qui s'exprime dans *Sein und Zeit* est contre l'humanisme. Mais cette opposition ne signifie pas qu'une telle pensée s'oriente à l'opposé de l'humain, plaide pour l'inhumain, défende la barbarie [*die Unmenschlichkeit*] et rabaisse la dignité de l'homme. Si l'on pense contre l'humanisme, c'est parce que l'humanisme ne situe pas assez haut l'humanitas de l'homme. (75)

> My sole aim is rather to show that the highest humanist determinations of the essence of man do not yet test the dignity proper to man. In this sense the thought which is expressed in *Sein und Zeit* is against humanism. But this opposition does not mean that such thought is directed against the human, that it speaks on behalf of the inhuman, that it defends barbarianism and belittles the dignity of man. If one thinks against humanism, it is because humanism does not place the humanitas of man high enough.

Heidegger's thought thus turns out to be a more radical, more fundamental humanism, 'un "humanisme" qui pense l'humanité de l'homme à partir de la proximité à l'Etre' (111) (a 'humanism' which thinks the humanity of man on the basis of the proximity to Being). And Heidegger is adamant that, all misgivings about humanism aside, his thought remains bound to the fundamental humanist concern: 'car l'humanisme consiste en ceci: réfléchir et veiller à ce que l'homme soit humain et non in-humain, "barbare" [*inhuman*], c'est-à-dire hors de son essence' (45) (for humanism consists in this: reflecting and paying attention so that man is human and not inhuman, 'barbarian', that is outside his essence).

So, instead of setting himself up 'against humanism', Heidegger reluctantly reclaims the humanist label; and this entails replicating the definition by exclusion through which metaphysical humanism had operated. The human is that which is opposed to what Heidegger calls in German the *inhuman*, the *barbar* or the *unmenschlich* (words which are inconsistently translated in the French version). The mutually exclusive identities of *homo humanus* and *homo barbarus* are just as central to Heidegger's redefined humanism as they are to the humanism he rejects. Essences are to be kept pure and uncontaminated by what lies outside them; thus the essence which Heidegger describes is 'plus essentiel dans l'essence' (109) (more essential in its essence), an essence washed whiter. If Man dwells in the proximity of Being, the Barbarian must be kept at a safe distance; and if Man is the shepherd of Being (77, 109), the Barbarian is presumably the wolf at the gate.

For all his explicit opposition to Sartre, Heidegger's *Lettre sur l'humanisme* reproduces some of the moves made in *L'Existentialisme est un humanisme*. In neither text does anti-humanism appear as an option which can realistically be considered; humanism must be redefined so that a more acceptable version of it may be embraced (albeit lukewarmly in Heidegger's case). Sartre distinguishes between two types of humanism and rejects one in favour of 'l'humanisme existentialiste' (93) (existentialist humanism); Heidegger distinguishes between metaphysical humanism and his own '"humanisme" d'une étrange sorte' (119) ('humanism' of a strange kind). Sartre and Heidegger also get into complementary, and perhaps inevitable, tangles over the problem of what lies outside the human. Sartre's humanism is all-inclusive: the human embraces all differences of race, age or epoch in a single, open-ended totality. But when the human has expanded to incorporate all possible decisions, projects, actions and moralities, the very word *human* risks becoming little more than a catch-all that can refer to virtually anything. On the other hand, Heidegger's exclusionary definition of the human anxiously preserves the existence of Others (for whom the Barbarian serves as emblem) in opposition to whom our own humanity may be measured and reaffirmed. But such exclusions are always open to the accusation of arbitrariness and violence: why is the Barbarian any less human than me, why should my values and culture serve as the standard for all others?

Through the texts of Sartre and Heidegger, it can be seen that one of the key issues of humanism is the manner in which it polices the frontiers between itself and its Others. Man needs the Barbarian to serve as his own negative image; and he also requires a barrier separating the territory of the Other from what is properly his own.[21] The barrier may be crossed, relocated and redefined; but humanism is a meaningful term only in as far as it maintains – whatever the cost in terms of violence – its barriers and the Others on the far side of them.

This exclusionary aspect of humanism emerges with particular clarity in the fiction of Marguerite Yourcenar. In *Mémoires d'Hadrien* Yourcenar takes as her protagonist the Roman emperor Hadrian, a ruler in a unique position to promote what is best in Man whilst restricting what is worst, to fortify the frontiers of Man's empire against the assaults of the Barbarian. The Others of humanism, however, come back to haunt the text and the emperor, exposing its underlying reliance on violent exclusions.

Imperium

Marguerite Yourcenar is something of an anachronism amongst major postwar French writers. Whilst writers of the artistic and intellectual avant-garde sought to reconceive the world through their engagements with existentialism, Marxism, structuralism, feminism, poststructuralism and beyond, Yourcenar remained aloof. In 1968, whilst France seemed to some to be on the verge of revolution, Yourcenar published *L'Oeuvre au noir*, a novel set in the sixteenth century about a doctor hounded to his death by superstition and stupidity. The warning against popular enthusiasms is immediately apparent. Yourcenar's writings stand as a testimony to non-dogmatic, humane, civilized values in a world all too ready to forget them. But the reverse side of these civilized values is an intellectual and aesthetic caution, even complacency; and there is no doubt that Yourcenar's reactionary attitudes on a whole range of philosophical, social and cultural issues were largely responsible for much of the enthusiasm of her admirers. Her election to the Académie française, rather than opening the door to women, may be thought to represent a recognition of her honorary maleness; it bears eloquent witness to her (perhaps regrettable) respectability. Nevertheless, there is something dignified and moving in the summary of Hadrian's endeavour offered in *Mémoires d'Hadrien*,[22] first published in 1951: 'j'avais lutté de mon mieux pour favoriser le sens du divin dans l'homme, sans pourtant y sacrifier l'humain. Mon bonheur m'était un payement' (181) (I had struggled as best I could to favour the sense of the divine in man, but without sacrificing the human in the process. My happiness was my reward).

Yourcenar continued to carry the flag for humanism long after its prestige had waned. She chose as the epigraph to the first part of her novel *L'Oeuvre au noir* the passage from Pico della Mirandola's *Oratio de hominis dignitate* describing the creation of Man as free: 'Je ne t'ai fait ni céleste ni terrestre, mortel ou immortel, afin que de toi-même, librement, à la façon d'un bon peintre ou d'un sculpteur habile, tu achèves ta propre forme' (I made you neither celestial nor terrestrial, mortal or immortal, so that you yourself, freely, in the manner of a good painter or a skilful sculptor, might determine your own form).[23] In the opening chapter of Yourcenar's novel, the aspiration expressed by the soldier Henri-Maximilien, 'Il s'agit d'être homme' (It is a question of being a man),[24] is rejected as not sufficiently ambitious by Yourcenar's protagonist Zénon: 'Il s'agit pour moi d'être plus qu'un homme' (For me it is a question of being more than a man).[25] This ambition, recalling the form of humanism described by Sartre in *L'Existentialisme est un humanisme* which exalts what is most admirable in Man, is constantly brought up against the ignorance and intolerance which finally lead to Zénon's death. Man's finest achievements are counterbalanced by his worst instincts. Yourcenar celebrates the former and condemns the latter.

Given the inherently decent humanism of Yourcenar's writing, it is perhaps unsurprising that critical studies of her work have been largely characterized by respect and admiration. Elaine Marks, however, has struck a discordant note. In an article reprinted in her book *Marrano as Metaphor*, Marks accuses Yourcenar's pre-war novel *Le Coup de grâce* of anti-Semitism; and the Yourcenar's denegatory preface of 1962, in which she plays down the judeophobia of her protagonist by attributing it to a 'natural' response of the aristocratic caste, does nothing to offset the charge.[26] If *Mémoires d'Hadrien* is read in the light of Marks's comments, disturbing evidence may certainly be found to support the charge of anti-Semitism. Hadrian readily adopts crude stereotypes: as he describes them, Jews are motivated by profit, they are fanatical, intolerant, impervious to reason and cannot be made to recognize civilized values. Hadrian's reference to the 600,000 Jews who are killed in the course of his campaign against them immediately puts the reader in mind of the six million Jewish victims of the Holocaust (268);[27] and Hadrian implies that these were necessary sacrifices, since execution is the only way of making a Jew see reason. The rebellious Jews are described as an abscess or a contagion ('l'abcès juif... la contagion zélote', 259) (the Jewish abscess... the zealot contagion), a sick member to be cauterized or amputated ('on pouvait sans danger cautériser ou amputer ce doigt malade', 259) (this sick finger could be cauterized or amputated without danger). Moreover, Hadrian echoes one of the most invidious racist commonplaces by implying that all Jews are the same: the moderates are merely timid or hypocritical fanatics, even the emperor's Jewish adviser is thought to be covertly opposed to him (260). Hadrian tells us that 'il avait fallu exécuter en masse les rebelles de Gaza' (259) (it was necessary to execute *en masse* the rebels at Gaza), though he does not feel the need to explain or to justify the necessity implied in *il avait fallu* (it was necessary). Hadrian endorses the view of his military commander that 'cet ennemi insaisissable pouvait être exterminé, mais non pas vaincu' (256) (this ungraspable enemy could be exterminated, but not defeated). The use of the word *exterminé* (exterminated), alluding unmistakably to the *camps d'extermination* (extermination camps), presents the death of the Jews as an unavoidable measure, ultimately their own fault. If it is already disturbing for Yourcenar to publish a novel (*Le Coup de grâce*) which adopts anti-Semitic discourse in 1939, to publish such comments in 1951, in full knowledge of the events of the war, is simply outrageous.

Hadrian's views cannot simply be identified with those of Yourcenar herself. At the same time it may be regarded as at the very least a weakness in Yourcenar's novel that it does nothing to question the racist stereotypes to which its narrator gives voice; and the very specific allusions to the Holocaust must be attributed to the author rather than to Hadrian, since the emperor died seventeen centuries before the Second World War. The issue here is not simply to denounce Yourcenar or her novel for anti-Semitism, but rather to ask whether its more discomforting aspects are merely blind spots in an otherwise solid humanism or fault lines through the whole edifice. More generally, what is at stake here is the status of the Other in humanist discourse; the anxious expulsion of alterity which was displayed in the humanism of Heidegger and Sartre is replicated in Yourcenar's novel. This can be seen, firstly, by examining the foundations of Hadrian's humanism in the harmony of self and empire, and then by considering the figures which seem to endanger those foundations.

*   *   *

As he approaches death, an ageing emperor looks back over his life to see if he can find order and meaning within diversity and flux. He is aware that such order may be a fiction, an effect of narrative without cognitive grounding; yet the act of narration serves to mask that initial awareness, as he repeatedly finds the traces of coherence and continuity in his experience of the world. This is illustrated in the status of Rome as the eternal city, constant in its changes, the seat of power capable of accommodating radical shifts, the reconciliation of stability and vicissitude: 'J'accepte avec calme ces vicissitudes de Rome éternelle' (314) (I accept calmly these vicissitudes of eternal Rome). Behind the multiplicity of religions also, there lies a single source; the different deities are 'mystérieusement fondues en un Tout, émanations infiniment variées, manifestations égales d'une même force; leurs contradictions n'étaient qu'un mode de leur accord' (183) (mysteriously dissolved in a Whole, infinitely varied emanations, equal manifestations of a same power; their contradictions were only a mode of their agreement). Jupiter, the centre of order and authority, is also Proteus, the ever-changing god (159). All beliefs elucidate an aspect of the divine, all truths are part of the Truth. Hadrian's narrative is the quest for totalities without residue, for seamless wholes to contain the plurality of the parts. Within the Heraclitean flux to which he claims allegiance, he always posits the organizing force of the Parmenidean One: one culture, the Greek culture, forms the model for all others (88); one divinity binds together the pantheon of the gods; one city and one state hold temporal authority over the civilized world; and one emperor rules over a single empire. And Hadrian dreams of extending that empire to cover the whole domain of human experience: 'J'aurais voulu que l'État s'élargît encore, devînt ordre du monde, ordre des choses' (124) (I would have wanted the State to become even larger, to become the order of the world, the order of things).

All this is possible because both the individual subject and humanity in general are ultimately unified and self-identical. The first problem for the aspiring autobiographer seeking order and unity is the apparent diversity of the self; yet Hadrian, whilst drawing attention to the multiplicity of the roles he has played (see 65–6), also emphasizes their all-inclusive nature: 'J'ai cru, et dans mes bons moments je crois encore, qu'il serait possible de partager de la sorte l'existence de *tous*' (15, my emphasis); 'J'ai occupé *toutes* les positions extrêmes tour à tour' (33, my emphasis) (I believed, and in my good moments I still believe, that in this way it would be possible to share the existence of everyone; I occupied all the extreme positions one after the other). Hadrian appears, then, not as a random collection of unrelated personae, but as a sort of Universal Subject, containing all possible subject positions at the level of potentiality, capable of entering the minds of others because they are variants on his own being, basing his understanding of others on analysis of the self (127).

Although, as I have already indicated, it would be wrong to make a simple equation between the views of Hadrian and those of Yourcenar herself, she does nevertheless encourage some degree of identification through the 'Carnet de notes de *Mémoires d'Hadrien*' which accompanies the text of her novel. In the 'Carnet', Yourcenar bluntly conflates all human subjects: 'Tout être qui a vécu l'aventure humaine est moi' (342) (Every being who has lived the human adventure is me). It is unclear whether she is speaking in her own voice here, or on behalf of her protagonist. But, of course, it makes no difference, if any subject is potentially any other. Echoing once again Sartre's *L'Existentialisme est un humanisme*, Yourcenar implies that all men are potentially all Man. In the 'Carnet' she describes the '*magie sympathique*' (sympathetic magic) which makes it possible for her to enter into the skin of her emperor (330), as Hadrian himself describes the 'sympathie' (sympathy) which allows him to share in the lives of others (15). Wittingly or not, in the word *sympathie* both Hadrian and his author are using the term which, in the German hermeneutic revival of the nineteenth century, was used to throw a bridge between ourselves and others, be they other selves or alien cultures; by means of sympathy (*Einfühlung* in German), inessential differences are bracketed off and the unity of humanity refound.[28]

This raises a difficult and delicate question: what place does such unity leave for the Other, the cornerstone of much modern thought in areas as diverse as anthropology, postcolonial studies, feminism, psychoanalysis and poststructuralist ethics? Hadrian accords to the Other the capital letter ('l'Autre', 20, 21, 22) which has come to signal the acknowledgement of it as something radically alien, unassimilable to the perspective of the self. Yet it is not clear that Hadrian maintains the respect that this implies, as can be seen for example in his discussion of sensuality, the paradigmatic site of encounter with alterity.[29] Hadrian imagines elaborating a system of knowledge in which 'le mystère et la dignité d'autrui consisterait précisément à offrir au Moi ce point d'appui d'un autre monde' (22) (the mystery and the dignity of others would consist precisely in offering the Self this point of contact with another world). The Other thus appears as an instrument, part of a technique ('une technique de plus', 22) (another technique) put in the service of the self. In fact, Hadrian's entire narrative project militates against the preservation of otherness: the search for patterns, order and coherence entails the elimination of those disruptions and slippages which might signal the appearance of the Other. As the text of Hadrian's life becomes a smooth narrative, traces of otherness are an unwanted residue. The effort of making a life coincide with a text consists in transforming encounters into self-encounters; others are variants of the self, and their stories serve only as stories of the self. Thus, at the end of his narrative, Hadrian can 'recognize' the story of Achilles and Patroclus as the key to his own life, and meaning emerges from disorder: 'l'aventure de mon existence prend un sens, s'organise comme dans un poème' (297) (the adventure of my existence acquires a meaning, becomes organized as in a poem).

Hadrian's story is a journey through chaos into order, or through otherness into self. This is illustrated, and its significance revealed, through his reference to Ulysses. Hadrian refers to himself as 'Ulysse sans autre Ithaque qu'intérieure' (138) (Ulysses whose only Ithaca is inside himself).[30] Ithaca is Ulysses' point of departure and return. Hadrian's Ithaca is internal; his spiritual journey is thus established as a return to the self. He belongs nowhere, he believes, because his true place of belonging, the true destination of his search, is his self. The distinction between Ulysses and the biblical Abraham drawn by Emmanuel Levinas throws an important light on this.[31] According to Levinas, Abraham gives up all that is familiar and leaves home never to return; he risks who he is in order to experience the world of the Other. The journey of Ulysses, on the contrary, is a return to the point of departure; the world of the Other is a hindrance or delay preventing him from reaching his real destination. Ulysses thus becomes emblematic of the dominant strain of Western thought which, according to Levinas, has consisted in a neglect of the Other in favour of the Same. The Other is assumed and subsumed as the subject moves towards self-possession and self-knowledge. The Other, thus, turns out to be merely a facet of the Same.

Levinas picks up on the connection between imperial politics and the struggle between self and world when he refers to the 'impérialisme du Même' (imperialism of the Same);[32] the subject seeks to extend its sovereignty over an alien environment by transforming the world into a support for its own needs and pleasures. Through this perspective, the humanist imperium of Yourcenar's emperor may be understood. The imperium is a homogenous space with closed borders (Hadrian's cities are criticized for being all identical; 143); it is commanded by stable, knowable principles of wisdom, reason, justice and order, with each subject open to others because all share in the same values and culture. It is, in other words, a nightmare.

But what of the residue, the remainder which is unaccounted for in the order of imperium? In the next section I want to discuss three manifestations of resistance: Barbarians, Jews and women.

Others

Every inside requires an outside; at the same time, the totalizing impulse requires that the outside must have the potential to form part of an enlarged, ultimately all-encompassing inside. This is indicated by Hadrian's dealings with the Barbarians. In *Mémoires d'Hadrien* as in Heidegger's *Lettre sur l'humanisme*, the Barbarians are defined in opposition to the civilized human; they represent the outside of civilization. The word *barbarian* is thought to derive from the meaningless sounds the Barbarians are deemed to utter; they inhabit a wild space, endangering the borders of the empire, threatening the order of imperium with chaos and nonsense.

However, these outsiders are only unenlightened, or unconquered, insiders. The *pax romana* operated by offering to conquered peoples the advantages of Roman civilization. This was an offer than no reasonable person was expected to refuse; and Hadrian hopes to extend the *pax romana* to all humanity: 'Je voulais que l'immense majesté de la paix romaine s'étendît à tous' (148) (I wanted the immense majesty of Roman peace to extend to all). The Barbarians are thus capable of being integrated into the world of imperial values ('J'entrevoyais la possibilité d'hélléniser les barbares', 88) (I glimpsed the possibility of hellenizing the Barbarians). They are embryonic or potential Romans, Others awaiting conversion to Sameness. Hadrian allows his soldiers on the frontiers of the empire to marry barbarian women, and he legitimizes their children (134). The possibility of civilizing the Barbarian is revealed most clearly when the emperor is attacked by a slave. Instead of punishing his assailant, Hadrian treats him humanely. The slave is thereby allowed to become 'ce qu'il était vraiment, un être pas moins sensé que les autres, et plus fidèle que beaucoup' (128) (what he truly was, a being no less endowed with sense than others, and more faithful than many). His real essence as a member of a unified humanity is disclosed. This leads Hadrian to envisage that all people may one day share the values of Roman civilization:

> Ce barbare condamné au travail des mines devint pour moi l'emblème de tous nos esclaves, de tous nos barbares. Il ne me semblait pas impossible de les traiter comme j'avais traité cet homme, de les rendre inoffensifs à force de bonté, pourvu qu'ils sussent d'abord que la main qui les désarmait était sûre.... J'aurais voulu reculer le plus possible, éviter s'il se peut, le moment où les barbares au-dehors, les esclaves au-dedans, se rueront sur un monde qu'on leur demande de respecter de loin ou de servir d'en bas, mais dont les bénéfices ne sont pas pour eux. Je tenais à ce que la plus déshéritée des créatures, l'esclave nettoyant les cloaques des villes, le barbare affamé rôdant aux frontières, eût intérêt à voir durer Rome. (129)

> This Barbarian condemned to work in the mines became for me the emblem of all our slaves, of all our Barbarians. It seemed to me not impossible to treat them as I had treated this man, to make them harmless through kindness, provided that they knew first of all that the hand which disarmed them was sure.... I would have wanted to push back as far as possible, to avoid if it could be done, the moment when the Barbarians outside and the slaves within will pour down on a world which they are asked to respect from afar or to serve from below, but whose benefits are not for them. I was keen that the most disinherited of creatures, the slave cleaning the town lavatories, the starving Barbarian roaming the frontiers, should have an interest in seeing Rome survive.

An important test case for the universality of Roman reason is provided by Hadrian's encounter with the Parthian emperor Osroès. Osroès presents the apparent paradox of 'un barbare raffiné' (156) (a refined Barbarian), a civilized Barbarian who recognizes the same values as Hadrian. Although he rules over a rival empire, his patterns of thought prove to be far from alien. Hadrian can understand his point of view ('je m'imaginais devenu Osroès marchandant avec Hadrien', 156) (I imagined myself in the role of Osroès haggling with Hadrian), and a lasting peace is concluded between them. The Barbarian turns out after all to be a reflection of the sovereign subject: his thought processes, interests and desires are discovered to be fundamentally identical.[33]

The Barbarians, then, occupy a position of alterity which is only relatively Other. They represent a sort of good alterity, one which does not endanger the integrity of imperium, but which, on the contrary, may be employed to reinforce it. The Jews are a different matter. As inhabitants of territories which belong to the Roman empire, they are already on the inside; however, for reasons incomprehensible to Hadrian, they do not recognize what he calls 'les solides avantages de la paix romaine' (259) (the solid advantages of Roman peace). Hadrian appears utterly mystified as to why the Jews should object to their beliefs being insulted, their rituals outlawed and their religious schools closed. The words *fanatique* (fanatic) and *fanatisme* (fanaticism) are used on numerous occasions in the passages of the novel referring to Jews. The words designate a set of practices and beliefs which are irreducible to our own models of reasonableness; a fanatic is not simply someone with whom I disagree, but more radically someone whose values are incomprehensible to me. In the struggle between what Hadrian calls 'le fanatisme et le sens commun' (254) (fanaticism and common sense), the fanatics place themselves outside the human community by rejecting common sense, the source of agreement which all reasonable subjects are expected to accept.

The Jews thus challenge the very limits of imperial tolerance and reveal the profound intolerance which lies behind it. The cults of conquered peoples were generally permitted to continue by the Romans in as far as they did not bring into question the imperially sanctioned polytheism. But Jewish monotheism, like its Christian offshoot which Hadrian also finds distasteful, is another matter. Monotheism represents a radically different way of thinking about divinity, one which cannot be reconciled with polytheism because it refuses its founding principles. The Jews believe in a single God to the exclusion of all others; Hadrian believes in a multiform divinity which contains everything ('la multiplicité du Dieu qui contient tout', 253) (the multiplicity of the God who contains everything).

Each view is equally totalitizing and totalitarian. The Romans and the Jews are opposed by what Jean-François Lyotard calls a *différend*, a disaccord which cannot be resolved because there is no common ground between the opponents.[34] Jews and Romans, then, must be intolerant of the others' intolerance. Hadrian is aware that, with the Jews, he is confronted with 'les différences irréconciliables, le point où deux pensées d'espèces opposées ne se rencontrent que pour se combattre' (260) (irreconcilable differences, the point where two thoughts of opposed kinds can meet only in order to combat one another).

Whereas the Barbarians represent a form of good alterity, the good Other beyond the frontiers whose assimilation will extend the empire, the Jews are purveyors of bad alterity, an already internalized but still recalcitrant Other which questions the empire from within. The series of corporeal metaphors to which I mentioned earlier, when Hadrian refers to the Jews as an abscess, a contagion, or a wounded finger to be cauterized or amputated (259), suggests that the Jews belong to a unified body, but that they are an infection or sickness which endangers its health. If it cannot be cured, if the Other cannot be reintegrated into an undiseased whole and restored to the self, then is must be amputated or destroyed. The self is thereby diminished but preserved. It will be clear, I hope, how sinister I find this line of thought.

If the Jews are the enemy within the gates, a more numerous and formidable fifth column brings into question the foundations of imperium: women. Yourcenar's preference for male, especially homosexual, protagonists and narrators can be related to a suppression of the feminine which, in the 'Carnet de notes de *Mémoires d'Hadrien*' Yourcenar attempts to justify in terms which are both aesthetically weak and intellectually suspect.[35] The key passage concerning women in *Mémoires d'Hadrien* itself deals with Hadrian's heterosexual affairs before he becomes emperor (73–8). If it is shocking to find Yourcenar's novel reproducing and sanctioning racist stereotypes, it is no less discomforting to find the discourse of misogyny so openly embraced here. The feminine is associated with chatter and superficiality:

> leur amour, dont elles parlaient sans cesse, me semblait parfois aussi léger qu'une de leurs guirlandes, un bijou à la mode, un ornement coûteux et fragile; et je les soupçonnais de mettre leur passion avec leur rouge et leurs colliers. (74)

their love, of which they spoke endlessly, sometimes seemed to me to be as light as one of their garlands, a fashionable piece of jewellery, an expensive and delicate ornament; and I suspected that they put on their passion with their lipstick and their necklaces.

Women's pleasure is 'tantôt feint, tantôt dissimulé' (sometimes feigned, sometimes hidden); and even in a quarrel they are playing roles: 'on attendait de moi une réplique prévue d'avance, et la belle éplorée se tordait les mains comme en scène' (74) (I was expected to give a reply which was laid out in advance, and the beautiful, grief-stricken woman would wring her hands as if she were on stage). Their beauty is a product of ruse (74–5); even when they are naked, they never appear 'sans parure' (75) (out of costume); they present different faces which it is hard to reconcile (76), they harbour a secret life which they do not reveal.

Women, then, are associated with cunning and ornament, deceit and dissimulation; they are always in disguise and playing roles. They thus offer the exact opposite of what Hadrian wants in erotic relationships: an authentic encounter with a partner who makes it possible to know and to possess an alien self (22–3). Any falsehood, or any elusiveness, is rejected outright: 'L'idée qu'un être, si peu que se soit, se contrefait en ma présence, est capable de me le faire plaindre, mépriser, ou haïr' (24) (The idea that someone might dissemble in my presence, however little, is capable of making me pity, despise or hate him). In this context it is perhaps hardly surprising that Hadrian takes a wife whom he neither likes nor desires, or that his most important relationships (with Lucius and Antinoüs) are homosexual. But in as far as Hadrian seeks in homosexuality a refuge from the inauthenticity which he associates with the feminine, he fails: his lover Lucius loves decoration, game playing and acting every bit as much as the women over whom he is preferred;[36] and with Antinoüs Hadrian again discovers 'tout ce qui m'avait irrité chez les maîtresses romaines: les parfums, les apprêts, le luxe froid des parures' (195) (everything that had irritated me in my Roman mistresses: the perfumes, the affected airs, the cold luxury of ornament).

Moreover femininity, as constructed by Hadrian, represents a more radical danger. The feminine confounds Hadrian's desire for authentic encounters, as his female lovers do not accept the values of Hadrian's masculine epistemology: 'Mais mes amantes semblaient se faire gloire de ne penser qu'en femmes: l'esprit ou l'âme, que je cherchais, n'était encore qu'un parfum' (75) (But my [female] lovers seemed to be proud of thinking only as women: the spirit or soul that I was searching for was no more than a perfume). The soul is not a knowable essence beneath a deceptive surface; rather, it is associated with subterfuge, being no more than a perfume like the 'parfums frottés sur la peau' (74) (perfumes applied to the skin) which contribute to the deceptive allure of the feminine. Nevertheless, Hadrian remains convinced that the feminine masquerade must conceal a secret life which he wishes to understand: 'Il devait y avoir autre chose' (75) (There had to be something else). In search for this elusive *autre chose* (something else) he takes to spying on his lovers when he believes they are unaware of his presence, 'dissimulé derrière un rideau, comme un personnage de comédie attendant l'heure propice' (75) (concealed behind a curtain, like a character in a play waiting for his cue). What is crucial here is that Hadrian has effectively succumbed to the dissolution of essences and identities which he saw as the scandal of femininity. The word *dissimulé* (hidden) and the image of the 'personnage de comédie' (character in a play) are picked up from the previous page, where they represented the subterfuge of the feminine. Hadrian here is effectively feminized (dissimulating, playing roles) through his endeavour to discover the secret of femininity; and the absence of depth beneath the surface has infected his own being. In other words, the question of femininity and the qualities that become attached to it are only partly to do with people biologically gendered as female. The suppression of the feminine in *Mémoires d'Hadrien* is most importantly derived from the fact that femininity discloses the radical fragility of an epistemological position which rests on secure distinctions between surface and depth, accident and essence, authentic and inauthentic, dissimulation and truth, male and female.

Humanism

The core of Hadrian's humanism is the desire for a flawless sublation of difference though which the accidents of particularity are integrated into a global harmony:

> Aux corps physiques des nations et des races, aux accidents de la géographie et de l'histoire, aux exigences disparates des dieux et des ancêtres, nous aurions à jamais superposé, mais sans rien

détruire, l'unité d'une conduite humaine, l'empirisme d'une expérience sage. Rome se perpétuerait dans la moindre petite ville où des magistrats s'efforcent de vérifier les poids des marchands, de nettoyer et d'éclairer leurs rues, de s'opposer au désordre, à l'incurie, à la peur, à l'injustice, de réinterpréter raisonnablement les lois. Elle ne périrait qu'avec la dernière cité des hommes. (125)

On the physical bodies of nations and races, on the accidents of geography and history, on the disparate demands of the gods and our ancestors, we would have superimposed for ever, but without destroying anything, the unity of human conduct, the empiricism of wise experience. Rome would live on in the most insignificant small town where magistrates attempt to check the weights of the shopkeepers, to keep the streets clean and light, to oppose disorder, negligence, fear, injustice, to reinterpret laws reasonably. It would only perish with the last city of men.

The unity of human conduct is to be achieved without destroying anything; wisdom, justice, reason and order will become the governing principles of a civilized, united world. Rome will be the measure of all locations, and the emperor will be the universal subject in which all others are contained.[37] This vision leaves no place for a residue of alterity which might represent a legitimate resistance to the totalizing project. However, the qualities of the suppressed Other come back to inhabit the humanist subject: thus the intolerance ascribed to Jews and the subterfuges and dissimulation of femininity are the consistent underside of Hadrian's actions. His humanism is built on, and can be defined as, the suppression of otherness.

For this reason Hadrian's anti-Semitism, an anti-Semitism never seriously questioned in Yourcenar's text, is not simply a blind spot in an otherwise coherent humanism. The blind spot reveals the truth about the vision, an ideology is unmasked by what it consigns to the place of the Other. As Slavoj Žižek puts it, 'the persecution of the Jews pertains to a certain repressed truth of our civilization'; this repressed truth may be brought to light by identifying with whatever indicates 'the intrusion into the social field of some "impossible" kernel that resists integration'. Thus, Žižek encourages his readers to assert that 'We are all Jews', 'We are all victims of Chernobyl', 'We are all boat people':

by means of such an identification with the (social) symptom, we traverse and subvert the fantasy frame that determines the field of social meaning, the ideological self-understanding of a given society, i.e., the frame within which, precisely, the 'symptom' appears as some alien, disturbing intrusion, and not as the point of eruption of the otherwise hidden truth of the existing social order.[38]

The Others who appear in the background of *Mémoires d'Hadrien* likewise reveal the novel's 'otherwise hidden truth' and the violence which inhabits its 'ideological self-understanding'. These Others are not threats from the outside; they occupy and define the inside. By serving as explanations for the evils of contradiction, resistance and dissension, they actually make possible the fantasy-image of humanity as a consistent, harmonious whole.[39] The exclusion of Jews and women from Yourcenar's universal humanism ensures that it is neither universal nor humane; its reality, its foundation in terror, is revealed through what is denies. And identification with the text's victimized Others may afford the most effective release from Hadrian's nightmare of Sameness.

* * *

The preceding chapters on Sartre, Camus, Beauvoir and Yourcenar have dealt with texts of a broadly humanist persuasion. Each of them displays an unease, even violence, towards the Other; and their attempts to establish secure ethical positions are endangered by the anxieties and exclusions which they seek to occlude, but which continue to inform their constructions of alterity. Violence towards the Other returns all the more insidiously when it is most repressed. The final two chapters of this book will examine texts by Duras and Genet which make little concession to the moral fortitude valued in the humanist lineage. Their bold and disturbing explorations of violence may allow a more complex, precarious and traumatized understanding of ethical relations than their more overtly moral counterparts.

7
Ethical Indifference: Duras

Marguerite Duras's *L'Amante anglaise* (1967) recounts a simple, everyday murder:

> Je me souviens d'un crime: c'était un ouvrier agricole des environs, très bien à tous les points de vue. Un soir il arrachait des pommes de terre dans un champ et une femme est passée. Il la connaissait depuis très longtemps. Peut-être la désirait-il, l'aimait-il sans l'avouer? Elle a refusé de le suivre dans la forêt. Il l'a tuée.[1]
>
> I remember a crime: it was an agricultural worker from around here, a good man from all points of view. One evening he was picking potatoes in a field and a woman came by. He had known her for a long time. Perhaps he desired her, loved her, without admitting it. She refused to follow him into forest. He killed her.

The murderer and his victim are identified only as *un ouvrier agricole* (an agricultural worker) and *une femme* (a woman), their story is recounted as a banal occurrence; a possible explanation is ventured ('Peut-être la désirait-il, l'aimait-il sans l'avouer?') (Perhaps he desired her, loved her, without admitting it), but it is given little authority. As in the novel as a whole, which revolves around the murder by Claire Lannes of her deaf-mute cousin Marie-Thérèse, the reader is neither required nor allowed to understand. Elsewhere in Duras's fiction, murder recurs in equally casual and passionate forms. *La Vie tranquille* (1944) begins with fratricide; in *Moderato cantabile* (1958) a man murders his lover and grieves over her corpse;

in *Dix heures et demie du soir en été* (1960) a man has killed his wife and her lover. These crimes reflect at the level of the *fait divers* other unimaginable acts which haunt Duras's writing: the explosion of the atom bomb in Hiroshima and the Holocaust.

In the texts discussed in previous chapters, the relationship with the Other is a topic of specifically ethical anxiety. The impulse to annihilate the Other is typically resisted or denied so that some sort of moral order can be maintained. Even in works where murder is intended as a liberating political act, such as Sartre's *Les Mouches* or Camus's *Les Justes*, it is not to be undertaken lightly; it must be justified in an anguished disquisition on ends and means, and probably paid for by the peace of mind or the life of the assassin. The characteristic tension of the texts I have discussed derives from the conflict between a deep-rooted adherence to the prohibition of murder ('Thou shalt not kill') and the impulse or political need to break it; the authority of the prohibition is reinforced whilst and because it is transgressed. To put it crudely, for the writers discussed in previous chapters murder is a moral issue; what is shocking about Duras's writing is that it isn't. Murder is, on the contrary, something very simple. To be given the opportunity to kill one's wife and her lover *in flagrante delicto* appears as almost enviable, an option that should and may be available to all:

> Tandis que se poursuit le dîner on parle du crime de Rodrigo Paestra. Des gens rient. A l'instar de Rodrigo Paestra qui, dans sa vie n'aurait pas l'occasion de tuer avec cette simplicité?[2]

> Whilst the meal continues the crime of Rodrigo Paestra is discussed. People laugh. In the manner of Rodrigo Paestra who in his life would not have the opportunity to kill with this simplicity?

Murder in Duras's texts is not yet the deliberate wickedness that it will become for Genet; it is rather a casual and irrevocable act, unexpected and inexplicable. It may be a way of freezing or arresting the traumatic circulation of desire, but it also serves as instigation to further desire, be it erotic or epistemological or both. Maria in *Dix heures et demie du soir en été* recognizes in the murder of the wife and lover a version of her own story as she anticipates her husband's infidelity; the unconsummated affair of Anne and Chauvin in *Moderato cantabile* progresses through their attempts to understand and re-enact the murder with which the novel begins; *L'Amante anglaise* consists in the attempts of an unnamed interviewer to understand why Claire has murdered and dismembered her cousin. In each case, the deferment of explanation and the short-circuit of desire are not provisional failures. For Duras they are the conditions of being human.

Duras's fiction is founded on the insight that the search to understand is both inevitable and inevitably frustrated. The murder in *Moderato cantabile* is never explained, though the novel derives its momentum from the desire to explain it. In *L'Amante anglaise* no particular event or resentment seems to have provoked the murder; the victim and even the perpetrator might have been someone else. Claire killed Marie-Thérèse, but might just as easily have killed her husband Pierre or herself. Pierre admits to having dreamt of killing Marie-Thérèse, but insists that neither she nor his wife was the real victim.[3] The roles of murderer and victim appear as radically fluid, interchangeable. Few writers illustrate better than Duras that, even if we have not committed murder, we are all murders in the reality of our dreams. Asked if he has dreamt of committing a crime, Pierre responds simply: 'J'ai dû lui répondre que ça arrivait à tout le monde, que ça m'était arrivé à moi aussi' (81) (I must have replied to him that it happened to everyone, that it had happened to me as well). According to Claire, others give the same response: 'J'ai demandé à Alfonso et à Robert, le soir, au café. Ils m'ont dit qu'eux aussi avaient rêvé de crime, que tout le monde rêvait de crime' (140) (I asked Alfonso and Robert in the evening at the café. They told me that they also had dreamt of crime, that everyone dreamt of crime). All that separates real murders from these imaginary ones is the occasion:

> Au fond, la cause de la plupart des crimes c'est peut-être ni plus ni moins la possibilité... dans laquelle on se trouve de les commettre. Supposez qu'on vive nuit et jour avec près de soi, par exemple... une machine infernale... qu'il suffise d'appuyer sur un bouton pour qu'elle se déclenche. Un beau jour on le fait. (36)

> Basically, the cause of most crimes is perhaps neither more nor less than the possibility... that you find yourself in to commit them. Imagine that you live day and night with, nearby, for example... an infernal machine... that all you have to do to set it off is press a button. One fine day you do it.

What is most disturbing here is the nonchalant separation of murder from criteria of moral judgement. The legal system pursues the murderer because that is its role; murderers must be apprehended, but their actions cause no outrage or even particular disapproval. Whereas Camus's Meursault had to be expelled from society as a moral monster, Duras's murderers seem banal or even enviable. In the case of Rodrigo Paestra in *Dix heures et demie du soir en été*, no one condemns his crime and most seem to wish for his escape. The prohibition on murder has simply evaporated; there seems to be no moral perspective available which would make it possible to condemn the taking of life. Characters live on in the wake of a catastrophe which disables ethical reflection and disqualifies moral principles. In *L'Amante anglaise* this catastrophe emerges through Claire's relationship with *l'agent de Cahors*:

> Nous nous sommes aimés à la folie pendant deux ans. Je dis à la folie. C'est lui qui m'a détachée de Dieu. Je ne voyais que par lui après Dieu. Je n'écoutais que lui, il était tout pour moi et un jour je n'ai plus eu Dieu mais lui seul. Et puis un jour il a menti.... Le ciel s'est écroulé. (152–3)

> We loved one another to the point of madness for two years. I say to the point of madness. He was the one who led me away from God. After God I could only see through his eyes. I listened only to him, he was everything for me and one day I no longer had God but just him. And then one day he lied.... The sky/heaven fell down.

The *agent de Cahors* functions here not as a Levinassian Other (the absolute stranger, desired and unknowable) but as the Lacanian Big Other, the guarantor of the coherence of the symbolic order. He replaces God, gives meaning to experience and bathes the subject in the certainty of being seen and approved. The realization that he has lied entails not only the loss of a cherished lover, but also the collapse of the moral and epistemological order which the Big Other had underwritten: 'Le ciel s'est écroulé' (The sky/heaven fell down). After the desertion of the Big Other, neither the purpose and intelligibility of actions nor the discriminations which sustain the symbolic order (right and wrong, good and bad) can survive. Claire can marry Pierre, or someone else; she can murder Marie-Thérèse, or someone else. The numerous references to her *folie* (madness) serve not to explain her crime, but as markers that all intelligible meaning and moral determination have been evacuated from her actions. The *folie* of her love for *l'agent de Cahors* is transformed by his betrayal into the defining madness of life outside the gaze of the Big Other.

The ethical interest and challenge of Duras lies in the very indifference of much of her fiction to ethics. Whereas, biographically, she was involved in numerous political and moral campaigns, her writing frequently approaches moral issues with a disturbing impassivity. She thus provides a counterpoint to the authors discussed in the previous chapters. Altericidal impulses are no longer resisted or denied; rather, they are depicted as ordinary, banal components of human relations. Duras distances herself from her humanist contemporaries by making it more difficult for the reader to find ethical significance in her writing. In the rest of this chapter I shall discuss the consequences of this by looking more closely at the links between Duras's *La Douleur* and the text of her one-time husband Robert Antelme, *L'Espèce humaine*; Duras's writing both recalls and subverts Antelme's resilient humanism, leaving both narrators and readers in a situation of ethical distress.

Duras and Antelme

Marguerite Duras's *La Douleur* (1985) is a text haunted by spectral presences and significant absences.[4] The first and longest section of the book, itself entitled 'La Douleur', recounts the period before and after the return of the narrator's husband, called here Robert L., from a German concentration camp. Before his return, the narrator imagines him dead, and is inhabited by his death: 'Sa mort est en moi.... Il est mort depuis trois semaines.... Il est mort en prononçant mon nom' (13–14) (His death is inside me.... He has been dead for three weeks.... He died with my name on his lips). But when he returns the narrator distances herself from him. At first she literally runs away from him: 'Je n'ai pas pu l'éviter. Je suis descendue pour me sauver dans la rue.... Il a dû me regarder et me reconnaître et sourire. J'ai hurlé que non, que je ne voulais pas voir. Je suis repartie, j'ai remonté l'escalier' (64) (I couldn't avoid him. I went downstairs to run away in the street.... He must have looked at me and recognized me and smiled. I shouted that no, I didn't want to see him. I left, I went back upstairs). And

136 *Ethical Issues in French Fiction*

later, as he begins to recover his strength, she informs him that she intends to divorce him:

> Un autre jour je lui ai dit qu'il nous fallait divorcer, que je voulais un enfant de D., que c'était à cause du nom que cet enfant porterait. Il m'a demandé s'il était possible qu'un jour on se retrouve. J'ai dit que non, que je n'avais pas changé d'avis depuis deux ans, depuis que j'avais rencontré D. Je lui ai dit que même si D. n'existait pas, je n'aurais pas vécu de nouveau avec lui. Il ne m'a pas demandé les raisons que j'avais de partir, je ne les lui ai pas données. (75)

> Another day I told him that we had to get divorced, that I wanted to have a child with D., that it was because of the name the child would have. He asked me if it was possible that one day we would get back together. I said no, that I hadn't changed my mind for two years, since I had met D. I told him that even if D. didn't exist, I wouldn't have lived with him again. He didn't ask me my reasons for leaving, I didn't tell him them.

Robert L., then, is desired when he is absent and rejected when he returns. The wife's desiring-rejecting is reproduced at the level of the text in the use of the name Robert L. to refer to the husband: this name effaces from the text – whilst also leaving clearly legible – the presence of Robert Antelme, Duras's real husband during the war, deported to Buchenwald as a member of the Resistance and later transferred to the camp at Gandersheim and finally to Dachau. The name 'Antelme' is raised on the very threshold of Duras's text by the fact that one of its dedicatees is a certain Frédéric Antelme (7). Later, the narrator refers to her husband's account of his experiences as a prisoner of the Nazi regime: 'Il a écrit un livre sur ce qu'il croit avoir vécu en Allemagne: *L'Espèce humaine*' (77) (He wrote a book on what he believed he experienced in Germany: *L'Espèce humaine*). After his return from Germany, Robert Antelme himself wrote a book of that title; and if Antelme is a spectral presence in *La Douleur*, Duras is also present-in-absence in *L'Espèce humaine*.[5] The prisoner thinks of home:

> Le pain est fini, on va rentrer, s'enfoncer en soi, ... s'enfoncer jusqu'à s'approcher de la figure de M..., de D..., là-bas. ... Je ne me vois que de dos là-bas, toujours de dos. La figure de M... sourit à celui que je ne vois que de dos. (113; see also 277)

The bread is finished, we are going to go inside, to sink into ourselves, ... to sink down to the point of approaching the face of M..., of D..., back there. ... Back there I can see myself only from the back, always from the back. The face of M ... smiles at the person I can see only from the back.

Perhaps incorrectly, I take M ... to be Marguerite, Antelme's wife, and D ... to be the same person as the D. of *La Douleur*, the friend for whom his wife will leave him.[6]

La Douleur and *L'Espèce humaine* contain, in fact, a number of significant echos and cross-references, so that the two works may be regarded to some extent as complementary texts.[7] The abbreviation of names is only one of the links. The narrator of *La Douleur* discovers from returning deportees that her husband had escaped, been recaptured, but not shot (49–53); *L'Espèce humaine* fills in the details of Antelme's almost inadvertent 'escape' and offers some explanation of why he was not executed (255–60). After Robert L.'s return, his wife's concentration on his bodily functions (*La Douleur*, 69–72) picks up one of the central concerns of *L'Espèce humaine* and echoes numerous passages in which Antelme describes eating and defecation. Parts of the texts of Duras and Antelme adopt a similar diary format, and both are written largely in the present tense, as if the experiences of their respective narrators were contemporary with the act of writing. Most importantly perhaps, *La Douleur* and *L'Espèce humaine* recount events from precisely the same period, narrated respectively from the standpoint of the wife waiting in liberated Paris and from the perspective of the husband still in captivity in Germany. 'La Douleur' begins with the heading '*Avril*' (11) (April), and the diary-like section of the narrative comes to an end with an entry dated '*28 avril*' (59) (28 April). This is the same period covered in the second and third sections of *L'Espèce humaine*, entitled 'La Route' and 'La Fin', which describe the journey from Gandersheim to Dachau, and the starvation and summary executions to which the prisoners were subjected. The first words of 'La Route' give the date '4 avril' (4 April); and the final date given in the text refers to '*30 avril*' (30 April), after the arrival in Dachau and the liberation of the camp (300).

L'Espèce humaine and *La Douleur* are, then, closely related texts.[8] Initially at least, *La Douleur* places itself in a position of secondarity and dependence: thematically it describes a woman almost completely absorbed in thoughts of her husband; and as a work of testimony it testifies not to the camps themselves, but to the ignorance of those awaiting the return of their loved ones.[9] However, *La Douleur* does not passively accept a position of dependence, as is made evident by the revisionary stance adopted by Duras's work towards Antelme's text. This can be seen thematically in the wife's intention to divorce her husband and thereby consecrate his removal from the centre of her attentions and her affections; more importantly, the revisionary stance of Duras's text operates in the radical misprision through which the ethical foundations or *L'Espèce humaine* are transposed into *La Douleur*. As I shall argue in the rest of this chapter, Duras's text takes on Antelme's robust, defiant humanism and subjects it to a disturbing rereading.

Shared Humanity

In an important essay printed in *L'Entretien infini*, Maurice Blanchot takes *L'Espèce humaine* as the instigation to a 'réflexion essentielle' (essential reflection) on the question: 'Qui est "Autrui"?' (Who is the Other?).[10] With an evident debt to Levinas and Levinassian vocabulary,[11] Blanchot describes how, in Antelme's account, the experience of being interned in a concentration camp strips the human subject of its private identity and leads to an encounter with alterity:

> L'homme peut tout, et d'abord m'ôter à moi-même, me retirer le pouvoir de dire 'Je'. Dans le malheur..., l'homme, frappé par les hommes, est radicalement altéré, il n'existe plus dans son identité personnelle... [La relation du bourreau à sa victime], c'est bien plutôt ce rapport sans pouvoir qui fait surgir, face à face et cependant à l'infini, la présence de l'Autre comme celle d'Autrui.[12]

> Man can do everything, and first of all he can take me away from myself, take away the power to say 'I'. In misfortune..., man, beaten by men, is radically altered, he no longer exists in his personal identity.... [The relationship between executioner and victim] is rather this relationship without power which makes appear, face to face and yet to infinity, the presence of the Other as that of Others.

For Blanchot, the significance of *L'Espèce humaine* does not lie principally in its testimony to the historical existence of the concentration camps; its most important aspect is the insight it offers into the nature of alterity, the irreducible place it occupies in human relations and the role that it might play in the demand for social justice. This reading informs Blanchot's attempt to explain the textuality of the work. Blanchot argues that the point of writing is not primarily to communicate an experience; *parler* (to speak) represents a movement towards the Other, a willingness to hear and respond to the alterity at the far side of identity:

> Ce n'est pas, je l'ai dit, ce n'est pas seulement un témoignage sur la réalité d'un camp, ni une relation historique, ni un récit autobiographique. Il est clair que pour Robert Antelme, et sans doute pour beaucoup d'autres, se raconter, témoigner, ce n'est pas de cela qu'il s'est agi, mais essentiellement *parler*: en donnant expression à quelle parole? Précisément cette parole juste où 'Autrui', empêché de se révéler pendant tout le séjour des camps, pouvait seul à la fin être accueilli et entrer dans l'entente humaine.[13]

> It is not, as I have already said, it is not only a testimony about the reality of a camp, nor a historical account, nor an autobiographical narrative. It is clear that for Robert Antelme, and probably for many others, to tell one's story, to bear witness, that wasn't what they wanted, but rather essentially *to speak*: by giving expression to what word? Precisely that just word in which 'the Other', prevented from revealing itself during the period in the camps, could alone finally be greeted and enter into human understanding.

Blanchot is making a number of moves which are, to say the least, questionable. The hesitation in his prose ('Ce n'est pas, je l'ai dit, ce n'est pas *seulement*...') (It is not, as I have already said, it is not *only*...) perhaps betrays a degree of unease about the reading of *L'Espèce humaine* which he offers. Claiming to take Antelme's experience of the camps and reveal 'l'essentiel de la situation, sa vérité' (the essence of the situation, its truth)[14] is in itself an act of considerable (and perhaps tasteless) hubris. Blanchot dehistoricizes the camps in the name of some untheorized transcendental reduction conducted in a rhetoric of truths, essences and 'la relation humaine dans sa primaute' (human relations in their primacy).[15] Moreover, he badly misreads the urgency of testimony, understood as bearing witness to real historical events, in *L'Espèce humaine*. It is true that Antelme's book is painfully aware of the pitfalls of testimony; but Antelme's knowledge of his own failure – potential or real – does not overwhelm the imperative to communicate. The mimetic project, however precarious, is affirmed in the opening paragraph of the book: 'Nous voulions parler, être entendus enfin. On nous dit que notre apparence physique était assez éloquente à elle seule. Mais nous revenions juste, nous ramenions avec nous notre mémoire, notre expérience toute vivante et nous éprouvions un désir frénétique de la dire telle qu'elle' (9) (We wanted to speak, finally to be heard. We were told that our physical appearance was eloquent enough on its own. But we were just returning, we were bringing back with us our memory, our still vivid experience. And we felt a frenetic desire to tell it as it was). And later, the narrator insists once again, 'Je rapporte ici ce que j'ai vécu' (11) (I am recounting here what I experienced).

Blanchot's transformation of *L'Espèce humaine* into a reflection on alterity and an expression of a Levinassian 'humanisme de l'autre homme' (humanism of the other man)[16] entails a significant distortion of the ethical stance adopted within the text itself. In particular, the Other does not have the centrality which Blanchot gives it in his reading. The Other appears, according to Blanchot, when the subject is no longer able to say 'I': 'Dans le malheur, nous nous approchons de cette limite où, privés du pouvoir de dire "Je", privés aussi du monde, nous ne serions plus que cet Autre que nous ne sommes pas' (In misfortune we approach that limit where, deprived of the power to say 'I', deprived also of the world, we would only be that Other that we are not).[17] However, it is not the case that the narrator of *L'Espèce humaine* loses his hold on the first person pronoun. In fact, in Duras's *La Douleur* the 'Je' (I) of the narrating subject is much more unstable, much more liable to slip into an alienating and alienated third person (see for example *La Douleur*, 46), than it is in *L'Espèce humaine*. In Antelme's book, on the contrary, the narrator clings doggedly to his use of the first person. He endeavours to maintain his 'Je' (I), even if the embattled self is reduced to little more than the subject of its own bodily functions. Indeed the text can be read as the triumph of the first person over the forces which aim to alienate it from itself. Curiously, Blanchot reverses what Levinas describes as the characteristic move of Western thought: rather than appropriating the Other from the standpoint of the Same, Blanchot rebaptizes Antelme's affirmation of the persistence of the Same as the emergence of the radical Other.

L'Espèce humaine gives voice to a much more conventional, mid-century Marxist humanism than the ethics of alterity sketched by Blanchot.[18] One of the central dramas of the text involves the attempt to preserve a basically hopeful sense of human value in the face of experiences which expose it to the maximum possible strain. The text documents a series of different responses to internment, some more ignominious than others. Even amongst the prisoners there are differences and stratifications: the political prisoners (*détenus politiques*) are pitted against the common criminals (referred to as *droit commun*), the Poles compete against the French, and each prisoner is set against all others in the struggle for food. A camp aristocracy develops, with the Kapos (block leaders, prisoners with authority over others), interpreters and kitchen workers receiving better treatment and more food as reward for their willingness to work with the camp authorities. Some prisoners beat and exploit their fellows with at least as much alacrity as the prison guards. Contrary images of German civilians are also offered: one man encourages the prisoners to work more slowly in order to preserve their strength, and he shakes their hand in a gesture of common, decent humanity (59, 80); another respectable middle-class civilian one day beats a prisoner for the first time and discovers in himself the bestial instinct behind the Nazi regime (197–8).

The SS and their collaborators explain the differences between men as insurmountable differences of *nature*: the common criminals attempt to present themselves to the SS as 'différents de nous par nature' (10) (different from us by nature), the Kapos become 'des hommes d'une nature différente de celle des détenus' (133) (men of a different nature from the prisoners); the 'cassure définitive' (148) (definitive gulf) between victims and victors is to be maintained through violence. But the consistent move of *L'Espèce humaine* is to insist that these differences of nature are in fact products of historical conditions. In this respect, Antelme's work echoes the Marxist analysis of the camps to be found, for example, in fellow Buchenwald internee David Rousset's *L'Univers concentrationnaire*.[19] The concentration camp system functions as a moment of privileged historical revelation when social relations under Capitalism are laid bare (see, for example, 56–7). But for Antelme, the endeavour to create and enforce differences in nature between men cannot alter the indivisibility of the human species. Repeatedly he returns to this theme. Whatever the attempts of the SS to dehumanize them, the prisoners remain men:

Mais il n'y a pas d'ambiguïté, nous restons des hommes, nous ne finirons qu'en hommes. La distance qui nous sépare d'une autre espèce reste intacte, elle n'est pas historique.... [Il] n'y a pas des espèces humaines, il y a une espèce humaine. C'est parce que nous sommes des hommes comme eux que les SS seront en définitive impuissants devant nous.... [Nous] sommes obligés de dire qu'il n'y a qu'une espèce humaine. Que tout ce qui masque cette unité dans le monde, tout ce qui place les êtres dans la situation d'exploités, d'asservis et impliquerait par là même, l'existence de variétés d'espèces, est faux et fou.... [Le bourreau] peut tuer un homme, mais il ne peut pas le changer en autre chose. (229–30)

But there is no ambiguity, we remain men, even at the end we will be men. The distance which separates us from other species remails intact, it is not historical.... [There] are not several human species, there is one human species. It is because we are men like them that the SS will be definitively powerless against us.... [We] are obliged to say that there is only one human species. That everything that masks this unity in the world, everything that puts men in the position of being exploited or enslaved and might imply by that fact that there might exist a variety of species, is false and mad.... [The executioner] can kill a man, but he can't change him into something else.

This affirmation cuts two ways: if the SS fail to rob the prisoners of their humanity, then it is also the case that prisoners and SS are or the same species, the crimes of the latter remain potentialities of the former. Even so, the dominant move of *L'Espèce humaine* is to emphasize the positive side of the affirmation. The text charts the endeavour to fracture the unity of the human species, to undermine the subjecthood of the prisoners; yet it affirms the unbreached wholeness of humanity and the survival of the self despite the threat of its annihilation.

Shared Crime

In his important book on Duras entitled *Marguerite Duras: Apocalyptic Desires*, Leslie Hill relates the passage from *L'Espèce humaine* quoted above to the following lines from *La Douleur*:

Si l'on fait un sort allemand à l'horreur nazie, et non pas un sort collectif, on réduira l'homme de Belsen aux dimensions du ressortissant régional. La seule réponse à faire à ce crime est d'en faire un crime de tous. De le partager. De même que l'idée d'égalité, de fraternité. Pour le supporter, pour en tolérer l'idée, partager le crime. (60-1)

If we make of the Nazi horror a German fate, and not a collective fate, we will reduce man in Belsen to the dimensions of a regional occurrence. The only response to make to this crime is to make it everyone's crime. To share it. In the same way as the idea of equality, fraternity. To make it supportable, to make the idea tolerable, share the crime.

Hill observes that Duras's response here 'accords most clearly with the view expressed by Antelme himself in his own memoir, *L'Espèce humaine*'.[20] In a more detailed account of the complex relations between *La Douleur* and *L'Espèce humaine*, Martin Crowley also insists that 'at no point do the implications of Duras's texts in fact exceed what is already implied – and occasionally highlighted – in *L'Espèce humaine.*'[21] However, although there is a clear link between the quoted passages of Duras and Antelme and between their texts more generally, the difference in emphasis between them is crucial. Antelme invokes the unity of the human species in order to affirm, against the efforts of the Nazis, the survival of the prisoners as human beings. There is no notion in Antelme's text that the prisoners should also *share* responsibility for the crimes of their oppressors. Duras's narrator goes much further than Antelme. She develops a possibility inherent in Antelme's position, but one which remains mainly in the background of *L'Espèce humaine*: the unity of the human species has the consequence that SS and prisoners, torturers and victims, perpetrators and bystanders are disturbingly indistinguishable in nature. Collective responsibility for the Holocaust extends beyond the Nazis and the German people in general to fall on everyone. We are confronted, as she insists, with 'un crime de tous' (61) (everyone's crime).

This conclusion is at a far remove from anything implied in Antelme's text. Yet Duras's narrator suggests that the knowledge of human potential *derives from* Antelme's writing. In 'Monsieur X. dit ici Pierre Rabier' the narrator refers to her fears for Robert L. and her ignorance about the Nazi concentration camps:

On ne sait pas encore pour les camps.... Rien n'a été encore découvert des atrocités nazies.... Nous sommes au premier temps de l'humanité. Elle est là vierge, virginale, pour encore quelques mois. Rien n'est encore révélée sur l'Espèce Humaine (118).

We don't yet know about the camps.... Nothing has yet been found out about the Nazi atrocities.... We are still in the first time of humanity. There it is, pure, virginal, for a few months yet. Nothing has yet been revealed about the Human Species.

The capitalization of 'Espèce Humaine' (Human Species) suggests that the phrase should be read as an allusion to Antelme's work, which is elevated to the status of a revelatory text capable of robbing humanity of its virginal naivety. This is confirmed in the final sentence of 'Monsieur X. dit ici Pierre Rabier' which refers to the summer of 1945, the return of the camp survivors and the consequences of discovering their narratives of suffering: 'L'été est arrivé avec ses morts, ses survivants, son inconcevable douleur réverbérée des Camps de Concentration Allemands' (131) (Summer arrived with its dead, its survivors, its inconceivable pain reverberating from the German Concentration Camps).

Fragments of the Marxist analysis which informs *L'Espèce humaine* can also be found in Duras's *La Douleur*: the text describes the restoration of social and political divisions in France after the relative levelling of the war, the re-emergence of a bureaucratic class conscious of its authority and privileges, and resentment against the carefully nurtured myth of De Gaulle as the saviour of the French, 'celui qui a sauvé notre honneur pendant quatre ans' (56) (the person who saved our honour for four years). There are also passages of unambiguous moral outrage provoked by accounts of Nazi atrocities:

Ils sont très nombreux, les morts sont vraiment très nombreux. Sept millions de juifs ont été exterminés, transportés en fourgons à bestiaux, et puis gazés dans les chambres à gaz faites à cet effet et puis brûlés dans les fours crématoires faits à cet effet.... Une des plus grandes nations civilisées du monde, la capitale de la musique de tous les temps vient d'assassiner onze millions d'êtres humains à la façon méthodique, parfaite, d'une industrie d'état. (60)

They are very numerous, the dead are really very numerous. Seven million Jews have been exterminated, transported in cattle waggons, and then gassed in gas chambers made for this purpose and then burned in crematorium ovens made for this purpose.... One of the largest civilized nations in the world, the music capital of all time, has just murdered eleven million human beings in the methodical, perfect manner of a state industry.

However, having begun from such a clear moral standpoint, this passage ends with the already quoted reference to Nazi atrocities as 'un crime de tous' (61) (everyone's crime). Duras crucially distorts the significance of Antelme's insistence on the oneness of the human species precisely at the moment when she seems to be coming closest to it. Antelme's text provides the intellectual and moral framework which informs Duras's work, but *La Douleur* teases out consequences of that framework which endanger the ethical foundations of *L'Espèce humaine*. The insistence on the indivisibility of the human species also entails the implicit acceptance that no fundamental moral barrier separates the victim from the persecutor. What remains a possible consequence of the thinking behind *L'Espèce humaine* becomes fully explicit in *La Douleur*: 'Nous sommes de la race de ceux qui sont brûlés dans les crématoires et des gazés de Maïdanek, nous sommes aussi de la race des nazis' (57) (We are of the same race as those who are burned in the crematoriums and those gassed in Maidanek, we are also of the same race as the Nazis).

In his *Marguerite Duras: Apocalyptic Desires*, Leslie Hill observes the intricacies of the relationship between Nazis (or collaborators) and Resistants in *La Douleur*: in 'Monsieur X. dit ici Pierre Rabier' the narrator befriends a collaborator with the full agreement of the Resistance; in 'Albert des Capitales' the central female character promotes an act of senseless torture; in 'Ter le milicien' she seems attracted to a member of the collaborationist *Milice*.[22] However, by conflating the texts of Duras and Antelme on precisely the issue which, in my view, separates them most fundamentally, and by proposing an account of Antelme's text which is heavily marked by the influence of Blanchot, Hill is able to give an affirmative twist to the potentially disturbing confusion of moral positions which he finds in the works of Antelme and Duras. In Antelme's text, the very act of writing is associated with the possibility of survival and the 'desperate capacity for apocalyptic affirmation':

Writing, then, is always already transgressive of authority; it always exceeds the law that seeks to impose limits and to police borders.... Even at the most extreme point of dereliction and despair there is room for the possibility of affirmation;... the ethics implied in *L'Espèce humaine* is an ethics founded on the transgressive value of writing, and much the same is arguably true of Duras's texts in *La Douleur*. Writing, here, has a strange status. It precedes the law of division and exclusion, and undermines the authority of the law by fusing together apparently irreconcilable opposites; and it dissolves all fixity of meaning by virtue of the fact that words always exceed whatever it is they appear to say. Writing here takes on the role of a radical force that overwhelms identity, and disperses all monolithic authority or power. It continually outlives its own finite character and survives as pure affirmation, as an attentiveness to otherness that eschews moral dogmatism and refuses to enclose meaning or alterity within the circular equations of dialectical identity.[23]

Hill's language suggests the positive moral significance of transgression: excess, undermining, otherness or alterity are to be valued, whereas laws, limits, authority, power, fixity, moral dogmatism and dialectical identity are rejected. Hill is demonstrating the relevance of Duras's text to a poststructuralist politics and ethics; as he observes, 'for Duras, the only politics consistent with the ethics of writing is a politics that rejects all forms of representation or external authority; it is a politics that is simultaneously a refusal of politics.'[24]

However, despite the surface hostility towards dialectical processes exhibited in the passage quoted above ('[Writing] refuses to enclose meaning or alterity within the circular equations of dialectical identity'), a movement of dialectical recuperation continues to inform Hill's reading of *La Douleur*. A positive ethical moment is observed: moral outrage at the concentration camps, participation in the Resistance, the commitment to social justice. This is contrasted with a negative ethical moment: the disrespect for traditional polarities, the dissolution of comfortable moral distinctions, the erosion of distinctions between collaborator and Resistant. These two moments are then combined, preserved and surpassed in the concluding affirmation of transgression as a positive ethical force. Hill conflates *L'Espèce humaine* and *La Douleur* in order, nervously ('and much the same is arguably also true of Duras's texts in *La Douleur*'), to associate the two texts with the same ethics of writing. This conflation entails a distortion of both texts and of the relationship between them: the role of transgression in *L'Espèce humaine* is exaggerated, when much of the drama and tension of the text consists in its attempt to preserve, in the face of brutal counter-evidence, a humanist faith in the inherent value of humanity; and the violent capability of human beings in *La Douleur* is underemphasized when its shocking potential is turned to the service of an affirmative, transgressive ethics of writing.

This violent capability is most starkly revealed in the third story of *La Douleur*, entitled 'Albert des Capitales'. This story narrates the beginnings of internal division within the previously unified group of Resistants. The split first becomes evident when the central character, Thérèse, finds herself in opposition to the rest of the group as she argues for the execution of German soldiers (140). The sense of common aims and values is further eroded when Thérèse presides over the savage and increasingly pointless torture of a suspected collaborator; some of the Resistants approve, whilst some leave in disgust: 'Le bloc des camarades s'est scindé. Quelque chose de définitif est en train de s'accomplir. De nouveau. En accord avec certains, en désaccord avec d'autres. Les uns suivent de toujours plus près. Les autres deviennent des étrangers' (153) (The bloc of comrades has split. Something definitive is happening. Again. With the agreement of some, with the disagreement of others. Some follow ever more closely. Others become strangers).

'Albert des Capitales' boldly reverses the victim's perspective adopted in Antelme's *L'Espèce humaine* and 'La Douleur' itself. Here, the protagonist is in a position of agency and power, and she abuses it just as surely as the Nazis and collaborators had in different circumstances. The title 'Albert des Capitales' refers to a name found in the diary of a suspected collaborationist informer; the name is presumed to refer to a contact and perhaps provides a lead into the whole collaborationist network. But within the story, Albert is also the name of one of the two Resistants who actually administer the beatings ordered by Thérèse; and the use of the same name perhaps gives a first indication that the differences between collaborators and Resistants are less marked than the profound similarities between them. The suspected collaborator implies that he is fundamentally the same as everyone else, and to a certain extent the text supports this implication. When forced to strip, the prisoner removes his tie 'comme les autres' (147) (like the others); he claims to have got into the Gestapo headquarters 'comme tout le monde' (like everyone), and the phrase is repeated two more times (150); and he claims to have been 'un bon patriote, comme vous' (151) (a good patriot, like you). This identity between victim and persecutor, collaborator and Resistant, is precisely what most infuriates those who wield power. In the analysis offered in Antelme's *L'Espèce humaine*, the SS were endeavouring to *denature* their victims, to establish and enforce a radical ontological difference between themselves and the prisoners. Thérèse aims to do the same in 'Albert des Capitales'. The attempt to discover the whereabouts of the mysterious Albert rapidly becomes peripheral to the interrogation; as the violence escalates, Thérèse's questions seek to discover only the colour of the card used to get into Gestapo headquarters, a question to which she already knows the answer. But as the substance of the interrogation becomes less important, the attempt to dehumanize the prisoner acquires its full significance. Rather than to gain information, the purpose of the torture is to establish a chasm between victim and torturer.

Duras's text collaborates in the dehumanizing of the prisoner by adopting a form of *style indirect libre* which avoids all analysis, explanation or justification and which offers no moral criteria by which to judge Thérèse's actions. As he is beaten and becomes increasingly bloody and incoherent, the prisoner ceases to be 'comme les autres' (like others), 'comme tout le monde' (like everyone) or 'comme vous' (like you); he is no longer of the same species as other men: 'Ce n'est déjà pas un homme comme les autres.... Mais maintenant on ne peut plus le comparer à rien de vivant. Même mort, il ne ressemblera pas à un homme mort' (156) (He is already not a man like the others.... But now he can no longer be compared to anything living. Even dead, he will not look like a dead man). The language of the text assists in the dehumanization of the prisoner. At first the Resistants use conventional insults: 'Salaud, cochon, fumier' (151) (Bastard, pig, dirt). Later, warming to the task as Thérèse warms to the torture, the narrator becomes more inventive. The man is likened to a flea ('Il veut vivre. Même les poux se raccrochent à la vie,' 154) (He wants to live. Even fleas cling to life). But even this is too animate, as the text fulfils its claim that 'on ne peut plus le comparer à rien de vivant' (156) (he can no longer be compared to anything living). The prisoner's inarticulate screech of pain is compared to that of a siren (160), and he is thrown around by his torturers like a ball:

Les gars le sortent du coin où il se réfugie sans cesse. Ils le sortent et l'y rejettent comme ils le feraient d'une balle.... Ils se le lancent comme une balle et frappent à coups de poing, à coups de pied. (158–9)

The lads take him out of the corner where he keeps taking refuge. They take him out and throw him back as they would a ball.... They throw him to one another like a ball and beat him with their fists, with their feet.

Finally Thérèse asks for the release of the prisoner, with no important information having been revealed. The claim is made that the torture is perpetrated in the name of justice: 'Plus il frappe, plus il saigne, plus c'est clair qu'il faut frapper, que c'est vrai, que c'est juste' (153) (The more he strikes, the more he bleeds, the more it is clear that one must strike, that it's true, that it's just). But the equation of justice with escalating violence and the victim's blood ('plus il saigne, plus c'est clair... que c'est juste') (the more he bleeds, the more it's clear... that it's just) hollows the ethical claim of the last trace of credibility. The irony of 'Albert des Capitales' is that, in showing that they are *different* from the collaborator, the Resistants show that they are *no better* than him, and if anything they are worse. The story comes dangerously close to replicating, and sanctioning, the annihilation or at least the denaturing of the Other which, according to Antelme's account in *L'Espèce humaine*, the SS attempted to achieve in the concentration camps.

Art without Ethics

Hill, like other critics who have written on *La Douleur*, observes the disturbing nature of 'Albert des Capitales' but does not dwell on it.[25] The transgression of comfortable moral distinctions between victims and persecutors is acknowledged, but transgression is itself given an ethical force. I suggest, on the contrary, that it is difficult to read Duras's erasure of ethics as itself ethical. Her writing leaves open no prospect that the negative insight can be understood as a step along the road leading to an ultimate ethical revelation.

The spectral presence of Robert Antelme and his text in *La Douleur* can also be described as the haunting, distressing absence of the moral fortitude of *L'Espèce humaine*. Antelme's text asserts the unity of species between victim and persecutor in order to affirm a basic core of ineradicable human value; the boldness of *La Douleur* resides in its readiness to explore the bleakest side of that insight, finding an absent centre where Antelme had sought real worth.[26] In Duras's writing, being in the right, being a Resistant rather than a collaborator, a victim rather than a torturer, is an historical accident without ethical significance. It provides no lesson to be learned, no moral improvement to be gained. To call this an ethics of writing is to obscure the point, or rather the absence of point; it *insinuates* an ethical significance where none can be *demonstrated*. In the liminary text to 'La Douleur' Duras refers to literature as a source of shame (10); but this is not the shame felt by Antelme, for example, on the train to Dachau, when he is robbed of his last shreds of human dignity.[27] Antelme's shame is an incitement to outrage, potentially resulting in real moral or political consequences. Duras's shame, on the contrary, is associated by her with the condition of literature, a condition which *La Douleur* does little to question. Kristeva, famously, has described Duras's writing as an art without catharsis.[28] It is also – and this is perhaps what makes it most difficult for us to accept – an art without ethics, a literature which holds open no prospect for the recovery of moral value.

This does not mean that the experience of reading Duras may not be in some sense ethical. Duras herself sometimes gestured towards an ethical justification of her writing: recognizing the human potential for violence is thus identified as a way of preventing its realization.[29] This effectively lets us off the hook by providing a sanitized way of interpreting the representation of horror. But there is some risk here: why should the recognition of violence not also or alternatively be perceived as sanctioning it, of making it seem attractive or acceptable? Current debates about the effects of horror films suggest that some viewers may be encouraged in acts of violence by seeing them represented on screen. The same film or text may be edifying for some, morally corrosive for others; the mistake would be to confuse our response with a quality inherent in the work itself. What I am resisting here is the hasty transformation of a disturbing corpus into something ultimately edifying and beneficial. The encounter with the otherness of literature does not take place if we do not permit the Other to say what we do not wish to hear. If Duras's ethical indifference is turned too rapidly into a new ethical revelation, then perhaps her disquieting voice has gone unheard. Just as sense-making is fundamental to our activities as readers and critics, so the discovery of value is a basic, defining factor in our response to literary texts, even when those texts offer little by way of sense or value on which to build. Ethical dissidence or disengagement obstructs the affirmation of value and arouses a deep-seated hostility; and the critical resistance to the otherness of the unethical text can be observed still more clearly through the writings of Jean Genet, with which the next chapter is concerned.

8
Readers, Others: Genet

> Les romans ne sont pas des rapports humanitaires. (Novels are not humanitarian reports)
> (*Miracle de la rose*, 271)

Reading Genet

Jean Genet's first novel, *Notre-Dame-des-Fleurs*, is described on its second page as written in honour of the crimes of murderers,[1] and his texts are punctuated by murders committed and described with almost casual detachment.[2] For the eponymous hero of *Notre-Dame-des-Fleurs*, becoming a murderer is all too easy:

> Tuer est facile, le coeur étant placé à gauche, juste en face de la main armée du tueur, et le cou s'encastrant si bien dans les deux mains jointes. Le cadavre du vieillard, d'un de ces mille vieillards dont le sort est de mourir ainsi, gît sur le tapis bleu. Notre-Dame l'a tué. Assassin. (104–5)

> Killing is easy, since the heart is placed on the left, just opposite the armed hand of the killer, and since the neck fits so neatly in his two joined hands. The corpse of the old man, of one of those thousand old men whose lot is to die in this way, lies on the blue carpet. Notre-Dame has killed him. Murderer.

Characters in later books kill with equal ease. Harcamone in *Miracle de la rose* murders a prison warden:

Je ne puis savoir comment Harcamone se trouva sur le passage du gâfe, mais on dit qu'il se précipita derrière lui, le saisit par l'épaule, comme s'il eût voulu, par-derrière, l'embrasser.... (A la main droite, il tenait un tranchet volé à la cordonnerie.) Il donna un coup. Bois de Rose s'enfuit. Harcamone courut après lui. Il le rattrapa, le ressaisit à l'épaule et cette fois, lui trancha la carotide. Le sang gicla sur sa main droite qu'il n'avait pas retirée à temps. (73-4)

I don't know how Harcamone came to be on the warden's route, but people say he threw himself behind him, grabbed him by the shoulder, as if he wanted, from behind, to kiss him.... (In his right hand he was holding a leather knife stolen from the cobbler's.) He struck a blow. Bois de Rose fled. Harcamone ran after him. He caught him, grabbed him by the shoulder again and this time cut his jugular. Blood spurted on to his right hand, which he hadn't withdrawn quickly enough.

In *Pompes funèbres* Erik commits an apparently unmotivated murder, justifying his repeated shooting with a rather poor play on words:

Je tirai. Je tirai trois coups.
 – Un garçon aussi joli peut bien me faire tirer trois coups.
 Du reste, le premier seul comptait. L'enfant tomba comme on tombe dans ces cas-là, en fléchissant sur les jambes, la face contre la terre. Je regardai immédiatement l'arme et connus que j'étais bien un assassin avec le canon de mon revolver, comme celui des gangsters, des tueurs, relatés dans les pages illustrées de ma jeunesse. (81)

I fired. I fired three times.
 – Such a pretty boy can make me fire/come three times.
 Besides, only the first shot counted. The child fell like people fall in those cases, his legs bending, his face against the ground. I looked immediately at the weapon and knew that I was really a murderer with the barrel of my revolver, like those of the gangsters, the killers, whose stories were told in the magazines of my youth.

154 *Ethical Issues in French Fiction*

At the end of the same novel, Erik is in turn murdered by Riton after their sexual encounter on the rooftops of Paris:

> Dans un angle, Riton boutonna sa braguette, puis il saisit doucement la mitraillette. Il tira un coup. Erik s'abattit, roula sur la pente du toit et tomba. (191)

> In a corner, Riton buttoned up his trousers, then he gently picked up the machine gun. He fired a shot. Erik collapsed, rolled down the slope of the roof and fell.

In *Querelle de Brest* Querelle is, like his predecessors in Genet's fiction, a skilled murderer; for example, he kills Vic, his accomplice in crime:

> Vif, Querelle lui serra la gorge, lâchant le paquet qui tomba sur le sentier. Quand il relâcha son étreinte, avec une aussi grande prestesse il tira de sa poche son couteau ouvert et il trancha la carotide au matelot. Vic ayant le col du caban relevé, le sang, au lieu de jaillir sur Querelle, s'écoula le long du vêtement, sur la veste. (248)

> Quickly, Querelle took him by the throat, dropping the package which fell on the path. When he released his grip, with equal speed he took his open knife from his pocket and cut the sailor's jugular. Since the collar of Vic's coat was raised, the blood, instead of spurting on to Querelle, ran down the coat, on to his jacket.

The profit motive which may lie behind some of these murders is completely absent from others. The narrator typically offers little by way of explanation. Harcamone's crime is 'un mystère aussi absurde que celui que propose une rose dans tout son éclat' (*Miracle*, 224) (a mystery as absurd as that proposed by a rose in all its beauty). The narrator of *Pompes funèbres* concedes that the explanations he will give for Erik's crime 'ne sembleront pas d'abord valables' (will not at first seem valid), though he proposes, perhaps unconvincingly, that the act may elucidate the rest of the novel (79). Whereas in Malraux, for example, murder is bound up with the passionate fascination for the experience of extreme, irrevocable acts,[3] Genet's prose is too cold, his narratorial stance too distanced, for such intense engagement. Murder may be 'l'acte symbolique du mal' (*Pompes funèbres*, 79) (the act which symbolizes evil); but, as Georges Bataille noted (with regret) in the 1950s, even Genet's taste for evil is half-hearted, never reaching the point of becoming a radical transgressive commitment.[4]

What is lacking in these descriptions of murder is any sort of ethical perspective. Genet's narrators are more interested in the prestige conferred on the murderer by his crime than by the moral judgement that his readers might be inclined to make. Genet thus poses an acute problem for ethical criticism, at least in its most humanist varieties. Wayne Booth argues that ethical criticism 'attempts to describe the encounters of a storyteller's ethos with that of the reader or listener';[5] in similar vein, Martha Nussbaum proposes a mutually respectful alliance of philosophy and literature based upon a commitment to shared values.[6] But Genet offers a less amicable partnership built on shifting sands of pretence, indifference and betrayal; his unedifying texts demonstrate that non-encounters and sham dialogues may be just as characteristic of the experience of reading as the encounter or the alliance described by Booth and Nussbaum. Genet's work requires a less placid, more anxious account of the relationship between literature and ethics; and reading his works will almost inevitably entail the experience of being offended. In particular it seems impossible to discuss *Pompes funèbres*, with its praise of the pro-Nazi *Milice* and its detailed descriptions of the homosexual activities of Adolf Hitler, without some concession to straightforward moral condemnation. The novel has been described as 'not particularly palatable';[7] aspects of it are 'hard to forgive' and as a whole it is 'disappointingly puerile';[8] more radically, the novel may be 'totally unacceptable', the depiction of Hitler and his activities being 'intensely repulsive',[9] or 'repellent'.[10]

Critics have inevitably felt obliged to grapple with the moral questions raised by their engagements with Genet.[11] The terms of the problem are largely set by Sartre in *Saint Genet, comédien et martyr* (1952), the monumental study published as the first volume of Genet's *Oeuvres complètes*.[12] In the final chapter of his book, entitled 'Prière pour le bon usage de Genet' (Plea for the proper use of Genet), Sartre acknowledges that Genet's work is dominated by elements which seem diametrically opposed to his own philosophical and political concerns: Genet refuses commitment and communication, and he privileges instead singularity, solitude and failure. However, Sartre converts each of these terms into its opposite through the operation of his own sophisticated dialectic: the blockage of communication effected by Genet's self-negating prose in fact communicates the opaque nature of language; despite himself, Genet shows how solitude is a part of social reality, proves that any analysis of humanity must also account for his absolute singularity, and transforms failure into a form of success (since it is the condition of his literary genius). He also confronts his bourgeois readers with the insight that Evil is a human possibility which they contain within themselves: 'aux vices qui nous répugnent chez les autres, il nous paraît qu'une chance incroyable seule nous a fait échapper;... il est notre vérité comme nous sommes la sienne; nos vertus et ses crimes sont interchangeables' (650) (from the vices which repel us in other people, it seems that only incredible good luck has saved us;... he is our truth as we are his; our virtues and his crimes are interchangeable). Genet thus effects an ultimately beneficial subversion of his readers' comfortable world-view, requiring them to reassess their self-serving repudiation of the criminal as Other. Sartre is well aware that this moral recuperation of Genet entails reading against the grain of Genet's apparent intentions. Indeed, 'Prière pour le bon usage de Genet' can be read as Sartre's defence of reading as betrayal, as the perhaps violent assimilation of text's otherness to the values of its reader. Given the inevitability of betraying Genet (and it is striking here how the theme of betrayal extends beyond Genet's texts to characterize his commentator's response to them), Sartre ultimately accepts that he will use Genet for his own purposes:

> Jugez de mon embarras: si je révèle qu'on peut tirer profit de ses ouvrages, j'invite à les lire mais je le trahis; que j'insiste au contraire sur sa singularité, je risque de le trahir encore: après tout, s'il a livré ses poèmes au grand public, c'est qu'il souhaitait d'être lu. Trahir pour trahir, je prends le premier parti: au moins serai-je fidèle à moi-même. (646)

> See my problem: if I indicate that we can gain some profit from his works, I encourage people to read them but I betray him; if on the contrary I insist on his singularity, I risk betraying him again; after all, if he has handed over his poems to the public, it must be because he wanted to be read. Betray or betray, I take the first choice: at least I will be faithful to myself.

Overwhelmingly, Sartre's successors have replicated this move of domesticating the otherness of Genet's texts by finding in them echoes of their own values, even if the particular values uncovered may be at a far remove from those proposed by Sartre. Specific acts of appropriation have ranged from the improbable to the ingenious. Philip Thody argues that, although Genet apparently writes in praise of homosexuality and crime, he in fact shows the abjection of homosexuality, the stupidity of crime and the self-defeating nature of Evil;[13] the conservative heterosexual reader thus finds in Genet a surprisingly common-sensical[14] confirmation of his own political and sexual commitments. At a more sophisticated level Leo Bersani shows how Genet's writing dissolves the very notion of relationality which grounds the oppositions between self and Other, subject and object, Good and Evil; he thereby anticipates (even though he may not be aware of it) a new, as yet unrealized relationality in which subjecthood and sociality may be reconstituted along less oppressive lines.[15]

None of these readings is self-evidently wrong; it is not clear, however, that they are compatible. Genet's writing poses in a particularly acute form the problem of the inherent ambiguity of literature and the diversity of possible interpretations. If Genet can appear variously as reactionary or revolutionary, as someone who subverts or confirms the values of his implied bourgeois reader, one wonders whether the critics are actually reading the same texts. A curious illustration of this is provided by the apparent disagreement that has arisen over the status of Genet's writing between gay and feminist critics. Some gay critics have shown a distinct hostility towards Genet. Bersani describes Genet as 'the least "gay-affirmative" gay writer I know'.[16] Christopher Robinson, drawing on comments by recent French gay writers, criticizes the negative image of homosexuals in Genet's writing; by associating homosexuality with crime, Evil, self-hatred and abjection, Genet implicitly reinforces the stereotypes of heterosexual orthodoxy: 'he is guilty of pandering to, intensifying, even giving new life to, the traditional heterosexual view of homosexuality as abnormal, morally depraved and socially destructive.'[17] Whilst some homosexual authors have repudiated one of the best-known gay writers of the twentieth century, feminists have seen him as a potential ally. Hélène Cixous, for example, takes him as a practitioner of *écriture féminine*, rejecting the scriptural and intellectual practices of patriarchy and adopting forms of writing which explore hitherto uncharted possibilities of experience, identity and knowledge.[18] From very different theoretical premises, Kate Millett also accords a revolutionary role to Genet in her groundbreaking *Sexual Politics* (1969). In the final chapter of her book Millett shows how Genet's prose texts expose the workings of sexual domination; and more importantly still, his plays indicate his identification with the situation of women: 'Alone of our contemporary writers, Genet has taken thought of women as an oppressed group and revolutionary force, and chosen to identify with them.'[19]

Genet has been accepted as an ally by feminists, but has been repudiated by some members of the gay movement to which he would more obviously seem to belong. Both appropriation and repudiation, I would suggest, are strategies of non-reading, forms of resistance to the potent force of Genet's writing. As Child Bickel suggests, critics have tended either to find positive value in Genet's writing or to denounce its corrupting influence: 'Mais partout, la stratégie est la même: rendre l'oeuvre socialement acceptable en lui attribuant une valeur positive, ou, au contraire, constater son effet corrupteur et la rejeter, l'expulser' (But in all cases the strategy is the same: to make his work socially acceptable by attributing a positive value to it or, on the contrary, to affirm its corrupting influence and to reject it, to throw it out).[20] The publication of Jacques Derrida's *Glas* in 1974 opened up new perspectives in Genet criticism in part through its endeavour to avoid global interpretations and recuperative moral judgements. Taking issue with the existential psychoanalysis of Sartre's study, especially its urge to uncover keys for the works in the life of the author, Derrida focuses on the textual complexity of Genet's writing without attempting to find in it thematic or aesthetic unity. Derrida is more interested in how textual features (such as the chain *glas, glaviot, glaïeul, glu, sigle, glace* (knell, gob, gladioli, glue, acronym, mirror) or the proliferation of references to flowers)[21] defer meaning rather than providing clues to what the texts might be taken to signify or to exemplify. Derrida thus seeks to describe the residue, *le reste*, which normally escapes critical attention but in which consists the singularity of Genet's work.[22] Hegel, whom Derrida discusses alongside Genet in *Glas*, posits the ideal of an Absolute Knowledge from which all residue is excluded; Genet, on the other hand, undermines the project of intellectual mastery and his texts constitute the residue which Absolute Knowledge cannot recuperate.[23]

Derrida is intensely sensitive to the textual features which Sartre and others concerned with the morality of Genet's writing tend to neglect. But Derrida's virtuoso demonstration that context is nonsaturable, that multiple links and associations can always be found, that the text is never fully self-present 'in itself', has its own problems. Genet's text, according to Derrida, makes it impossible to say, 'ceci est le sujet, ceci n'est pas le sujet' (277) (this is what it is about, this is not what it is about). Derrida offers no criteria for arresting the dissemination of meaning; and by showing how it is never possible to say *everything* about the text, he conspicuously fails to say *anything* about the moral shock occasioned in most readers by, for example, the praise of Hitler and the *Milice* in *Pompes funèbres* or the prestige attached to murderers in *Notre-Dame-des-Fleurs*. In reference to Bataille's essay on Genet, Derrida is scathing about 'l'académisme sentencieux de ce discours édifiant' (277) (the sententious academicism of this edifying discourse), but he remains oddly reticent about the ethics of reading Genet and of his own commentary in particular. More damagingly for the prospects of ethical criticism, his attempts to avoid critical mastery (see 285) foreshadow a potential collapse of any critical project; the markers of caution with which he refers to writing 'about' Genet[24] suggest a disowning of the hermeneutic act of faith which underpins any critical practice: criticism requires the belief that we are *at least in some sense* writing about (not just 'about') the texts we cite, but Derrida's cautions and quotation marks indicate serious reservations in respect of even this belief. His slightly embarrassing statements of enthusiasm for Genet's writing ('Écriture merveilleuse. Incroyablement précieuse', 204) (Marvellous writing. Incredibly precious) signal an anxiety over how to proceed or, once proceeding, how to stop. Genet leaves his readers insecure about even local questions of critical protocol; and Derrida expresses an anxiety about being unfaithful to Genet which is remarkably similar in formulation to that voiced by Sartre (though Sartre is more sanguine about the inevitability of betrayal): 'Je suis donc de toute façon jugé et condamné, c'est ce qu'il a toujours cherché a faire: si j'écris pour son texte, j'écris contre lui, si j'écris pour lui, j'écris contre son texte' (279) (So in any case I am judged and condemned, that is what he always sought to do: if I write in favour of his text, I write against him, if I write in favour of him, I write against his text).

The fact that both Sartre and Derrida share a sense of unease about their appropriations of Genet's text looks too consistent to be entirely coincidental. Genet's relationship with his readers is particularly elusive; his texts lend themselves to scenes of self-recognition in which we find our own reflections rather than anything specific about Genet: 'Genet, c'est nous' (Genet is us), as Sartre concludes his study (661). Derrida in particular is acutely aware that the peculiar self-consciousness of Genet's writing lies in its ability to anticipate, facilitate and ultimately frustrate the reader's desire for meaning (see 299). Genet's texts, then, stage an encounter with a critic or reader which takes place on treacherous ground; rather than an experience of otherness, they seem to provoke an anxious, defensive self-assertion.

The interest of Genet from the perspective of this study is that he puts into question the very possibility of encountering the text as Other, of remaining receptive when what it says or does swerves too far from what we are prepared to confront. The rest of this chapter will be concerned with encounters and murders, first as themes of Genet's writing, and then as aspects of the reader's relationship with the text; finally, a confrontation between the fundamental ethical encounter described by Levinas and the murderous encounter described by Genet will illuminate the harsh morality of Genet's writing.

Encounters

A passage from near the beginning of *Journal du voleur* recounts an imaginary encounter in which the ethics of the text and its relationship with the reader are adumbrated. In a long parenthesis, the narrator describes what he might do if he were to meet his mother; the passage is prompted by his description of a tube of vaseline found on him on an occasion when he has been arrested by the police:

> (En le décrivant, je recrée ce petit objet, mais voici qu'intervient une image: sous un réverbère, dans une rue de la ville où j'écris, le visage blafard d'une petite vieille, un visage plat et rond comme la lune, très pâle, dont je ne saurais dire s'il était triste ou hypocrite. Elle m'aborda, me dit qu'elle était très pauvre et me demanda un peu d'argent. La douceur de ce visage de poisson-lune me renseigna tout de suite: la vieille sortait de la prison.
> – C'est une voleuse, me dis-je. En m'éloignant d'elle une sorte de rêverie aiguë, vivant à l'intérieur de moi et non au bord de mon esprit, m'entraîna à penser que c'était peut-être ma mère que je venais de rencontrer. Je ne sais rien d'elle qui m'abandonna au berceau, mais j'espérai que c'était cette vieille voleuse qui mendiait la nuit.

– Si c'était elle? me dis-je en m'éloignant de la vieille. Ah! Si c'était elle, j'irais la couvrir de fleurs, de glaïeuls et de roses, et de baisers! J'irais pleurer de tendresse sur les yeux de ce poisson-lune, sur cette face ronde et sotte! Et pourquoi, me disais-je encore, pourquoi y pleurer? Il fallut peu de temps à mon esprit pour qu'il remplaçât ces marques habituelles de la tendresse par n'importe quel geste et même par les plus décriés, par les plus vils, que je chargeais de signifier autant que les baisers, ou les larmes, ou les fleurs.

– Je me contenterais de baver sur elle, pensais-je, débordant d'amour. (Le mot glaïeul prononcé plus haut appela-t-il le mot glaviaux?) De baver sur ses cheveux ou de vomir dans ses mains. Mais je l'adorerais cette voleuse qui est ma mère.) (21–2)

(As I describe it, I recreate that small object, but here is an image which intervenes: under a street light, in a street in the town where I am writing, the pale face of a small old woman, a face flat and round like the moon, very pale, of which I could not say if it was sad or hypocritical. She came up to me, told me that she was very poor and asked me for a little money. The gentleness of that fish-moon face informed me immediately: the old woman was just out of prison.

– She's a thief, I said to myself. As I walked away from her a sort of acute reverie, living inside me and not at the edge of my mind, led me to think that it was perhaps my mother that I had just met. I know nothing about the woman who abandoned me at birth, but I hoped that it was that thieving old woman who begged at night.

– What if it was her? I said to myself as I walked away from the old woman. Oh! If it was her I would go and cover her with flowers, with gladioli and roses, and kisses! I would go and cry with tenderness over the eyes of that fish-moon, on that round and stupid face! And why, I said to myself, why cry about it? It took just a moment for my mind to replace these normal signs of tenderness by any other gesture, and even the most disparaged, the most vile, to which I gave the role of signifying as much as kisses, or tears, or flowers.

– I would be happy to slobber over her, I thought, brimming over with love. (Was it the word gladioli used above which made me think of the word gob?) To slobber over her hair or to vomit in her hands. But I would worship that thief who is my mother.)

With some inaccuracies and elisions (which I shall discuss in a moment), Sartre quotes this passage in *Saint Genet, comédien et martyr* and uses it to illustrate Genet's relationship with his reader (561-3). The reader at first responds favourably to the discreet appeal for pity of the abandoned child. The narrator's dream of meeting his mother and treating her with proper filial affection seems to comply with the expectations of society; even the twist towards the end of the passage, when the narrator suggests that the humble might show affection by signs in accordance with their poverty, seems reasonable. But the reader has now been duped into accepting, if only for a moment, an unacceptable conclusion, which Sartre paraphrases as, 'Vomir sur les mains de sa mère c'est lui rendre le plus bel hommage' (561) (To vomit in the hands of one's mother is to pay her the finest tribute). The reader's initial recognition of his (Sartre's reader is male) own values in the text facilitates an identification which, at the end of the passage, leaves him compromised by Genet's inverted morality: 'Et voilà l'honnête homme en train de dégueuler sur sa vieille mère' (563) (And there you have the decent man throwing up over his old mother).

In *Glas* Derrida quotes the same passage rather more accurately than Sartre, and with greater sensitivity to its context within *Journal du voleur* (*Glas*, 203-5). The passage constitutes a parenthesis within an episode which is already a digression from the main narrative: the description of life in Barcelona is interrupted by the account of a scene 'qui précéda celle par quoi débute ce livre' (*Journal du voleur*, 20) (which preceded the one with which this book begins), and which describes how the Spanish police once discovered a tube of vaseline on the narrator; this account is in turn interrupted by the passage quoted above. So the meeting with the old woman is doubly embedded in the text, part of a narrative present located after the incident with the tube of vaseline which took place before the events previously recounted. In Derrida's presentation a convoluted textual chain has priority over narrative coherence or thematic pattern: the contents of the tube make the narrator think of 'une veilleuse' (21) (night light), which then leads to the image of 'une petite vieille' (a little old woman), the 'voleuse' (thief) who then becomes a 'vieille voleuse' (old thief). Similarities of sound ('glaïeul'/'glaviaux') (gladioli/gob) contribute to a series of metonymic and metaphoric relations which link this passage to other parts of Genet's text: connections are established between flowers and spit, the phallus and sperm, swords and semen (208); the tube of vaseline is linked with the mother, who in turn is associated with the Virgin Mary, the phallus, the clitoris (225). Derrida amply demonstrates that this series of associations and developments could be extended indefinitely, or else described quite differently; formal and semantic features are produced by a practice of writing which emerges like vaseline from a tube.

Although Derrida is not directly engaged in a critique of Sartre at this point, his response to the passage prompts two series of comments on Sartre's reading:

(1) Sartre's silence about the context of the passage weakens his analysis of it. He requires a reader who can identify – even if only temporarily – with the values apparently espoused by the narrator; only on the basis of this identification can the later reversals have their full effect. Sartre's analysis depends upon the existence of a reader who is prepared repeatedly to suspend his distaste, however recently it has been aroused. In this instance at least, it seems unlikely that the reader would be so gullible. Immediately before the imagined encounter with the mother, Genet's narrator describes a tube of vaseline 'dont la destination paraissait au monde' (21) (of which the purpose was clear to everyone); this would surely forewarn Sartre's self-righteous heterosexual reader in a fairly unambiguous fashion that the values of the text were in conflict with his own.

(2) The inaccuracies and elisions in Sartre's quotation of the passage support his reading of the text but omit important aspects of it. He leaves out the first sentence which refers to the tube of vaseline and which describes the old woman as 'une image' (an image); he begins instead with a much more solid assertion: 'Une petite vieille m'aborda' (561; Genet's text reads: 'Elle m'aborda' (22)) (An old woman came up to me/She came up to me). Sartre subsequently elides phrases which, presumably, he regards as unimportant; in the following quotation I have italicized phrases omitted by Sartre (In each case he acknowledges the omission by use of elision marks):

En m'éloignant d'elle, une sorte de rêverie aiguë, *vivant à l'intérieur de moi et non au bord de mon esprit*, m'entraîna à penser que c'était peut-être ma mère *que je venais de rencontrer*. Je ne sais rien d'elle qui m'abandonna au berceau, mais j'espérai [Sartre has *espérais*] que c'était cette vieille voleuse *qui mendiait la nuit*.
— Si c'était elle? *me dis-je en m'éloignant de la vieille*

As I walked away from her a sort of acute reverie, *living inside me and not at the edge of my mind*, led me to think that it was perhaps my mother *that I had just met*. I know nothing about the woman who abandoned me at birth, but I hoped that it was that thieving old woman *who begged at night*.
– What if it was her'? *I said to myself as I walked away from the old woman.*

Genet's text emphasizes right from the beginning that it is describing an event of which the primary importance is private and imaginary. It is 'une image' (an image), amplified by 'une sorte de rêverie aiguë, vivant à l'intérieur de moi' (a sort of acute reverie, living inside me); the narrator demonstrates that he has no desire for a real encounter with his mother by the repetition of 'en m'éloignant' (as I walked away). Sartre suppresses this, as he suppresses the repetition of 'me dis-je' (I said to myself), which occurs twice in the passage: if the narrator speaks, it is for himself only, he is both the source and destination of his own message. The first speech recorded in *Journal du voleur* is similarly self-addressed ('– Il a bien fallu, me dis-je, que le crime hésite longtemps', 12–13) (It was necessary, I said to myself, for crime to hesitate for a long time), and throughout the text the narrator shows a particular fondness for the first-person reflexive pronoun. More consistently than Sartre implies, the narrator keeps his reader at a distance; we are permitted to observe and be shocked, but not to share an experience or understand a thought process which advances as if motivated by rigorous but unspecified principles.[25]

Sartre's account of the passage depends upon a reader who misreads, who fails to observe the warning signs that would preserve him from becoming the text's fool; and in his own reading of the passage, Sartre repeats the error he diagnoses. He suppresses or overlooks contextual and internal features which are discordant with his account; and rather like the Bourgeois reader whom he describes reading Genet, he opens himself up to the text's mockery when he finds in it a reflection of his own concerns. Misreading, in detail and in general, appears then as an inevitable step in making acceptable sense out of Genet's writing;[26] and misreading is itself a counterpart to the missed encounter which is the thematic stake of Genet's text. The passage forms a parenthesis within a digression at the centre of which is a non-event, the description of a meeting that does not take place. The narrative obstructs the expected relay between text and world, or between narrator and reader, by excluding both experiential referent and communicative intention: it is concerned with an image or a reverie in the course of which the narrator establishes himself as his own principal addressee ('me dis-je') (I said to myself). This does not make the passage uninterpretable, but it does divest the reader of any security as privileged addressee in a closed communicative circuit. The reader's position is also made uncertain by the extreme fluidity of meaning and values. The text effects a series of inversions typical of Genet's writing: the tube of vaseline is an object of shame reinvested as an object of pride; dribbling and vomiting are charged with the same meaning normally attributed to conventional signs of affection.[27] But the inversion can hardly be taken as definitive. Vomit is likely to retain its ordinary sense for the reader whilst being ennobled by the narrator; dribbling on the mother appears disrespectful, or at best infantile, whilst being qualified in the passage as a sign of love. The characteristic strangeness of Genet's text depends upon the tension established between the new values explicitly espoused and their more conventional counterparts. Adoration and vilification are both signified by the same actions; as Genet wrote in his late essay on Dostoyevsky's *The Brothers Karamazov*, 'Tout acte a donc une signification et la signification inverse' (So every act has a meaning and the opposite meaning).[28]

The passage describing the narrator's non-encounter with his mother reveals an urge to retain control over both event and interpretation which is characteristic of Genet's writing and which lies at the heart of its ethical significance. The narrator of *Journal du voleur* refuses to be surprised by an unexpected meeting or a fortuitous meaning; his narrative may be ambiguous, but its ambiguity is contrived and controlled. The narrator aggressively asserts his command over text and reader; and this may serve to compensate for a loss of control experienced at a thematic level in the events narrated in *Journal du voleur*, in particular through erotic fascination. The experience of desire undermines the secure self-possession of the narrator: when he falls for Stilitano, he first blushes, then describes himself as 'Détruit' (36) (Destroyed), 'dominé' (37) (dominated), 'perdu' (38) (lost); he feels 'trouble' (36) (trouble), 'un vide' (36) (a void), 'panique' (panic) and 'détresse' (39) (distress); he compares the encounter to 'un rapport d'oiseau cruel à victime' (39) (a relationship of a cruel bird to its victim). The self is transformed by the encounter; but its endangered sovereignty is reaffirmed through the manner in which the encounter is presented in *Journal du voleur*. Several passages have already forewarned us of Stilitano's importance in the book. We are told that he has only one hand and that he is a coward (14); his spit has been described (17–18), and the narrator has recorded his reflections on Stilitano's penis (24–5). The encounter is anticipated and deferred: 'Pour mieux parler de Stilitano, le manchot, j'attendrai quelques pages' (27) (To speak better of Stilitano, the one-armed man, I will wait a few pages). When the narrator finally meets Stilitano, it entails for both him and the reader an act of recognition rather than an unexpected encounter: 'Immédiatement je reconnus Stilitano' (35) (Immediately I recognized Stilitano). Then, in an apparent digression which narrates a chronologically earlier episode, it is revealed that the narrator had in fact already encountered Stilitano after the murder by Pépé of a street gambler (43). The chronological priority of this first encounter is overturned in the text as the description of it is preceded by accounts of later meetings and reflections. Even the reliability of the narrator's recollections is brought into question by a typically casual disclaimer: 'Ce qu'alors j'éprouvai je l'ignore' (39) (What I felt then I do not know). Genet's *Journal du voleur* masters the shock of desire by asserting the primacy of the text itself over the traumatic experiences it records; the act of narration is privileged over narrated events: 'Ce que j'écris fut-il vrai? Faux? Seul ce livre d'amour sera réel' (113) (What I write was it true? False? Only this book of love will be real).[29]

When surprised by the Other, the narrating self reassembles a sovereignty which was temporarily dispersed. The story of the relationship between the narrator and Stilitano entails a gradual reaffirmation of the former's ascendancy. After the initial shock of desire, the narrator begins to assert control: he encourages Stilitano to become a thief (61) and is delighted when he witnesses his cowardice (71–2). He describes himself as Stilitano's 'valet' (servant), yet he insists that he owns the object to which he is subservient: 'J'étais le valet qui doit entretenir, l'épousseter, le polir, le cirer, un objet de grand prix, mais qui par le miracle de l'amitié m'appartenait' (64) (I was the servant who must maintain, dust, polish, wax, an object of great value, but which by the miracle of friendship belonged to me). When he meets Stilitano again in Antwerp, the narrator implies that he allows himself to love him ('je me laissais l'aimer', 136) (I let myself love him), rather than succumbing to an uncontrolled emotion. Even when obeying Stilitano's orders after a drug smuggling incident, the narrator insists that it is he who is in control: 'car je savais déjà que Stilitano était ma propre création, et qu'il dépendait de moi que je la détruisisse' (144) (for I knew already that Stilitano was my own creation, and that it depended on me to destroy him). In a footnote he describes how he feels no emotion when he reads of Stilitano's arrest (144); and finally he leads Stilitano to demonstrate his repressed homosexuality in an unambiguous act (301–4).

The text becomes a site for the construction of a sovereign self, impervious to the surprise of chance encounters. The potentially shocking confrontation with the Other is at least in part avoided by the consistent gesture of seeing each person as a new version of an already familiar category. The narrator concedes that his lovers and characters resemble one another (106, 219; see also *Pompes funèbres*, 74); and his endeavour is to reduce all experience and all new acquaintances to the already-known, to deny any remnant of irreducible otherness in the encounter with the Other. Even his use of the future perfect tense suggests a future that is already in a sense past because it can only repeat what has already been seen; the narrator refuses to be surprised: 'A tout comportement, le plus étrange en apparence, je connaissais d'emblée, sans y réfléchir, une justification. ... J'aurai donc traversé les pénitenciers, les prisons, connu les bouges, les bars, les routes sans m'étonner' (114–15) (In all behaviour, even what seemed to be the strangest, I immediately knew, without thinking about it, a justification. ... So I will have passed through penitentiaries, prisons, known dives, bars, roads, without being surprised).

Genet's text seeks to maintain a solipsistic self-absorption which excludes the unforeseen and the accidental. In an extraordinary passage the narrator describes how the self becomes its own companion, establishes the external world as a divinity of which it is the privileged creation, and finally draws this divinity into itself and identifies with it:

> Tant de solitude m'avait forcé à faire de moi-même pour moi un compagnon. Envisageant le monde hors de moi, son indéfini, sa confusion plus parfaite encore la nuit, je l'érigeais en divinité dont j'étais non seulement le prétexte chéri, objet de tant de soin et de précaution, choisi et conduit supérieurement encore qu'au travers d'épreuves douloureuses, épuisantes, au bord du désespoir, mais l'unique but de tant d'ouvrages. Et, peu à peu,

par une sorte d'opération que je ne puis que mal décrire, sans modifier les dimensions de mon corps mais parce qu'il était plus facile peut-être de contenir une aussi précieuse raison à tant de gloire, c'est en moi que j'établis cette divinite – origine et disposition de moi-même. (96)

So much solitude had forced me to make of myself a companion for myself. Regarding the world outside myself, its indeterminate nature, its confusion which was even more perfect at night, I set it up as a divinity of which I was not only the beloved pretext, the object of so much care and precaution, chosen and led by a higher force even through painful, exhausting trials, but the unique goal of so much work. And, little by little, by a sort of operation that I can only describe badly, without modifying the dimensions of my body but because it was perhaps easier to contain such a precious reason for so much glory, it is in myself that I established this divinity – origin and disposition of myself.

The narrator of *Journal du voleur* appears as weak ('je suis corruptible à l'extrême', 235) (I am corruptible in the extreme) and hazardously susceptible to desire and longing, but also as divinely strong ('je suis mon propre dieu', 24) (I am my own god). He is the 'conscience réfléchissante' (reflecting consciousness) of his companions (295), in full possession of the world and experiencing it only as a region of himself ('cette région de moi-même: la Guyane', 16; 'cette contrée de moi que j'ai nommée l'Espagne', 306) (this region of myself: Guiana; this region of myself that I have called Spain); he establishes himself as incapable of surprise, the source of his own inscrutable principles and commandments.

The self-founding, self-legislating subjecthood to which Genet's narrators aspire entails a rejection of the encounter with alterity. The extreme lengths to which this is taken in Genet's writing are a repudiation of the Other, but also a tacit acknowledgement of its power over the subject, and furthermore of its insistent presence as part of the subject. In 'Ce qui est resté d'un Rembrandt déchiré en petits carrés réguliers, et foutu aux chiottes' Genet recounts a devastating encounter on a train which reveals to him the fundamental equivalence of everyone. Singularity, the uniqueness and sovereignty of the subject, are corroded by the discovery that, as Genet puts it,

'Chacun est l'autre et les autres' (Everyone is the other and the others).[30] Even as it asserts its ability to contain the whole of the real, the subject is riven. 'La scène fut en moi, j'y assistai' (The scene was inside me, I was present at it), writes the narrator of *Miracle de la rose* (26). He thereby says two things at once: he contains the real within himself, but at the same time he is a witness to and thus separated from his own innermost being. The solipsistic subject contains everything, but is also internally fissured.

The exclusion of alterity is, then, also an extreme susceptibility to it. This is most evident in *Pompes funèbres*, a work written in mourning for a dead lover which repeatedly demonstrates how the passionate, traumatized subject is inhabited and constituted by the lost Other. From the beginning the text is characterized as a locus where seemingly independent and mutually obscure agencies compete within and for the self: 'Il est troublant qu'un thème macabre m'ait été offert il y a longtemps, afin que je le traite aujourd'hui et l'incorpore malgré moi à un texte chargé de décomposer le rayon lumineux, fait surtout d'amour et de douleur, que projette mon coeur désolé' (*Pompes funèbres*, 10) (It is troubling that a macabre subject was offered to me a long time ago, so that I might deal with it today and incorporate it despite myself in a text charged with decomposing the ray of light, made up especially of love and pain, which my sorrowful heart projects). The narrator describes himself as troubled by material imposed from outside himself with some apparent, but unspecified purpose; yet the outside world is itself the projection of his most intimate emotions. His text is both absolutely his own possession, and dictated by some authority of which he has no knowledge. This convergence of conflicting agencies within the text and self amounts to a fracturing of the solipsistic project. If I contain the Other, the Other also contains me. This confusion is suggested by the fact that both the narrator and his dead lover share the forename Jean. Moreover the *je* (I) of Jean, and of *Pompes funèbres*, is free-floating, shifting on occasion from sentence to sentence as it is adopted in turn by the narrator, Erik Seiler, Hitler or Riton. The narrator's fantasy of consuming his lover's dead body entails Jean eating Jean, Jean incorporating the Other who is also himself, permitting the alterity of the Other to become part of the alterity of the self.[31] The fantasy of consuming the Other signals the ineradicable presence of the Other as a traumatic loss within the self.

170 *Ethical Issues in French Fiction*

My (Br)Other's Keeper

Genet's fiction, then, is articulated around a double drama of weakness and strength; he is, as he reportedly described himself, 'le plus faible de tous et le plus fort' (the weakest of all and the strongest),[32] dominated and dominant, solipsistically self-contained and disastrously susceptible to the desire of the Other. In *The Existential and its Exits* Dobrez has shown how murder is one of the responses in Genet's writing to the subject's troubled engagement with alterity.[33] Adopting a Sartrean vocabulary, Dobrez describes how the Genetian subject is wounded and dispossessed by the look of the Other; the murderer responds by destroying the Other, but thereby only confirms his submission to the Other's authority, finally realizing through his own actions the identity as outcast which had been imposed upon him.

The struggle between sameness and alterity which comes to a violent head in murder can be seen at its clearest in the conflict between the identical twins in *Querelle de Brest*, Genet's fourth novel. *Querelle de Brest* is the story of two brothers who fail to kill one another. In the fight which is at the centre of the novel, both thematically and structurally, neither of the identical twins, Querelle and Robert, actually succeeds in murdering his opponent. But if Querelle doesn't succeed in killing his biological brother, he is nevertheless a serial assassin; and the murders he commits have a clear fratricidal element. This is stressed by the narrator, for example, after Querelle has killed his accomplice Vic: 'Il est facile de faire le meurtrier visiter par l'image de son frère. De le faire tuer par son propre frère. De lui faire tuer ou condamner son frère' (253) (It is easy to have the murderer visited by the image of his brother. To have him killed by his own brother. To make him kill or condemn his brother). The narrator even goes so far as to imagine an extended, almost universal fraternity (from which only women are excluded), which ensures that there are plenty of brothers to betray or murder: Gil, whom Querelle will hand over to the police, is described as his brother (329); after his fight with the policeman Mario (which echoes his struggle with his twin), the pair disappear into the fog 'fraternellement' (357) (fraternally); and later the narrator speaks of 'une fraternité secrète, énigmatique' (393) (a secret, enigmatic fraternity) established through language, and of the 'toute-puissante fraternité des pédérastes' (399) (all-powerful fraternity of pederasts). But this near-universal fraternity should not be taken as a positive value. Fraternity is rather an abhorrent proximity of self to Other;[34] and following what Freud calls 'the narcissism of minor differences',[35] hatred is exacerbated when the Other's resemblance to me is most apparent.

The fundamental question confronted in *Querelle de Brest*, 'Why kill one's brother?', discreetly alludes to the story of Cain and Abel, and the first murder in the history of humanity. According to tradition (although this is not made explicit in the Bible itself), Cain and Abel were born on the same day, and so (at least according to the normal rules of biology) they are twins like Querelle and Robert.[36] The biblical account of the antagonism between the brothers is extremely rapid. Cain and Abel each make an offering to God, who accepts Abel's but rejects Cain's. Later, the brothers fight:

And Cain spoke to Abel his brother. And as they were in the fields, Cain rose up against Abel his brother, and killed him.
And the Lord said to Cain: Where is Abel your brother? And he replied: I do not know; am I my brother's keeper?
And the Lord said: What have you done? The voice of your brother's blood cries out from the earth to me. (Genesis 4, 8–10)

The narrative is to say the least elliptic, even for a text in which the practice of ellipsis is so frequent. Too many questions are left unanswered. Why does God prefer Abel's offering to Cain's? What is the object of the brothers' dispute? Why does God reign ignorance when he asks Cain about his brother? Such questions give rise to a whole series of hypotheses which are explored in the Jewish collections of commentaries and interpretations known as Midrash. Midrashic interpretation takes as its starting point gaps or moments of indeterminacy within the text in order to speculate upon otherwise unexplained motivations. In the case of the struggle between Cain and Abel, interpreters have found, or imposed, varied and surprising meanings. The dispute is said to concern their parents' inheritance, or a woman, or the division of the spiritual world. The villain of the piece is said to be either Cain, who chooses violence, or Abel, who provokes his brother and shows him no pity, or God himself, who manipulates the action and fails in his duty of protection towards the world.[37]

According to at least one commentator, the true theme of the narrative is responsibility,[38] and this is perhaps why Emmanuel Levinas has shown an interest in it. For Levinas, the key to the story is not

172 *Ethical Issues in French Fiction*

to be found in the ambiguity of motives, but in Cain's question: 'Am I my brother's keeper?' Despite the apparent facetiousness of this response, Levinas insists that Cain is sincere.[39] Cain is speaking as a philosopher who sees all beings as ontologically separate; no one is bound to anyone else, so the well-being of the Other need be of no concern to me. What is lacking in Cain's response, according to Levinas, is an ethical perspective. Misunderstanding Levinas's basic notion that the Other solicits my responsibility, Cain speaks only for himself.

Implicit in the story of fratricide, then, are the questions of self and Other, of separateness and responsibility, and of the sovereignty of the subject or its submission to an external authority. Although the names of Cain and Abel do not appear in Genet's *Querelle de Brest*, it is none the less clear that the text alludes to their story. The very title of the novel, whilst referring to the protagonist's surname, also hints at the conflict at its centre: *les frères Querelle* (the Querelle brothers) become engaged in *la querelle des frères* (the brothers' quarrel). And when the two brothers fight, the narrator emphasizes the biblical nature of the scene: 'La rue devenait un passage de la Bible où deux frères dirigés par deux doigts d'un seul Dieu s'insultent et se tuent pour deux raisons qui n'en sont qu'une' (295) (The street became a passage from the Bible where two brothers directed by two fingers of one God insult and kill one another for two reasons which are only one).[40]

In the central scene of *Querelle de Brest* the brothers nearly kill one another during a brutal fight interrupted by a police patrol. This scene can be read as a sort of primal encounter in which fundamental ethical choices are taken. The apparent absurdity of the fight is accompanied by a sense of freedom. 'C'est en décidant de frapper son frère que Robert connut le plus pur instant de liberté' (It is in deciding to strike his brother that Robert knew the purest moment of freedom), the narrator tells us (295). Dédé, the police informer who watches the scene, also feels what is called 'la conscience révélée... de sa liberté' (296) (the revealed consciousness... of his freedom). In the Bible, the murder of Abel takes place before the revelation of Sinai, and so before the imposition of laws and prohibitions. In other words, when Cain kills his brother, murder is not formally forbidden (and as the Midrash shows, Cain can even claim that he could not have known that his act would lead to the death of his brother; because he has never seen a human corpse, he does not know from his own experience that people can die).[41] The importance of fratricide in this context is that it represents a moment of absolute choice when all options are open. In the fratricidal scene, nothing is prohibited, everything is possible and permissible. Ethics, not yet being established, is to be invented. Writing at the highpoint of French existentialism, Genet has the courage, or effrontery, to celebrate freedom in violence much more radically than humanist contemporaries such as Sartre and Camus.[42]

Typically, the description of violence in Genet's text carries a heavy erotic charge. Robert reproaches his brother with being a 'Sale enculé' (295) (Dirty bugger) because he has been to bed with Norbert, the owner of the brothel where much of the action of the novel takes place. And in the fight between the brothers, the antagonists behave as if they are attempting to reproduce the homosexual act of which Robert is accusing his brother. The narrator underlines the erotic implications of fraternal violence:

> Plutôt que de se détruire, ils paraissaient vouloir se joindre, se confondre dans une unité qui, de ces deux exemplaires, obtiendrait un animal beaucoup plus rare. Le combat qu'ils menaient était plutôt une lutte d'amour où personne n'osait sérieusement intervenir. On devinait que les deux combattants se fussent ligués contre le médiateur qui – au fond – n'eût désiré d'intervenir qu'afin de participer à cette partouze.... [Les deux frères] se tordaient, se malaxaient, se défaisaient, pour s'incorporer mutuellement: leur double résistait. (297)

> Rather than destroying one another, they seemed to want to join one another, to become confused in a unity which, from these two people, would create a much rarer animal. The fight in which they were involved was rather a lover's fight in which no one would dare to intervene. The spectators could see that the two fighters would join against anyone who interfered who, basically, would only have wanted to intervene in order to take part in this orgy ... [The two brothers] were writhing, kneading one another, taking each other to pieces, in order to become incorporated with the other: but their double resisted.

Given such an eroticised description, it is not surprising that some of the women present at the scene think of going to fetch 'un seau d'eau qu'elles jetteraient sur ces mâles comme on les jette sur des chiens lubriques' (298) (a bucket of water to throw over these men as one throws water over dogs on heat). In the passage quoted above, the narrator alludes to the Platonic myth of love as the search for the other half of oneself which has been cut away; in this account love is understood as the urge to recapture a lost plenitude and unity.[43] Genet inverts the terms of this scenario: rather than the reconstruction of lost unity, his characters prefer division and separation. If the sexual act makes it possible to glimpse the fusion of partners, then it must be rejected for that very reason. Rather than the joy of unity refound, in sexuality Genet's characters seek shame, abjection and solitude. As the narrator tells us unequivocally, the lover does not want romantic fusion, he rejects it with all his force: 'leur double résistait' (297) (their double resisted).

The uncanny resemblance of the twins to one another is the cause both of the erotic fascination of the spectators and of the antagonism between Robert and Querelle. With characteristic ambiguity, Genet presents resemblance as the source of desire and violence, to the point that both are confused in the central fratricidal struggle. The narrator tells us that 'Querelle semblait se battre contre soimême' (Querelle seemed to be fighting against himself); in the course of the fight, 'De plus en plus les deux frères se ressemblaient' (297) (More and more the two brothers resembled one another). In wanting to kill his double, the fratricidal brother is seeking to rid himself of what prevents him from being himself: 'Ces deux visages si exactement les mêmes venaient d'engager une lutte héroïque et idéale – dont ce combat n'était que la projection grossière visible aux yeux des hommes – pour la singularité' (297) (These two faces, so exactly the same, had just begun an heroic and ideal struggle – of which this battle was only the crude projection visible to the eyes of men – for singularity). Before all else Genet's characters seek singularity, that which distinguishes them from all others. Through the drama of fascination and desire, it is necessary to find – in order to destroy – that which endangers the separate, autonomous existence of the subject. And the absolute Other, paradoxically, is that which is closest to me: the identical twin. It is the twin, much more than the complete stranger, who threatens to rob me of my fragile sovereignty over a world which resists me.

So, the stakes of the fratricidal scene crystallize around the relation with alterity. In Genet's novel, Querelle's project consists in the endeavour to attain full self-possession and a position of mastery with respect to the external world. Querelle constantly feels threatened by the presence of the Other: when he meets a sailor who is wearing a cap poised at the same angle at which he (Querelle) customarily wears his own, Querelle feels that he has been robbed of something essentially his; he beats up the sailor in order to give him his deserved punishment (227). After the murder of Vic, Querelle conducts his own imaginary trial, and even inflicts on himself what he judges to be a suitable punishment: to be sodomized by Norbert (249–55). Through crime and betrayal, Querelle attempts to constitute a world in which he will be the only point of reference, in which he alone will have the right to act, to judge, to condemn and to expiate. He wants to drag those around him into crime 'afin de les y figer, afin qu'ils ne puissent aimer ailleurs ou autrement qu'à travers lui seul' (410) (in order to fix them there, so that they cannot love elsewhere or otherwise than through him alone).

Querelle wants to preserve at all costs his absolute sovereignty in the direction and interpretation of his own experience. In order to protect his fragile singularity, he feels obliged to react through either violence or ruse towards anything which seems to resist him. When he meets Norbert and Mario, he is conscious that their power and authority are greater than his; he 'sentit trembler, vaciller, sur le point de s'abolir dans un vomissement, ce qui était proprement lui-même' (224) (he felt that which was properly himself tremble, vacillate, on the verge of being abolished). His sense of self-preservation leads him to submit to the authority of the Other by offering himself as a sexual object to those in a position of command. But the apparent submission and passivity are inverted and turn into real mastery. Norbert becomes attached to Querelle, but sees himself betrayed by him with Mario; and when Mario is unable to penetrate Querelle, the latter turns around and performs oral sex on the policeman. From being passive, he becomes active, engaging in an act which, later, will make Mario anxious that Querelle might bite off his penis (400). So Querelle submits to the desire of the Other, but then takes the initiative and becomes the one who gives his partner reason for fear. Seeing what is called the 'abjection' of the policeman, Querelle finds in himself 'une présence impérieuse, dominatrice, invincible et bonne' (400) (a presence which was imperious, dominating, invincible and good). By swallowing, making his own, the sperm of Mario, Querelle attempts to incorporate the essence of the policeman into himself,[44] in a manner which is at once literal and magic; he robs the policeman of the attributes of his power and appropriates his authority.

In the fratricidal scene, all the tensions which characterize the relations between self and Other in Genet's texts are at play. It is as if what we are observing is the repetition of an original ethical moment in which are taken, or revealed, the options which determine the work in its totality. Querelle stands as the fundamental altericidal subject, either literally in as far as he is a serial murderer, or by extension as he attempts to rob the Other of its initiative and dominance, to secure the citadel of subjecthood against the unforeseen assaults of alterity. From this it should be clear that altericide is not just an act of physical violence against other subjects, but that it is also a relationship to meaning and to the interpretation of one's own acts. It is in this respect that Querelle's relationship to others and to the Other exactly parallels Genet's relationship to his reader.

Murderous Books

In 1960 George Jackson, a seventeen-year-old black American, was imprisoned for an indefinite period after being convicted of involvement in the theft of 70 dollars. In prison he secretly joined the Black Panther Party and began writing the letters that would be published in *The Brothers of Soledad*. In 1970 he was accused with two other prisoners of the murder of a white prison warden; in August 1971, two days before the trial was due to begin, he was killed whilst allegedly trying to escape from prison. After his death he and his two co-defendants were found to be innocent of the warden's murder. Before Jackson's death Genet, who was by this time closely involved with the Black Panther movement, had written a preface for *The Brothers of Soledad* as well as an article, 'Le Rouge et le noir', which insisted on Jackson's innocence of the murder.[45] In this article Genet distinguishes between *l'assassinat* (assassination), the actual murder of the prison warden, and *le meurtre par le livre* (murder by the book), the absolute negation of the real effected by the revolutionary writer. The former is a luxury and a distraction; Jackson cannot have killed the warden because of the more radical crime in which his writing had engaged him:

> Le livre de George Jackson est un meurtre, ... c'est un meurtre radical, ... c'est le meurtre systématique et concerté de tout le monde blanc avide de se parer des dépouilles des peuples non blancs, c'est le meurtre – espérons-le définitif – de la bêtise agissante.[46]

George Jackson's book is a murder, ... it is a radical murder, ... it is the systematic and concerted murder of the entire white world which is avid to deck itself out with the spoils of non-white peoples, it is the murder – let us hope definitive – of effective stupidity.

It is not difficult to see why Genet might have identified with the imprisoned, victimized writer. In the current context, it is the notion of the book as a murder, as 'un acte de violence extrême' (an act of extreme violence),[47] which is most illuminating. Jackson's letters are written less *for* fellow black militants than *against* a repressive white ruling class. Similarly, Genet's texts are written less for sympathetic readers than against hostile ones. In Genet's writing murder is not just one theme amongst others because it is what the book does as much as what it describes; the murderer is an artist of sorts, and the artist is a murderer of sorts. Genet's narrators are characteristically highly intrusive; and one of the most important functions of their intrusions is to define their readership, to anticipate and to circumscribe the range of their readers' responses to the text in front of them. Genet's reader is an Aunt Sally set up to be provoked, offended, assaulted or mocked; as the text's Other, the reader must be denied the freedom of response or interpretation which might rob the text of its self-possession. The text, then, is engaged in the same struggle for dominance with the reader as the murderer confronted with the loathed and desired Other.

The opposition between self and Other is reproduced at the level of narration in the opposition between the *je* (I) of the narrator and the *vous* (you) of the addressee. The reader is established as the repository of values antithetical to those espoused in the texts. The narrator of *Journal du voleur* practises 'une morale inverse de celle qui régit ce monde' (206) (a morality opposite to the one which rules this world), he decides to be 'à l'inverse de vous-même' (opposite to you) and to explore 'l'envers de votre beauté' (110) (the reverse of your beauty). His theological virtues (theft, betrayal, homosexuality) are chosen in opposition to the presumed values of the implied reader. Constructed by society as its negative image (see 198), the narrator in turn attempts to construct the reader as his own inverted reflection. He acknowledges the need for the complicity and recognition of the reader ('J'aspire à votre reconnaissance, à votre sacre', 306; see also 17) (I aspire to be recognized, to be crowned, by you); but the Other, rather than an independent self, is characterized as an alter ego, a mirror image whose gaze confirms the narrator's ascendancy.

To a large extent the reader's role is simply to be offended by the sexual practices or moral attitudes described in the texts. The opening sentence of *Pompes funèbres*, written in the immediate aftermath of the liberation of Paris, refers to the 'héroïsme puéril' (puerile heroism) of the period (9). Later in that novel the narrator describes his pleasure at seeing the French terrorized by the hated *Milice* during the Occupation (59) or in drawing attention to the shame of the French (133); he describes homosexual acts in intricate detail, expresses admiration for Hitler and compares him to Joan of Arc, the symbol of French nationhood (119). In such passages Genet sends back to his readers an inverted image of what he presumes to be their values; and because of this, as many of Genet's critics have suggested, Genet's defence of Evil remains curiously reactionary, since it implicitly respects the morality and social order which it opposes. Genet acknowledged this conservatism within his revolt in an interview given in 1975: 'Mon point de vue est très égoïste. Je voudrais que le monde, mais faites bien attention à la façon dont je le dis, je voudrais que le monde ne change pas pour me permettre d'être contre le monde' (My point of view is very egoistical. I would like the world, but pay close attention to the way I say this, I would like the world not to change so that I can be against the world).[48]

In as far as the text merely inverts its readers' presumed values, it is in a losing position in the struggle against the reader-Other; it submits to the Other's ideology, remains a product of it even as it opposes it. Initiative is restored to the text by its ability to take a further self-reflexive step back from the scene of the struggle and to ironize the terms in which it is conducted. When the narrator of *Pompes funèbres* declares himself in favour of Evil, the reader's values may be offended but not brought into question; when the narrator describes himself as passionately attached to Good (160), we may suspect that he is no longer playing the same game. Inconsistencies throw into doubt the seriousness of one or both statements, creating a suspension of the text's declarative function. Stability of perspective or meaning simply evaporate. The narrator now becomes, not an inverted reflection of the reader's values, but a sly, vindictive agent which treats the reader as an object to be mocked and cajoled. The narrator tells the reader to pay attention

('Je demande que le lecteur me prête une grande attention,' *Miracle*, 347) (I ask the reader to pay close attention), insists on his rights as narrator ('Le lecteur doit nous permettre d'utiliser ce détestable lieu commun que nous condamnons,' *Querelle*, 395) (The reader must allow us to use this detestable commonplace which we condemn), anticipates the reader's responses ('Reparler de sainteté à propos de relégation fera crisser vos dents inhabituées aux nourritures acides,' *Miracle*, 57) (To speak again of sainthood in reference to relegation will make your teeth grate, unaccustomed as they are to acidic foods), and abandons the reader when he feels fit ('Nous abandonnons le lecteur dans ce désordre d'entrailles,' *Querelle*, 253–4) (We abandon the reader amidst this mess of entrails). Acknowledging that his book will disappoint its reader, he offers to recount some amusing anecdotes '[afin] d'en rompre la monotonie' (*Journal*, 115) (in order to break the monotony). Fifteen pages from the end of *Querelle de Brest*, the narrator announces that he has lost interest in his text: 'Ce livre dure depuis trop de pages et nous ennuie' (*Querelle*, 399) (This book has been going on for too many pages and is boring us). This leaves the reader in an impossible position. Should we stop reading and risk missing something important, or read on at the risk of wasting our time? Genet's text poses the dilemma and gives us no means of resolving it.

Most importantly, Genet's narrator insists that the meaning of his text is his own possession, to be shared or withheld at his whim. He offers explanations with offhand rapidity ('Voici quelques explications,' *Querelle*, 387) (Here are a few explanations), or weakens the force of his explanation even as he gives it: 'Dans le cas de Querelle, s'il faut une explication, hasardons celle-ci, ni meilleure ni plus détestable qu'une autre' (*Querelle*, 396) (In the case of Querelle, if an explanation is needed, let us try this one, neither better nor more detestable than any other). The narrator of *Pompes funèbres* warns that the explanations he will give of the murder committed by Erik may not seem valid (*Pompes*, 79), but then pushes the bluff even further by failing to offer any real explanation anyway. Typically, Genet's narrator explains in order to explain nothing, reserving for himself a command over meaning which is only imperfectly shared with the reader. The narrator of *Miracle de la rose* declares that 'les mots ont le sens qu'on leur donne et, à vrai dire, tout notre langage était chiffré' (*Miracle*, 194) (words have the meaning that they are given and, to tell the truth, our entire language was coded). We are only privy to the code in as far as the narrator allows us to be. Implicitly and explicitly, we are taunted with our inability to understand: 'Tout ce que je vous dis ne vous renseigne pas' (*Miracle*, 232) (Everything I tell you does not inform you).[49]

In *Notre-Dame-des-fleurs* Culafroy is described as 'un poème écrit seulement pour lui, hermétique à qui n'en a pas la clé' (*Notre-Dame*, 342) (a poem written only for him, hermetic for anyone who does not have the key). This could stand as a description of all Genet's writing. The reader is put in the position of the prison governor in *Miracle de la rose* questioning Harcamone about the murder of the warden; the brute facts do not make sense, and the author of the crime offers no explanation (*Miracle*, 224). And the characteristic stance of Genet's narrator is to imply that he has a secret which he is withholding, that he possesses a higher understanding which the reader may only glimpse. Whether or not there actually is a secret to be revealed is, of course, part of the secret. The sense that some readers have that they have missed the point of Genet's text, that they have failed to grasp what he is getting at, is precisely the point they are supposed to grasp. The text escapes us, not by accident or by our contingent inability to make necessary connections, but by its concerted retention of its own significance. The reader is expelled, and is made aware at every stage of his or her expulsion. In this way, Genet achieves a remarkable feat: the reader is inscribed and defined in his writing as an imaginary addressee, but is also excluded from the text's significance and denied any reality except as part of Genet's own imaginary world.[50] With an intense awareness of the presence of his reader, Genet writes for no one except himself: 'C'est qu'en art on est solitaire, on est seul en face de soi-même' (The thing is that in art one is solitary, one is alone in face of oneself).[51]

Genet with Levinas

Writing, then, is an act of murder in which the struggle for singularity, moral solitude and secure self-presence sought through crime by Genet's characters is reenacted at a textual level. Genet does what he can to frustrate the desire of readers and critics to be edified by what they read, either by their ability to find perhaps unexpected moral value in it, or by condemning it and thereby strengthening their own moral options, or by some subtle combination of both these moves. Both the text's stance towards its readers and the readers' stance towards the text are characterized by a resistance to otherness. At this point a final confrontation with Levinas should bring out the ethical significance of this resistance.

As outlined in Chapter 1, the mature thought of Levinas revolves around an original ethical encounter: the self, confronted by the face of the Other, discovers that it is not alone in the world and thereby finds itself and its possession of the universe put into question. The encounter with the Other reveals alterity as such, irreducible to thematization, knowledge, experience or totalization, all of which are ruses of the ego to establish its authority over what resists it. What is most important for Levinas is the ethical nature of the encounter: 'L'étrangeté d'Autrui – son irréductibilité à moi – à mes pensées et à mes possessions, s'accomplit comme une mise en question de me spontanéité, comme éthique' (*Totalité et infini*, 33) (The strangeness of the Other – his irreducibility to me – to my thoughts and to my possessions, is accomplished as a putting into question of my spontaneity, as ethics). The crux of Levinas's thought is that the encounter occasions a *mise en question* (putting into question), challenging the primacy of the Same, of consciousness, of Being or of knowledge; and through this challenge I discover the fundamental ethical relationship of obligation and responsibility for the Other summarized in the commandment 'Tu ne commettras pas de meurtre' (Thou shalt not kill) (see *Totalité et infini*, 217).

The discovery of the Other confronts me with a choice. I am, of course, hardly delighted to find my sovereignty over the world brought into question. Levinas acknowledges that I can respond to the presence of the Other by violence. In other words, I can attempt to destroy the Other; but, according to Levinas, when I kill others, it is always the Other (with a capital) which I am attempting to suppress, and the Other inevitably escapes me to reappear elsewhere. I can kill others, but the Other is invincible. From this follows one of the paradoxes of Levinassian ethics: the Other is beyond my grasp, it is both absolutely inviolable and utterly vulnerable, it calls on me to safeguard its wellbeing. In other words, Levinas's answer to the question 'Am I my brother's keeper?' is a resolute yes. This makes it possible to understand the scandal represented by the murder of Abel for Levinas's thought. Levinas describes fraternity as lying at the basis of human identity, society and ethics:

> Le moi humain se pose dans la fraternité: que tous les hommes soient frères ne s'ajoute pas à l'homme comme une conquête morale, mais constitue son ipséité. Parce que ma position comme

moi s'*évertue* déjà dans la fraternité, le visage peut se présenter à moi comme visage.[52]

The human self is revealed in fraternity: the fact that all men are brothers is not something added to man like a moral conquest, but it constitutes his very nature. Because my position as a self is maintained in fraternity, the face can be presented to me as a face.

Levinassian ethics are founded on the possibility of an encounter with the Other to which the self responds with generosity and responsibility. Cain misunderstands the nature of the encounter; he fails to realize that his own identity and worth are at stake in his relationship with his brother. Levinas endeavours to describe a mode of contact with the Other which does not entail the assimilation of its alterity to structures which are already familiar to me, so which does not reduce the Other to a mere projection of the self.

The word *rencontre* (encounter) is as much a keyword in Genet's texts as it is in Levinas's; but the surprise, discovery and transformation of the self inherent in the Levinassian encounter are entirely lacking in the version offered by Genet, as Sartre has shown in *Saint Genet, comédien et martyr*. According to Sartre, Genet refuses to be surprised by an Other existing independently of him; so, he accepts alterity inside himself in order the better to anticipate its appearances and effects: Genet will be his own interlocutor, occupying the place of the Other whilst also remaining himself. This project entails a radical rejection of history, or surprise, and of the encounter:

> La vérité c'est que Genet ne *rencontre* jamais personne. Il ne voit jamais du fond d'un bar, du fond de la nuit, s'avancer vers lui une créature contingente et singulière qu'il lui faudrait observer, apprendre, déchiffrer: qu'un beau Mac apparaisse ou un matelot, du premier coup il les *reconnaîtra*, il saisira l'essence qu'ils manifestent: il voit *le* dur du dur, *le* marin; l'avenir et le passé s'identifient dans une sorte d'intuition prophétique, fataliste et lasse. (349; all emphases are Sartre's)

The truth is that Genet never *meets* anyone. At the other end of a bar or in the dark of the night, he never sees some contingent and singular creature advancing towards him, someone whom he would have to observe, learn, decipher; if some handsome pimp or a sailor were to appear, at the first glance he will *recognize* them, he will grasp the essence which they manifest; he sees *the* tough guy, *the* sailor; the future and the past are identified with one another in a sort of intuition which is prophetic, fatalistic, and weary.

In Genet's text there is no encounter and no beginning; there is only repetition. This does not mean that the word *rencontre* (encounter) does not appear in his texts; on the contrary, it appears with great frequency. But there is no encounter in the Levinassian sense. This is evident, for example, in *Querelle de Brest* when Querelle goes to meet Gil in the abandoned prison where he is hiding. Querelle becomes aware that he 'allait rencontrer, pour la première fois, un autre criminel, un frère' (329) (he was going to meet, for the first time, another criminal, a brother). The phrase *pour la première fois* (for the first time) seems to promise that this encounter offers something genuinely new. But the person he is about to meet is 'un autre criminel, un frère' (another criminal, a brother), that is, another self who, in as far as he may be described as a brother, is perhaps not entirely unknown. The hypothesis is confirmed a few lines later: 'Vaguement déjà, il avait rêvé de se trouver en face d'un assassin de sa taille... Un garçon ressemblant, ayant sa grandeur et sa carrure... ayant pour sa gloire des crimes différents de ceux de Querelle, mais aussi beaux, aussi lourds et réprouvés' (329) (Vaguely already, he had dreamed of finding himself face to face with an assassin of his stature.... A youth like himself, having the same height and build... having to his glory crimes different from those of Querelle, but just as beautiful, just as grave and reprehensible). So, this encounter is the realization of a dream, played out in the presence of a brother who is the same size and build as the dreamer. His crimes and his attributes will be equivalent to those of Querelle, even if they are not strictly identical; and later Querelle will consider making Gil become 'pareil à lui-même' (366) (similar to himself). What Querelle is going to encounter *for the first time* is something that he has already seen many times before, at least in fantasy; he is aiming to encounter what he has always already known: himself.

For Levinas the key issue of ethics is what he calls 'le choc de la rencontre entre le Même et l'Autre' (32) (the shock of the encounter between the Same and the Other). The most consistent move in Western ontology, according to Levinas, has been to reduce the

Other to the Same; anything new or alien is classified as an aspect of Being or an object of knowledge, and thereby its otherness is eliminated. Western philosophy has been an Odyssey which, like the journey of Ulysses, ultimately leads back to its point of departure; it explores alterity only to rediscover sameness. As we have already seen in Chapter 6, Levinas prefers the story of Abraham to that of Ulysses: 'Au mythe d'Ulysse retournant à Ithaque, nous voudrions opposer l'histoire d'Abraham quittant à jamais sa patrie pour une terre encore inconnue et interdisant à son serviteur de ramener même son fils à ce point de départ' (To the myth of Ulysses returning to Ithaca, we would like to oppose the story of Abraham, leaving his homeland forever for a country still unknown, and forbidding his servant to take even his son back to this point of departure).[53] In the story of Abraham the ultimate destination is not known in advance; the encounter with the unknown takes precedence over the reappropriation of the familiar.

From a Levinassian perspective, Genet's writing does not so much reject traditional ethics as reproduce in a particularly extreme form a gesture inherent in Western philosophical discourse. Genet dramatically refuses exposure to alterity and affirms the demands of the self over the claims of the Other. Levinas's account of ontology highlights crucial features of Genet's attitude:

> Elle n'est donc pas une relation avec l'autre comme tel, mais la réduction de l'Autre au Même. Telle est la définition de la liberté: se maintenir contre l'autre, assurer l'autarcie d'un moi. La thématisation et la conceptualisation, d'ailleurs inséparables, ne sont pas paix avec l'Autre, mais suppression ou possession de l'Autre. La possession, en effet, affirme l'Autre, mais au sein d'une négation de son indépendance. <<Je pense>> revient à <<je peux>> – à une appropriation de ce qui est, à une exploitation de la réalité. (37)

> So it is not a relation with the other as such, but the reduction of the Other to the Same. This is the definition of freedom: to maintain oneself against the other, to assure the autarky of a self. Thematization and conceptualization, which anyway cannot be separated, do not represent peace with the Other, but rather suppression or possession of the Other. Possession, in effect, affirms the Other, but within a negation of its independence. 'I think' boils down to 'I can' – to an appropriation of what is, to an exploitation of reality.

For Levinas the encounter with the Other entails an approach, an acknowledgment of the proximity of Same and Other that does not imply the denial or annihilation of either; Genet's narrator, on the other hand, *distances himself* from the Other. The encounter is avoided because it takes place only in the imaginary, entirely within the confines of the self. Meaning is bestowed by the narrator rather than accepted from elsewhere. The narrator turns out to be Ulysses rather than Abraham. His story is one of rediscovery and recognition. Dispossessed of himself through extreme susceptibility to desire for the Other, the narrator repossesses himself through writing, affirming his ability to create and destroy the agent of his dispossession. Rather than an encounter with alterity, Genet's texts recount the struggle for the recovery of selfhood which involves a solipsistic negation of the non-self.

If Levinas lays the ground for an ethical critique of Genet's writing, Genet can nevertheless furnish the basis of a searching response. From Levinas's point of view, the encounter in Genet is not an encounter at all because alterity is not respected; from Genet's point of view, the encounter in Levinas's sense is something that never occurs because the cost to the self of respecting alterity is too high to pay. Reading Levinas through Genet also serves to highlight Levinas's difficulties in respecting the alterity of the Other. Especially after *Totalité et infini*, though also in that text and previous essays, Levinas's prose bears traces of a major struggle with language. Levinas's problem is to find a way of speaking of alterity without reducing it to the already-known. All thematization, all reference to a relationship with the Other, all knowledge or experience of the Other end up by eliminating the alterity of what should be totally outside the competence and power of the self. More and more, Levinas's philosophical project consists in the endeavour to dislodge or dismantle language in order to achieve a philosophical practice in which it may be possible to glimpse the still unheard shock of the encounter with alterity. Levinas is looking for what he calls 'un dire qui doit aussi se dédire', a saying which must also unsay itself.[54] Genet, on the other hand, readily (perhaps all too readily) embraces the failure which Levinas's thought cannot escape: the Other has no language, all encounters end by suppressing alterity, it is better to accept or to desire the disappearance of the Other than to search for a utopian idiom. In the terms of *Querelle de Brest*, Levinas is like Gil, the unwitting murderer who regrets his crime and seeks to deny it; Genet's writing, on the other hand, occupies the position of Querelle, the deliberate, self-conscious murderer who has taught himself to desire his own crimes. Genet functions, perhaps, as a sort of repressed unconscious to Levinassian discourse, never ceasing to remind his readers of what Levinas knows without wishing to acknowledge.

There is in Genet an ethical solipsism which rejects all reference to any authority outside the self. The search for singularity, the reconquest of the self, goes together with an irresistible distrust of the Other. Whereas Levinas proposes an ethics of generosity, substitution and responsibility, Genet's texts adopt a cruel lucidity which takes account, more than Levinas possibly could, of the hatred for the Other. His work embodies a malicious wisdom: the Other represents a threat to the wholeness of the self which can be countered with betrayal or violence. Levinas's protestation that such action is not in accord with the fundamental ethical relationship does nothing to exclude its possibility. Indeed, Levinas seems distinctly uneasy when it comes to explaining why we should accept responsibility for the Other rather than loyalty to the self, why we should respect the commandment not to kill rather than defending ourselves with violence. Levinas acknowledges that it is just as possible to kill the Other as it is to obey the commandment not to kill:

> Il serait inutile d'insister sur la banalité du meurtre qui révèle la résistance quasi nulle de l'obstacle. Cet incident le plus banal de l'histoire humaine correspond à une possibilité exceptionnelle – puisqu'elle correspond à la négation totale d'un être. (217)

> It would be pointless to insist on the banality of murder, which reveals the nearly nonexistent resistance of the obstacle. This most banal incident in human history corresponds to an exceptional possibility – since it corresponds to the total negation of a being.

A curious tension is established here when murder is qualified as both banal and exceptional: it occurs all the time but tells us nothing about fundamental ethical relationships; it appears as ethically unimportant because it represents a possibility rather than a responsibility, it is a sign of our lack of power over the Other rather than our sovereignty; there is no point in discussing it further ('Il serait inutile d'insister') (It would be pointless to insist). War is possible, Levinas argues, but peace, 'la présence préalable et non-allergique d'Autrui' (the prior and non-allergic presence of the Other), is originary (218). The 'banal' occurrences of murder and war are excluded from consideration because they are 'exceptional'; and Levinas's philosophy offers no means of establishing a regulative link between ethical responsibility and actual behaviour, between fundamental ethical experiences and ordinary acts of violence. Levinas criticizes Heidegger for preferring Being to beings, yet perhaps he is guilty of committing an equivalent error in focusing more on the inviolability of the Other (whom I cannot kill) than on the mortality of others (whom I can kill). He tells us a great deal about our responsibility, but very little about our possibilities.

The theological virtue of betrayal proposed by *Journal du voleur* involves an implicit acknowledgement of the priority of its opposite: only where responsibility is expected can betrayal be possible. Curiously, then, Genet rejoins Levinas in the implication that the relationship with the Other is characterized by obligation; where he differs is in his concentration on the fact that responsibility does not entail compulsion. In some respects, then, the texts of Genet and Levinas confirm one another's assumptions whilst challenging one another's priorities. Read from the perspective of Levinas, Genet's writing appears dangerously solipsistic in its relegation of the Other to a mere bit player in the drama of the self. But by comparison Levinas appears utopian in his unconditional respect for the alterity of the Other, concentrating as he does on obligation, respect, responsibility, hospitality and generosity. Reading Genet in conjunction with Levinas can serve to focus attention on the pervasive but often occluded knowledge in Levinas's texts that ethical obligation does not regulate moral choice; I am just as likely to respond to the Other with violence as with respect, to banish him from my house as to invite her to enter (see *Totalité et infini*, 188). *Autrement qu'être ou au-delà de l'essence*, Levinas's most important work along with *Totalité et infini*, is movingly dedicated to the victims of the Holocaust,[55] yet the book itself has nothing to say about those victims; in the face of its own tragic knowledge, it can appear at moments like an exercise in wishful thinking. As Blanchot observes, 'Comment philosopher, comment écrire dans le souvenir d'Auschwitz... C'est cette pensée qui traverse, porte, toute la philosophie de Levinas et qu'il nous propose sans la dire, au-delà et avant toute obligation' (How can one philosophize, how can one write in the memory of Auschwitz... This is the thought that traverses, carries, the entire philosophy of Levinas and which he proposes to us without saying it, beyond and before all obligation).[56] Levinas has described his life as dominated 'par le pressentiment et le souvenir de l'horreur nazie' (by the presentiment and the memory of the Nazi horror);[57] yet his life's work on ethics seems reticent or struck dumb when faced with the areas of human cruelty charted with chilling intelligence by Genet.

As much as the works of Levinas, Genet's writing can be read as a sustained and challenging ethical enquiry; but we would be foolish to expect or to hope for any edification from his texts. Genet has the courage, or perhaps just the *je-m'en-foutisme*, to envisage the most daring and unacceptable conclusions: for me to exist, the Other must disappear, I must make of myself the agent of its disappearance. In this light, altericide appears as a path to salvation; and if this is the case, perhaps the most difficult task for us is to learn to prefer not to be saved.

Conclusion: Tarrying with the Negative

The title of this concluding section comes from Hegel via Žižek. In the Preface to his *Phenomenology of Spirit*, Hegel writes of the power of the negative:

> Lacking strength, Beauty hates the Understanding for asking of her what it cannot do. But the life of Spirit is not the life that shrinks from death and keeps itself untouched by devastation, but rather the life that endures it and maintains itself in it. It wins its truth only when, in utter dismemberment, it finds itself.... This tarrying with the negative is the magical power that converts it into being.[1]

Hegel's point is that negativity is not something that alters Spirit from the outside; rather, Spirit is a movement of becoming-other which arrives at its truth only through a process of alienation, loss and return. The 'devastation' and 'utter dismemberment' which Spirit must endure to arrive at its truth are thus in no way incidental to what it discovers itself to be: they are indispensable to the possibility of discovery and they determine its outcome. Žižek will accuse Hegel of only feigning to tarry with the negative because he finally converts it back into being;[2] even so, in principle at least, Hegel's phenomenology requires a readiness to dwell with the negative, made risky (and exciting) by the knowledge that its effects and consequences cannot be controlled or calculated in advance. What returns from the sojourn in negativity may not be what we had expected or wanted.

Tarrying with the negative as a model of reading might entail focusing unflinchingly on what is most disturbing in literary texts, what is most likely to make us other than ourselves if we take the risk of reading it without resistance. Unfortunately, old habits of reading die hard. My interest in Genet derives in large measure from the repeated gestures of critical repudiation which his texts occasion, as can be seen in an openly 'ethical' reading of *Querelle de Brest*. Monica Johnstone observes that '[n]either Genet nor *Querelle*'s implied author is our friend even in the most tolerant conception of friendship', and she concedes that 'the seductions in *Querelle* lead to betrayal and murder'.[3] However, the dangers of Genet's text are offset by 'an ironic twist not intended by the novel': 'Genet's antisocial claims are undercut to some extent by the act of his writing and publishing them.... Ultimately, he is unsuccessful in conveying the norms he espouses because to convey them he must communicate with us, rendering his position of isolation meaningless' (67). This allows the crucial reversal. Genet's anti-values make it possible to see all the better the real values to be found in other literary works, and thus help us recognize and formulate our own: 'Genet intends me no good, but reading *Querelle* does me some good. My perception of *Querelle* as an inherently inconsistent epistemology is, ironically, its value for me' (67). *Querelle de Brest* thus becomes, if 'not particularly palatable', at least 'digestible', with 'a hidden medicinal purpose'; such texts help us make 'fewer mistakes', reach 'fewer dead ends', because we make 'fewer faulty assumptions about the norms implicit in texts or the range of values possible in people' (68). Genet deserves heartfelt thanks for being so unpleasant.

The critical move of acknowledging the disturbing aspects of a text before relegating their importance is too widespread for it to be dismissed as an individual aberration. Nussbaum's reading of Beckett is instructive in this respect. Whilst observing Beckett's nihilism and search for silence, she finds the emotion he expresses to be 'particularly sterile', based on 'religious prejudice', offering 'not a convincing picture' of how individuals or society develop; she effectively advises Beckett to go back and reread Henry James and Virginia Woolf in order to find a more satisfactory vision.[4] Nussbaum learns less than she claims from the literary works she discusses since her core beliefs and commitments are already in place, she knows the sort of lesson she expects to be taught by her favoured texts, and she repudiates those works which offer something different. Reading results in no encounter in Levinas's sense, since it is the familiarity, not the strangeness, of the text which is implicitly valued. Moreover, ethical criticism as practised by Nussbaum and others has for the most part disregarded literary works which explore the darker side of experience and desire. It has participated too unquestioningly in what Leo Bersani has called a 'culture of redemption' which expects its privileged texts to encapsulate redemptive virtues;[5] in similar vein, with reference to Holocaust narratives, Laurence Langer has described a 'culture of consolation' which insists on finding uplifting or edifying messages in even the bleakest material.[6] Does this mean that texts that are not morally or cognitively enriching are in some sense radically unreadable? Part of what is at stake here is the nature of the reader's encounter with literature and the extent to which any such encounter is falsified or disqualified by the reader's resistance to the text's otherness. Wolfgang Iser gives an appealing account of how the encounter with literature allows readers to 'think the thoughts of someone else' whilst remaining themselves;[7] their understanding is thereby extended and strengthened. However, this exposure of the reader to the text inevitably entails an element of risk which Iser himself tends to neglect; the experience of reading as he conceives it concerns only the right sort of text which will make of us the right sort of person. As with the ethical critics, the values we want to learn and the texts which will promote them are pretty much known in advance.

Other critics (though not many) have been less reticent in considering the potential dangers of reading. Emma Wilson, for example, has shown how literary accounts of sexuality might disrupt and disorient the reader's sense of secure sexual identity; and the title of Susan Rubin Suleiman's *Risking Who One Is: Encounters with Contemporary Art* suggests the danger of letting one's own identity be overwhelmed by the work of art. Both Wilson and Suleiman affirm the positive aspects of this risk:

> But if it is recognized that fiction may be formative, may we not suggest that its effect might be positive and ... its force might be seen, in liberating terms, to disrupt the regulatory function of the compulsory matrix of heterosexuality?[8]

> Potentially, every genuine reading experience is a life-changing encounter, even though few individual books can be said to have truly transformed one's life. The transforming effects are cumulative, each new work contributing its own small parcel.[9]

However, the risk involved in exposure to literary otherness might just as easily turn out to have no positive benefits. Wilson is careful to avoid the conflation of sexuality and violence; she insists that the liberating disruptions effected by the depiction of the former have no explicit bearing on the latter;[10] and Suleiman warns that exposing oneself to the influence of art may lead to 'temptation and error' as much as to 'beatitude and bliss'.[11] The encounter is a risk in that its results cannot be known in advance. The risk has been circumvented, and the encounter with the literary text missed, if its outcome entails a reaffirmation of pre-established beliefs, values, norms and identities. The text has not been allowed to be fully Other, and its critical recuperation is another version of altericide: the refusal to concede the Other's (text's) potential to say what we are most unwilling to hear. One might say that ethical reading, at least in its most widely practised forms, is a reluctance to tarry with the negative, a refusal to face the 'dismemberment' and the 'utter devastation' which Hegel describes, and which some literary texts offer us as the terrifying consequence of reading.

Žižek, however, gives a Lacanian spin to the notion of tarrying with the negative which Hegel could not have anticipated, and which permits a final reflection on the threatening and endangered proximity of the Other. Throughout this study I have concentrated on texts that stage the encounter with alterity in terms of conflict; contrary to the Levinassian model in which the encounter is characterized by openness, respect and generosity, the works I have been discussing enact violent reassertions of the primacy of the Same through the annihilation of the Other. The Other threatens me with an incursion into parts of my identity which I had held to be most private and unassailable; Žižek describes this in terms of a 'theft of enjoyment':

> We always impute to the 'other' an excessive enjoyment: he wants to steal our enjoyment (by ruining our way of life) and/or he has access to some secret, perverse enjoyment. In short, what really bothers us about the 'other' is the peculiar way he organizes his enjoyment, precisely the surplus, the 'excess' that pertains to this way: the smell of 'their' food, 'their' noisy songs and dances, 'their' strange manners, 'their' attitude to work.[12]

These 'others' encroach on our private space in so far as we suspect them of an enjoyment which exceeds our own; Žižek goes on to argue, however, that the fantasy of other people's excessive enjoyment is in fact a way of organizing our own enjoyment as mediated by the Other:

> The Lacanian thesis that enjoyment is always enjoyment of the Other, i.e., enjoyment supposed, imputed to the Other, and that, conversely, the hatred of the Other's enjoyment is ultimately always enjoyment of one's own enjoyment, is perfectly exemplified by this logic of the 'theft of enjoyment.' What are fantasies about the Other's special, excessive enjoyment – about the black's superior sexual potency and appetite, about the Jew's or Japanese's special relationship toward money and work – if not *so many ways, for us, to organize our own enjoyment?* Do we not find enjoyment precisely in fantasizing about the Other's enjoyment, in this ambivalent attitude toward it? Do we not find satisfaction by means of the very supposition that the Other enjoys in a way inaccessible to us? Does not the Other's enjoyment exert such a powerful fascination because in it we represent to ourselves our own innermost relationship toward enjoyment? . . . [The] fascinating image of the Other gives a body to our own innermost split, to what is 'in us more than ourselves' and thus prevents us from achieving full identity with ourselves. *The hatred of the Other is the hatred of our own excess of enjoyment.*[13]

Žižek's argument moves on from resentment towards 'others' to the desiring-hating relationship with the Other through which my own enjoyment is mediated and my most private being constituted as always already fractured. We thus encounter the spectre of the Lacanian Big Other, the commanding agency which structures our desires with its imperatives and prohibitions. However the crucial point which Žižek, following Lacan, repeatedly underscores, is that *the Big Other does not exist*. To paraphrase Orwell, the Big Other is *not* watching you; but the hole in the symbolic order which this insight produces may be more disturbing than the servitude to which belief in the Big Other condemns us. The task which Žižek assigns to the critical intellectual is, as he puts it, 'precisely *to occupy all the time . . . the place of this hole,* i.e., to maintain a distance toward every reigning Master-Signifier.'[14] This is the sense which Žižek gives to Hegel's 'tarrying with the negative': 'Perhaps, however our very physical survival hinges on our ability to consummate the act of assuming fully the "nonexistence of the Other," of *tarrying with the negative.*'[15]

This view of the Other as nonexistent, as a fantasy formation which enables enjoyment whilst guaranteeing order in the field of meaning, allows a final insight into altericidal narratives, for example (and pre-eminently) Camus's *L'Etranger*. One of the unexplained aspects of the murder in Camus's novel is why Meursault shoots (moreover: shoots a total of five times) the Arab, who is armed only with a knife and thus represents a relatively innocuous threat to Meursault with his revolver. The Other, here, is impotent; and perhaps it is the knowledge of the Other's impotence which is finally so intolerable to Meursault. At the end of the first half of *L'Etranger*, Meursault effectively opts out of the senseless world in which he has been living and puts himself under the harsh but definitive tutelage of the law courts and the prison. Paradoxically, the murder of the Other reinstates its command over him, a command which had been distressingly at strain in the first half of the novel. Meursault accepts and desires his imprisonment because in prison the Other, as the despotic guarantor of meaning, finally exists. In this account, the altericidal act is not an attempt to destroy the Other, to blind its powerful, alienating gaze, but on the contrary it is a desperate reaffirmation of the Other's authority. The brothers in Freud's *Totem and Taboo* obey their father more strictly once they have killed him. Altericide thus maintains the Other's power; as much as it entails a violent response to the hold the Other has over me, it bears witness to the need for the sense and security which only the Other can supply. In as far as it entails a profession of faith in the victim's symbolic mandate, killing the Other is a failure to tarry with the negative.

Finally, I am put in mind of the emperor's new clothes. In the familiar interpretation of the story, the boy who says the emperor is naked has seen through the crowd's self-mystification and recognized things as they really are; his insight then leads to the demystification of the rest of the crowd and gives rise to a new consensus. But perhaps this new consensus in turn masks a more distressing knowledge. It is bad enough that the emperor should be naked, but *what if there were no emperor*? What if the story's insistence on the emperor's existence, be he clothed or unclothed, is its most fundamental mystification? Žižek's 'tarrying with the negative' entails seeing, in a permanent tension and distress, that the space occupied by the emperor is empty.[16] Perhaps such distress is too much to endure. At the same time, belief in the Other, and the identification of specific others (be they defined by race, gender, religion, social position or sexual inclination) as occupying the position of alterity, continues to produce real, violent effects. The texts I have been discussing here choose acts of murder which serve to disguise the knowledge that the Other does not exist, that it is a fantasy formation with which no actual subject coincides. They implicitly recommend a course of action from which it is not easy to draw ethical lessons or moral comfort: we should kill the emperor in order to hide from ourselves the appalling knowledge that he does not exist.

Notes

Introduction

1. Richards, *Science and Poetry*, 90, quoted in Docherty, *Alterities*, 3. Full references to works cited in this book are given in the Bibliography.
2. On difficulties in Levinas's thought over the nature of the Other, see for example Derrida, 'Violence et éthique', in *L'Ecriture et la différence*, 184–7.
3. Prominent examples of ethical criticism include the following: Booth, *The Company We Keep*; Siebers, *The Ethics of Criticism* and *Morals and Stories*; Rorty, *Contingency, Irony, and Solidarity*; Nussbaum, *Love's Knowledge*; Goldberg, *Agents and Lives*; Greene, *Just Words*; Norris, *Truth and the Ethics of Criticism*; Parker, *Ethics, Theory and the Novel*; McGinn, *Ethics, Evil, and Fiction*; Goodheart, *The Reign of Ideology*. The charge made in most of these texts that poststructuralist criticism overlooks or cannot deal with ethics is eloquently refuted by a number of fine works from within poststructuralism, or sympathetic to it; see especially Hillis Miller, *The Ethics of Reading*; Nouvet (ed.), *Literature and the Ethical Question* (edition of *Yale French Studies*); Laub and Felman, *Testimony*; Johnson, *A World of Difference*; Newton, *Narrative Ethics*; Caruth, *Unclaimed Experience*; Docherty, *Alterities*; Keenan, *Fables of Responsibility*. For an account of the relevance of Levinas to ethical criticism, published after the draft of this book was completed, see Eaglestone, *Ethical Criticism: Reading After Levinas*.
4. For fairly typical expressions of such views, see Siebers, *The Ethics of Criticism*, 2; Norris, *Truth and the Ethics of Fiction*, 108–9; Nussbaum, *Love's Knowledge*, 21, 231; Parker, *Ethics, Theory and the Novel*, 3–4; Goodheart, *The Reign of Ideology*, 117; McGinn, *Ethics, Evil, and Fiction*, 173–4.
5. Hirsch, *The Deconstruction of Literature*, 165, 117.
6. Throughout this book I follow the convention of capitalizing 'other' when it is used in the broadly Levinassian sense of the embodiment of irreducible alterity; lower case 'others' refers to 'other people' in the more ordinary sense.
7. Levinas, *Totalité et infini*, 25.
8. Levinas, *Totalité et infini*, 25.

Chapter 1

1. Docherty, *Alterities*, 1; subsequent references are given in the text.
2. For a useful account of the importance of Same and Other in twentieth-century French thought, see Descombes, *Le Même et l'autre*. In an account of recent French thought, Keith Reader also insists on the importance of otherness: 'If there is one theme that can be said to have dominated

contemporary French thought, it is assuredly that of *otherness*.... [In] one form or another it haunts most of the major conceptual adventures that have taken place in France since 1968, and even well before' ('The Self and Others', 213).

3 It would be wrong, however, to suggest that there is any consistency in the use of these terms, even within the works of particular authors. On the distinction between *autre* (other) and *Autre* (Other), see Lacan, 'Introduction du grand Autre', in *Le Moi dans la théorie de Freud et dans la technique de la psychanalyse*, 275–88.

4 On the civilizing function of art, see Benda, *La Trahison des clercs*, for example 148, 240.

5 On Sartre's literary theory and his changing view of commitment, see Howells, *Sartre's Literary Theory*, and Goldthorpe, *Sartre: Theory and Literature*, especially 159–97.

6 Blanchot, 'Enigme', 5–7; references are given in the text.

7 See Alexandre Kojève, *Introduction à la lecture de Hegel*, containing notes taken at lectures between 1933 and 1939. For an account of the influence of these lectures, see Descombes, *Le Même et l'autre*, 21–70.

8 Kojève, *Introduction à la lecture de Hegel*, 14–15; Kojève is commenting on Hegel, *Phenomenology of Spirit*, Chapter 4, section A.

9 Cited in Kojève, *Introduction à la lecture de Hegel*, 18, from Hegel, *Phenomenology of Spirit*, 113.

10 Sartre, *L'Etre et le néant*, 481; subsequent references are given in the text.

11 Bowie, *Lacan*, 82–3.

12 See Lacan, *Les Quatre Concepts fondamentaux de la psychanalyse*, 211: 'le sujet n'est sujet que d'être assujettissement au champ de l'Autre, le sujet provient de son assujettissement synchronique dans ce champ de l'Autre' (the subject is only subject by being subjected to the field of the Other, the subject comes from its synchronic subjection in this field of the Other).

13 On the analyst as 'le sujet supposé savoir' (the subject supposed to know), see *Les Quatre Concepts fondamentaux de la psychanalyse*, 256–71.

14 Lacan, *Les Quatre Concepts fondamentaux de la psychanalyse*, 211.

15 Žižek, *Enjoy your Symptom!*, 39.

16. For Lacan's account of the Schreber case, and of psychosis in general, see 'D'une question préliminaire à tout traitement possible de la psychose', in *Ecrits II*, 43–102.

17 See Bowie, *Lacan*, 109–10.

18 Sartre, *Cahiers pour une morale* (1983), notebooks originally written in 1947 and 1948. For attempts to formulate Sartre's uncompleted ethics, see Bell, *Sartre's Ethics of Authenticity*; Anderson, *Sartre's Two Ethics*; Renaut, *Sartre, le dernier philosophe*.

19 Lacan, *L'Ethique de la psychanalyse*, 361.

20 For a fuller introduction to Levinas's thought, see my *Levinas: An Introduction*.

21 Levinas, *En découvrant l'existence avec Husserl et Heidegger*, 188.

22 The following comments are based on the section of Levinas's *Totalité et infini* entitled 'Visage et éthique' (Face and Ethics), 211–42.

23 See also Critchley, *Very Little... Almost Nothing*, 80; Critchley shares my view that Levinas is not decisive on this point: 'Why is alterity ethical? Why is it not evil, or anethical, or neutral?'
24 Lacan, *L'Ethique de la psychanalyse*, 208.
25 Freud, *Group Psychology and the Analysis of the Ego*, in *Civilization, Society and Religion*, 154. References to Freud's *Totem and Taboo* are given in the text.
26 Brooks, *Reading for the Plot*, 277.
27 As the editor of *Totem and Taboo* points out, the quotation here refers to Goethe's *Faust*, in which Faust proposes 'In the beginning was the Deed' as a translation for the opening line of the Gospel of St John.
28 See Girard, *La Violence et le sacré*, 297: 'On nous objectera que nous dépassons la pensée de Freud, que nous prétendons la rectifier. Et c'est bien vrai...' (It will be objected that we are going beyond the thought of French, that we aim to put it right. And this is true). Further references to Girard are given in the text.
29 Freud's misunderstanding of his own insight in *Totem in Taboo* consists in the chronological hierarchization of different forms of altericide: thus, parricide precedes, and gives rise to, the prohibition of fratricide, which later is generalized in the imperative 'Thou shalt not kill' (207–8). My point here is that each of these forms of murder can be understood as altericidal desire, and that none can be given chronological or epistemological priority over the others.
30 Žižek, *The Metastases of Enjoyment*, 7–8.
31 Žižek, *Looking Awry*, 16.
32 See, for example, Lacan, *Les Quatre Concepts fondamentaux de la psychanalyse*, 261.
33 See Levinas, *Totalité et infini*, 23.
34 References to Malraux's *La Condition humaine* are given in the text.
35 Compare Garine in Malraux's first novel *Les Conquérants* (1928), who describes how the world of people who have killed would be transformed by their acts: 'Dans la réalité, je crois qu'ils verraient le monde se transformer complètement, changer ses perspectives, devenir non le monde d'un homme qui "a commis un crime", mais celui d'un homme qui a tué.... Pour un assassin, il n'y a pas de crimes, il n'y a que les meurtres – s'il est lucide, bien entendu' (84) (In reality I believe they would see the world completely transformed, its perspectives changed, becoming not the world of a man who 'has committed a crime', but that of a man who has killed.... For an assassin, there are no crimes, there are only murders – if he is lucid, of course).
36 It is a subject of disagreement whether Malraux's text exposes or implicitly endorses such attitudes to women; for discussion see Greene, *Just Words*, 73–92, and 73 note 2 for further references.

Chapter 2

1 See Heidegger, 'Der Ursprung des Kunstwerkes', in *Holzwege*, 1–74.
2 Plato's *Phaedrus* is one of the most frequent points of reference in Levinas's

work; see for example the section of *Totalité et infini* entitled 'Rhétorique et injustice' (Rhetoric and Injustice), 66–9.
3   References to the first two volumes of Gadamer's complete works, *Hermeneutik I: Wahrheit und Methode, Grundzüge einer philosophishen Hermeneutik* and *Hermeneutik II: Wahrheit und Methode, Ergänzungen, Register*, are given in the text with volume and page numbers.
4   Gary Aylesworth, 'Dialogue, Text, Narrative: Confronting Gadamer and Ricoeur', in *Gadamer and Hermeneutics*, edited by Hugh Silverman, 81.
5   See Abrams, 'Coping with Loss in the Human Sciences', especially 79.
6   See Joel Weinsheimer, 'Foreword' to Peter Szondi, *Introduction to Literary Hermeneutics*, xiii.
7   Friedrich Ast, *Grundlinien der Grammatik, Hermeneutik und Kritik* (1808), as quoted in Szondi, *Introduction to Literary Hermeneutics*, 101.
8   For Hirsch's criticisms of Gadamer, see *Validity in Interpretation*, 245–64.
9   For Gadamer's rejection of 'hermeneutischer Nihilismus' (hermeneutic nihilism), see *Hermeneutik I*, 100.
10 For the relation of this to the encounter with the work of art, see Gadamer, 'The Play of Art', in *The Relevance of the Beautiful and Other Essays*, 123–30, especially 130: 'the play of art is a mirror that through the centuries constantly arises anew, and in which we catch sight of ourselves in a way that is often unexpected or unfamiliar: what we are, what we might be, and what we are about.'
11 For discussion of the Habermas–Gadamer debate, see Graeme Nicholson, 'Answers to Critical Theory', and Dieter Misgeld, 'Modernity and Hermeneutics: A Critical-Theoretical Rejoinder', in *Gadamer and Hermeneutics*, 151–62 and 163–77.
12 See Haidu 'The Semiotics of Alterity: A Comparison with Hermeneutics', especially 679.
13 See Levinas, *Totalité et infini*, 79, 329.
14 See Levinas, *Quatre lectures talmudiques, Du sacré au saint: Cinq nouvelles lectures talmudiques, L'Au-delà du verset: Lectures et discours talmudiques* and *A l'heure des nations*. Many of the papers contained in these collections were originally delivered orally at the annual meetings of the Colloque des intellectuels juifs de langue française.
15 Levinas, *L'Au-delà du verset*, 136–7; translation as in *Beyond the Verse*, 110 (slightly modified).
16 Levinas, 'La Réalité et son ombre', in *Les Temps modernes*, 38 (1948), 771–89; references, given in the text, are to the reprinting in *Les Imprévus de l'histoire*, 123–48.
17 See Robbins, 'Aesthetic Totality and Ethical Infinity: Levinas on Art', 67–9.
18 Heidegger, 'Der Ursprung des Kunstwerkes', 59: '*Art then is the becoming and happening of truth*' (translation from *Poetry, Language, Thought*, 71).
19 Levinas writes: 'La critique l'*arrache* à son irresponsabilité ... elle *rattache* à l'histoire réelle cet homme dégagé et orgueilleux ... cette statue immobile *il faut* la mettre en mouvement et *la faire parler*' ('La Réalité et son ombre', 147; my emphasis) (Criticism tears it from its irresponsibility ... it binds that disengaged and arrogant man to real history ... that immobile statue must be put to movement and made to speak).

20 See 'La Réalité et son ombre', 147: 'La critique, en interprétant, choisira et limitera' (Criticism, as it interprets, will choose and limit).
21 See Llewelyn, Chapter 5 in *The Middle Voice of Ecologigal Conscience*, 89–113. Llewelyn draws attention to Levinas's article of 1972, 'Paul Celan: De l'être à l'autre', in *Noms propres*, 49–56. On changes in Levinas's views on art, see also Hayat, 'Epreuves de l'histoire, exigence d'une pensée', in *Les Imprévus de l'histoire*, especially 22, note 22.
22 Hand, 'Shadowing Ethics: Levinas's View of Art and Aesthetics', in *Facing the Other*, edited by Hand, 63–89, especially 81, 84.
23 Robbins, 'Aesthetic Totality and Ethical Infinity', 76.
24 Robbins makes a similar suggestion in reference to 'good' and 'bad' exteriority; see Robbins, 'Aesthetic Totality and Ethical Infinity', 77.
25 Caputo, *Against Ethics*, 80–1.
26 Heidegger, *Sein und Zeit*, 153.
27 On the hermeneutics of suspicion, see Ricoeur, *De l'interprétation*, 40–4.
28 Fish, *Is There a Text in this Class?*, 327: 'Interpretation is not the art of construing but the art of constructing. Interpreters do not decode poems; they make them.'
29 On this issue, see Finkielkraut, *Sagesse de l'amour*, for example 50–81.
30 References to Gide's *Les Faux-Monnayeurs* are given in the text.
31 Hartman, 'The Struggle for the Text', in *Midrash and Literature*, edited by Hartman and Budick, 16.

Chapter 3

1 Michel de Montaigne, 'De l'expérience', quoted by John D. Lyons, 'Circe's Drink and Sorbonnic Wine: Montaigne's Paradox of Experience', in Gelley (ed.), *Unruly Examples*, 87.
2 See Gelley, 'Introduction', in Gelley (ed.), *Unruly Examples*, 1–2. The distinction between *paradeigma* as model and as individual instance is echoed by Kant in the distinction between *Muster* and *Beispiel*; see David Lloyd, 'Kant's Examples', in Gelley (ed.), *Unruly Examples*, 255–76.
3 See Suleiman, *Authoritarian Fictions*, 25–65. For discussion, see Gelley, 'The Pragmatics of Exemplary Narrative', in Gelley (ed.), *Unruly Examples*, 142–61.
4 See Gelley's discussion of Derrida on exemplarity, in 'Introduction', 10–13.
5 Žižek, *Tarrying with the Negative*, 70–1.
6 See Kant, *Grundlegung zur Metaphysik der Sitten*, 27–8.
7 Kant, *Critique of Practical Reason*, 156–8. On the pedagogical use of examples in Kant's *Critique of Judgement*, see David Lloyd, 'Kant's Examples', in Gelley (ed.), *Unruly Examples*, 255–76.
8 Kant, *Critique of Practical Reason*, 30.
9 I shall not quote the second example here since it would take the discussion too far from its present aims. It seems to me, however, that Lacan's rereading of Kant's second example in both 'Kant avec Sade' and *L'Ethique de la psychanalyse* is less decisive than his account of the first; he envisages cases which might test the duty of truthfulness but does not, I suspect, fundamentally dissent from Kant's assessment of

what would constitute the right ethical choice. See 'Kant avec Sade', *Ecrits II*, 140–1, and *L'Ethique de la psychanalyse*, 222–3.
10 Kant, *Critique of Practical Reason*, 30.
11 Lacan, *L'Ethique de la psychanalyse*, 129; translated by Dennis Porter, *The Ethics of Psychoanalysis, 1959–1960*, 108. See also 'Kant avec Sade', 138.
12 Lacan, *L'Ethique de la psychanalyse*, 130–1; *The Ethics of Psychoanalysis, 1959–1960*, 109.
13 Lacan, *L'Ethique de la psychanalyse*, 223; *The Ethics of Psychoanalysis, 1959–1960*, 189 (translation slightly modified.)
14 See Žižek, *For they know not what they do*, 239.
15 See Hillis Miller, *The Ethics of Reading*, 3: 'Without storytelling there is no theory of ethics. Narratives, examples, stories... are indispensable to thinking about ethics.'
16 Hillis Miller, *The Ethics of Reading*, 2. For his reading of Kant, which to a large extent lies behind the comments in the current chapter, see 13–39.
17 See Kermode, *The Genesis of Secrecy*, for example 24–5.
18 The connection between 'Le Mur' and Kant's paper is signalled in the Pléiade edition of Sartre's *Oeuvres romanesques*, 1822. The connection is discussed in Sweeney, 'Lying to the Murderer: Sartre's Use of Kant in "The Wall"'. Sweeney regards Sartre's story as 'a developed, philosophical argument' (1) or a 'didactic story' (14) in which, despite his disagreements with Kant, Sartre follows his precursor over the issue of Pablo's responsibility for the death of Ramon. The meaning of 'Le Mur' seems to me to be rather less clear; as I shall argue, I believe the story is less didactic and more ambiguous than Sweeney suggests.
19 Kant, *Critique of Practical Reason*, 30.
20 See Kant, *Grundlegung zur Metaphysik der Sitten*, 21.
21 Kant, 'On a Supposed Right to Tell Lies from Benevolent Motives', 362–3.
22 Kant, 'On a Supposed Right to Tell Lies from Benevolent Motives', 363.
23 References to Sartre's 'Le Mur', are given in the text.
24 Kant, 'On a Supposed Right to Tell Lies from Benevolent Motives', 362.
25 See Kant, *Critique of Practical Reason*, 159–60.
26 Sweeney, 'Lying to the Murderer', 12.
27 Sweeney, 'Lying to the Murderer', 14.
28 See Howells, *Sartre: The Necessity of Freedom*, 30.
29 The Kantian formulation of Sartre's views is especially evident in *L'Existentialisme est un humanisme* (1946), a text with which Sartre was himself dissatisfied. For discussion, see Howells, *Sartre: The Necessity of Freedom*, 27–45.
30 Johnson, *The Critical Difference*, 146.
31 Kant, 'On a Supposed Right to Tell Lies from Benevolent Motives', 362.
32 See Freud, *The Interpretation of Dreams*, 180–98.
33 Sartre's 'Erostrate' builds a narrative around Breton's definition of the surrealist act in his *Second Manifeste du surréalisme*; see Breton, *Manifestes du surréalisme*, 78: 'L'acte surréaliste le plus simple consiste, revolvers au poing, à descendre dans la rue et à tirer au hasard, tant qu'on peut, dans la foule' (The most simple surrealist act consists in going into the

street, revolvers in hand, and shooting randomly, as much as one can, into the crowd).
34 Sartre, *La Mort dans l'âme*, 244.
35 Sartre, *Situations II*, 328.
36 Quoted by Tournier, *Le Vent Paraclet*, 145. See also Oscar Wilde, 'Lying, the telling of beautiful untrue things, is the proper aim of art' (quoted in Booth, *The Company We Keep*, 11). On the relation between fiction and lying, see Barbedette, *L'Invitation au mensonge*, especially 11–31.
37 I have discussed this in relation to storytelling in the fiction of Elie Wiesel in my *Elie Wiesel's Secretive Texts*, 97.
38 See Sartre, *Situations, II*, 105: 'Ainsi la lecture est un pacte de générosité entre l'auteur et le lecteur; chacun fait confiance à l'autre, chacun compte sur l'autre, exige de l'autre autant qu'il exige de lui-même' (Thus reading is a pact of generosity between the author and the reader; each places his confidence in the other, each counts on the other, expects of the other as much as he expects of himself).
39 See Barthes, 'La Mort de l'auteur', in *Le Bruissement de la langue*, 61–7, especially 67: 'la naissance du lecteur doit se payer de la mort de l'Auteur' (The birth of the reader much be at the price of the death of the Author).
40 Quoted in Johnson, *The Critical Difference*, 140, from Hartman, *The Fate of Reading and Other Essays*, 206.
41 See Mauriac, *Thérèse Desqueyroux*, 81: 'Elle s'est tue par paresse, sans doute, par fatigue.... Elle demeura muette: éprouva-t-elle seulement la tentation de parler?' (She kept silent out of laziness, perhaps, or tiredness.... She said nothing: did she so much as feel tempted to speak?). Only after this scene when she watches her husband inadvertently take an overdose does Thérèse begin to administer the poison herself.
42 Hillis Miller, 'Parabolic Exemplarity: The Example of Nietzsche's *Thus Spake Zarathustra*', in Gelley (ed.), *Unruly Examples*, 174.
43 Robbe-Grillet, *Un régicide*, 172.
44 Robbe-Grillet, *Un régicide*, 178.
45 Žižek, 'Two Ways to Avoid the Real of Desire', in *Looking Awry*, 48–66; references are in the text.

Chapter 4

1 See Sartre's 'Réponse à Albert Camus' and 'Albert Camus', in *Situations, IV*, 90–125, 126–9; on the lack of humour in Camus, see Bloom, 'Introduction', Bloom (ed.), *Modern Critical Views: Albert Camus*, 7; on Camus as a white colonialist, see Henri Kréa, quoted by Alec Hargreaves in History and Ethnicity in the Reception of *L'Etranger*', in King (ed.), *Camus's 'L'Etranger': Fifty Years On*, 107. Writing in 1961, Kréa describes the murder of the Arab as 'la réalisation subconsciente du rêve obscur et puéril du petit Blanc que Camus ne cessa jamais d'être' (the subconscious realization of the dark and childish dream of the little white man that Camus never stopped being). For more admiring assessments of Camus, see Guérin, *Albert Camus: Portrait de l'artiste en citoyen*, and Judt, *The Burden of Responsibility*, 87–135.

2 See, for example, Catherine Savage Brosman, 'Strangers and Brothers in the Works of Albert Camus and Jules Roy', in *Camus's 'L'Etranger': Fifty Years On*, 234; Brosman describes the Arab as 'the quintessential other, by whom one acquires a sense of the self'. In the same collection of essays, see also Peter Schofer, 'The Rhetoric of the Text: Causality, Metaphor, and Irony', 150. See also Cloonan, 'The Workings of Power: Foucault and *L'Etranger*'.
3 See Felman, 'Camus's *The Fall*, or the Betrayal of the Witness', in Felman and Laub, *Testimony*, 171, 189.
4 On the enigma of the murder and different readings of it, see Fitch, *'L'Etranger' d'Albert Camus*, 105–9; on interpretations of the crime within the novel itself, see Showalter, *'The Stranger': Humanity and the Absurd*, 49–54.
5 See for example Fitch, *'L'Etranger' d'Albert Camus*, 105: 'le texte nous a toujours semblé très clair à cet égard et . . . nous n'avons jamais éprouvé d'hésitation à accepter l'explication donnée par Meursault lui-même' (the text always seemed to me to be very clear in this respect and . . . I have never had any hesitation in accepting the explanation given by Meursault himself).
6 See Fitch, *'L'Etranger' d'Albert Camus*, 107.
7 For discussion of racial attitudes in *L'Etranger*, see the essays in *Camus's 'L'Etranger': Fifty Years On*, especially Alec Hargreaves, 'History and Ethnicity in the Reception of *L'Etranger*', 101–12; Michel Grimaud, 'Humanism and the "White Man's Burden": Camus, Daru, Meursault and the Arabs', 170–82; and Jan Rigaud, 'The Depiction of Arabs in *L'Etranger*', 183–92.
8 There is always, of course, the further option of seeing the novel as an allegory of its own interpretation. For such a reading, see Fitch, *The Narcissistic Text: A Reading of Camus' Fiction*, 67; Fitch describes *L'Etranger* as 'a text wherein the reader reads the story of his own activity. The experience provided by *L'Etranger* is paradoxically that of its own reading.'
9 References to *L'Etranger* and *La Chute* are given in the text, from Camus, *Théâtre, récits, nouvelles*.
10 See also the words of Céleste at Meursault's trial: 'il a répondu que j'étais un homme' (1191) (he replied that I was a man).
11 This is suggested, for example, by the dedication of Levinas's *Autrement qu'être ou au-delà de l'essence*, which refers to the six million Jewish victims of Nazism and other 'victimes de la même haine de l'autre homme, du même antisémitisme' (5) (victims of the same hatred of the other man, of the same anti-Semitism).
12 On the racial significance of the murder, see note 7, above; for a psychoanalytical explanation of Meursault's murder of the Arab, see in particular Costes, *Albert Camus ou la parole manquante: étude psychanalytique*.
13 See for example Grimaud, 'Humanism and the "White Man's Burden"', 174; Rigaud, 'The Depiction of Arabs in *L'Etranger*', 189.
14 Raymond Gay-Crosier, 'Algérianité et marginalité: Le Cas d'Albert Camus', paper delivered at the MLA convention, 1988; reference given in Brosman, 'Strangers and Brothers', 234, 241.
15 See Camus, *Le Mythe de Sisyphe*, 11; *L'Homme révolté*, 21. Subsequent references to *L'Homme révolté* are given in the text.

16 The term 'dissonance' is taken from Felman ('The Betrayal of the Witness', 170); however, she gives only one example of it (Cottard's violence at the end of *La Peste*) and seems to find it relatively restricted in scope. I believe that its presence in *La Peste* is far more widespread, as I have argued in 'Interpreting *La Peste*'.
17 It is unclear whether this episode occurs before or after the incident on the bridge; whatever the case may be, it is suggested that its *significance* is only understood much later (28).
18 Cerdan was a French boxer who won the world middleweight championship in 1948.
19 References to Felman's 'Camus's *The Fall*, or the Betrayal of the Witness' are given in the text.
20 For Felman's reading of *La Peste*, see 'Camus's *The Plague*, or a Monument to Witnessing', in *Testimony*, 93–119.
21 Felman, *What Does a Woman Want?*, 7.
22 Felman, *What Does a Woman Want?*, 6.
23 See Felman and Laub, Foreword to *Testimony*, xviii; literature is described as 'a witness, and perhaps the only witness, to the crisis within history which precisely cannot be articulated, witnessed in the given categories of history itself.'
24 See Camus: 'il ne joue pas le jeu' (1928) (he doesn't play the game); Meursault: 'il ne faut jamais jouer' (1182) (you should never play) (see also *La Chute*, 1506). Camus: 'Il répond qu'il éprouve à cet égard plus d'ennui que de regret véritable' (1928) (he replies that in this respect he feels more bothered than truly regretful); Meursault: 'j'ai dit que, plutôt que du regret véritable, j'éprouvais un certain ennui' (1176) (I said that, rather than truly regretful, I felt bothered to a certain extent).
25 See Fitch, *The Narcissistic Text*, 52–6.
26 King, 'Introduction', in King (ed.), *Camus's 'L'Etranger': Fifty Years On*, 12.
27 King, 'Introduction', 13.
28 Showalter, *The Stranger*, 32.
29 Fitch, *The Narcissistic Text*, 51.

Chapter 5

1 Beauvoir's obsession with death is foregrounded in the first English-language study of her work, Marks's *Simone de Beauvoir: Encounters with Death*.
2 Beauvoir, *L'Invitée*, 8.
3 Beauvoir, *Tous les hommes sont mortels*, 161–2.
4 See Jardine, 'Death Sentences: Writing Couples and Ideology'; Hughes, 'Murdering the Mother: Simone de Beauvoir's *Mémoires d'une jeune fille rangée*'; Moi, *Simone de Beauvoir: The Making of an Intellectual Woman*, especially 118–24.
5 See Moi, *Simone de Beauvoir*, 97.
6 Moi, *Simone de Beauvoir*, 124.
7 References to Beauvoir's *Le Sang des autres*, are given in the text.
8 Beauvoir, *La Force de l'âge*, 625.

9 In Dostoyevsky's *The Brothers Karamazov* the Elder Zosima learns from his dying brother that 'each of us is guilty before the other for everything, and I more than any' (332). Beauvoir omits the final phrase 'and I more than any' from her epigraph; Levinas, on the other hand, makes of it the cornerstone of his conception of responsibility: 'Vous connaissez cette phrase de Dostoïevski: "*Nous sommes tous coupables de tout et de tous devant tous, et moi plus que les autres.*" Non pas à cause de telle ou telle culpabilité effectivement mienne, à cause de fautes que j'aurais commises; mais parce que je suis responsable d'une responsabilité totale, qui répond de tous les autres et de tout chez les autres, même de leur responsabilité. Le moi a toujours une responsabilité *de plus* que tous les autres' (*Ethique et infini*, 95) (You know that phrase from Dostoyevsky: 'We are all guilty for everything and everyone before everyone, and myself more than others.' Not because of such and such a guilt that is actually mine, because of faults that I might have committed; but because I am responsible with a total responsibility, which is responsible for all others and for everything about them, even their responsibility. The self always has a responsibility *more* than all others).
10 See Blanchot, *La Part du feu*, 196–8; and for Beauvoir's acceptance of Blanchot's judgement, *La Force de l'âge*, 622: 'Je suis d'accord avec lui. Mais le défaut qu'il dénonce n'entache pas seulement les dernières pages du roman: d'un bout à l'autre, il lui est inhérent' (I agree with him. But the fault he denounces does not only spoil the final pages of the novel: from beginning to end it is inherent in the whole novel). A little later, Beauvoir adds: 'Une oeuvre à thèse non seulement ne montre rien mais elle ne démontre jamais que des fadaises' (*La Force de l'âge*, 624) (Not only does a work with a thesis show nothing, but it only ever demonstrates trifling things).
11 See Atack, *Literature and the French Resistance*, 123–30; on the 'structure of unity', see 8.
12 Suleiman, *Authoritarian Fictions*, 54. Atack expresses important misgivings concerning Suleiman's 'rather narrow definition of didacticism in narrative'; see *Literature and the French Resistance*, 13. Later parts of Suleiman's study draw attention to ways in which ambiguities or elements of self-questioning may be present within didactic narratives; see for example 199–238.
13 Suleiman, *Authoritarian Fictions*, 22.
14 Keefe, *Simone de Beauvoir: A Study of her Writings*, 169, 167.
15 Hughes, *Simone de Beauvoir: 'Le Sang des autres'*, 57.
16 Hughes, *Simone de Beauvoir: 'Le Sang des autres'*, 27.
17 See also Keefe: 'the concept of Blomart as essentially a man *obsessed* with guilt may make us less inclined to take the Resistance message as such as the key to the ending' (*Simone de Beauvoir*, 168).
18 Fallaize, *The Novels of Simone de Beauvoir*, 64.
19 Fallaize, *The Novels of Simone de Beauvoir*, 64.
20 Burrell, 'The Problem of Individual Responsibility in *Le Sang des autres*', 19.
21 Burrell, 'The Problem of Individual Responsibility in *Le Sang des autres*', 36.

22 This possibility is foreshadowed in *The Brothers Karamazov*. As the Elder Zosima's dying brother explains how 'each of us is guilty before the other for everything', his doctor comments that 'he is lapsing from illness into madness' (332).
23 Beauvoir, *L'Invitée*, 502–3.
24 See Moi, *Simone de Beauvoir*, 95–124.
25 For discussion of the relationship between self and Other in *L'Invitée* and *Le Sang des autres*, see Atack, *Literature and the French Resistance*, 124–5.
26 It has been argued that Sartre developed the ideas in *L'Etre et le néant* from reading a draft of *L'Invitée*; see Fullbrook and Fullbrook, *Simone de Beauvoir and Jean-Paul Sartre: The Remaking of a Twentieth-Century Legend*, 100–1. Recent work has contested the view of Beauvoir's thought as dependent on that of Sartre, emphasizing instead how it differs from or influences Sartre's philosophy; see Simons, 'Beauvoir and Sartre: The Philosophical Relationship'. On Beauvoir's differences from Sartre over *Mitsein* and conflict, see Kruks, *Situation and Human Existence*, 87, and 'Gender and Subjectivity: Simone de Beauvoir and Contemporary Feminism', 105.
27 References to *Pyrrhus et Cinéas* and *Pour une morale de l'ambiguïté*, given in the text, are to the joint edition, *Pour une morale de l'ambiguïté, suivi de Pyrrhus et Cinéas*.
28 See Kant, *Kritik der Urteilskraft*, 196–200.
29 Kant, *Critique of Practical Reason*, 90.
30 On this view in what he calls 'postmodern ethics', see Bauman, *Postmodern Ethics*, 80.
31 Fallaize comments on the continuing controversy surrounding this calculation; see *The Novels of Simone de Beauvoir*, 65.
32 For this reading, see Green, 'Writing War in the Feminine: de Beauvoir and Duras', 225. Green does also note the possibility that *Le Sang des autres* may have 'subversive ends' (226), but she seems unsure about this, and finds subversion of dominant narratives much more readily in Beauvoir's autobiographical writings.
33 Fallaize, *The Novels of Simone de Beauvoir*, 64.
34 Freud illustrates this in discussion of the excessive self-reproaches characteristic of pathological mourning: 'We find that in a certain sense these obsessive self-reproaches are justified.... It is not that the mourner was really responsible for the death.... None the less there was something in her – a wish that was unconscious to herself – which would not have been dissatisfied by the occurrence of death and which might actually have brought it about if it had had the power'; see Freud, *Totem and Taboo*, 116.
35 Keefe comments that Blomart's experience of killing is 'not easy to reconcile with his normal sensitivities' (*Simone de Beauvoir*, 164).
36 This phrase recalls the deliberately shocking sentence from the opening paragraph of Radiguet's *Le Diable au corps* (1923), in which the narrator describes the First World War as 'quatre ans de grandes vacances' (45) (four years of holiday).
37 Suleiman, *Authoritarian Fictions*, 10.

38 The point is made, with reference to Suleiman, in Fallaize, *The Novels of Simone de Beauvoir*, 51–2.
39 See Suleiman, *Authoritarian Fictions*, 141–8.
40 Suleiman, *Authoritarian Fictions*, 10.
41 Suleiman, *Authoritarian Fictions*, 54.
42 The narrator who uses both the first- and third-persons in these chapters is sometimes taken to be Blomart; see for example Fallaize, *The Novels of Simone de Beauvoir*, 46. Whilst this view is reasonable enough (and supported by Beauvoir herself; see *La Force de l'âge*, 621), it is no more certain than the assumption that *je* (I) and *il* (he) should be attributed to different, constantly alternating narrators.
43 Green, 'Writing War in the Feminine: de Beauvoir and Duras', 25–6.
44 Low, 'Simone de Beauvoir's Wartime Novel *Le Sang des autres* et les yeux de l'auteur', 25.
45 Hughes, *Simone de Beauvoir: 'Le Sang des autres'*, 3.
46 Hughes, *Simone de Beauvoir: 'Le Sang des autres'*, 60.
47 Low, 'Simone de Beauvoir's Wartime Novel *Le Sang des autres* et les yeux de l'auteur', 31.
48 Suleiman, *Authoritarian Fictions*, 237.

Chapter 6

1 References to Sartre's *L'Existentialisme est un humanisme* and Heidegger's *Lettre sur l'humanisme* are given in the text. On the philosophical relations between these texts, see in particular Fell, 'Humanism: The Lecture and the Letter', in *Heidegger and Sartre*, 152–84.
2 Rockmore, *Heidegger and French Philosophy*, 187.
3 See Tournier, *Le Vent Paraclet*, 156–7.
4 Benda, *La Trahison des clercs*, 154.
5 Benda, *La Trahison des clercs*, 154: 'J'ajoute que cet humanitarisme, qui honore la qualité abstraite de ce qui est humain, est le seul qui permette d'aimer *tous* les hommes' (I add that this humanitarianism, which honours the abstract quality of what is human, is the only one that allows us to love *all* men).
6 See Foucault, *Les Mots et les choses*, 15: 'l'homme n'est qu'une invention récente, une figure qui n'a pas deux siècles, un simple pli dans notre savoir, et [il] disparaîtra dès que celui-ci aura trouvé une forme nouvelle' (man is only a recent invention, a figure which is not two hundred years old, a simple fold in our knowledge, and he will disappear as soon as the latter has found a new form).
7 Throughout this chapter I follow the practice of nearly all French writers of the 1940s (even authors such as Simone de Beauvoir, from whom one might have hoped for better) by referring to *Man* rather than to some gender-neutral term. This should not be taken as an endorsement of such an exclusionary term: in the context of my argument, the imperialism involved in taking a part of humanity to represent the whole should become explicit. On the logic of identifying 'man' with 'humanity', see Agacinski, *Critique de l'égocentrisme*, 138.

8 See Derrida, 'Les Fins de l'homme', in *Marges de la philosophie*, 138–9.
9 On this translation of Dasein, see Rockmore, *Heidegger and French Philosophy*, 73–5; Derrida, 'Les Fins de l'homme', 136.
10 Derrida, 'Les Fins de l'homme', 139.
11 On humanism in French thought, see Rockmore, *Heidegger and French Philosophy*, especially 60–9, and Soper, *Humanism and Anti-Humanism*. On the importance of the three Hs in French thought, see Descombes, *Le Même et l'autre*, 13.
12 On the *Lettre sur l'humanisme* and Heidegger's attempt to influence the French reception of his thought, see Rockmore, *Heidegger and French Philosophy*, 88–98.
13 See Sartre, *La Nausée*, 147–74. In his critique of Sartre's humanism, Derrida refers to this passage, but entirely fails to take account of it; see 'Les Fins de l'homme', 136–7.
14 Kant *Critique of Practical Reason*, 30.
15 Kant *Critique of Practical Reason*, 19.
16 Kant *Critique of Practical Reason*, 32.
17 On the problems of steering a course between universalism, ethnocentrism and relativism, see Finkielkraut, *La Défaite de la pensée*, and Todorov, *Nous et les autres*.
18 On the circumstances under which the *Lettre sur l'humanisme* was published, and in particular on its significance in the French debate on humanism, see Rockmore, *Heidegger and French Philosophy*, 81–103.
19 The connection between the inhuman and the barbarian is further reinforced by the French translation of the German *inhuman* as *barbare* (45, 46). For discussion of the status of Barbarians as outsiders, see Kristeva, *Etrangers à nous-mêmes*, 74–83.
20 Derrida reproduces this move in his discussion of Heidegger in *De l'esprit*; Derrida insists that he is not criticizing the 'téléologie humaniste' (humanist teleology) of Heidegger's writing because it remains 'le prix à payer dans la dénonciation éthico-politique du biologisme, du racisme, du naturalisme, etc.' (87) (the price to pay in the ethico-political denunciation of biologism, racism, naturalism, etc). Humanism is thus recognized as being questionable but, for the moment at least, indispensable. Considering whether this situation may change in the future, Derrida comments simply, 'Je ne le sais pas' (88) (I don't know).
21 On problems involved in getting to the 'outside' of humanism, see Derrida, 'Les Fins de l'homme', 162.
22 References to Yourcenar's *Mémoires d'Hadrien* are given in the text.
23 Yourcenar, *L'Oeuvre au noir*, 10.
24 Yourcenar, *L'Oeuvre au noir*, 17.
25 Yourcenar, *L'Oeuvre au noir*, 18.
26 Marks, 'Getting Away with Murd(h)er – Author's Preface and Narrator's Text: Reading Marguerite Yourcenar's *Coup de grâce* "After Auschwitz"', in *Marrano as Metaphor*, 85–95. For Yourcenar's comments in her 1962 preface to *Le Coup de grâce*, see 130: 'le lecteur naïf risque de... prendre pour un antisémite professionnel cet homme chez qui le persiflage à l'égard des Juifs fait partie d'un conformisme de caste' (the naive reader

risks... taking for a professional anti-Semite that man in whom mocking Jews is part of a caste conformism).
27 Dio Cassius, Yourcenar's principal source on the war against the Jews, gives the figure of 580,000 for the number of Jewish victims; see Johnson, *A History of the Jews*, 142. So Hadrian's reference to 'près de six cent mille hommes' (nearly six hundred thousand men) is in line with this figure. This does not prevent the reference from evoking, deliberately or otherwise, the victims of the Holocaust.
28 For illustration and discussion of this in hermeneutic thought, see Szondi, *Introduction to Literary Hermeneutics*, 101.
29 On the encounter with alterity through eroticism, see Levinas, *Le Temps et l'autre*, 77–84, and *Totalité et infini*, 286–99.
30 The quotation is used in the title of Harris, *Marguerite Yourcenar: Vers la rive d'une Ithaque intérieure*.
31 See for example Levinas, *En découvrant l'existence avec Husserl et Heidegger*, 191.
32 Levinas, *Totalité et infini*, 28.
33 On the 'good' Barbarians who have the potential to acquire civilized values, see Kristeva, *Etrangers à nous-mêmes*, 77.
34 See Lyotard, *Le Différend*.
35 The passage is worth quoting in full to demonstrate the remarkable unquestioned assumptions which lie behind it: 'Impossibilité aussi de prendre pour figure centrale un personnage féminin, de donner, par exemple, pour axe à mon récit, au lieu d'Hadrien, Plotine [The wife of Trajan, Hadrian's predecessor and adoptive father]. La vie des femmes est trop limitée, ou trop secrète. Qu'une femme se raconte, et le premier reproche qu'on lui fera est de n'être plus femme. Il est déjà assez difficile de mettre quelque vérité dans une bouche d'homme' (329) (Impossible also to take as central character a female figure, to make, for example, Plotina instead of Hadrian the axis of my story. The lives of women are too limited, or too secret. If a woman tells her story, the first reproach that will be made to her is that she is no longer a woman. It is already hard enough to put some truth into the mouth of a man).
36 Hadrian refers to Lucius's 'manies absurdes et délicieuses: la passion de confectionner à ses amis des plats rares, le goût exquis des décorations florales, le fol amour des jeux de hasard et des travestis' (122) (absurd and delicious obsessions: the passion of preparing rare dishes for his friends, the exquisite taste for floral decorations, the mad love for games of chance and travesties). Amongst the meanings of *travesti*, the Petit Robert gives 'un acteur qui se travestit, et *spécialt.* qui joue un rôle féminin' (an actor who travesties himself, and in particular who plays a woman's role) and 'Homosexuel habillé (fardé) comme une femme et qui a parfois des caractères secondaires féminins, naturels ou provoqués' (Homosexual dressed (made up) like a woman and who sometimes has secondary female characteristics, either natural or assumed).
37 On the dangers of universalist humanism turning into racism, see Agacinski, *Critique de l'égocentrisme*, especially 133–58. Agacinski describes the results of trying to impose a single model on all Others: 'Non

seulement [l'humanisme] entre alors dans le particulier, mais il fait de ce particulier (tel idéal culturel ou humain) un modèle universel. A la limite, il est tenté d'imposer ce modèle à tous de façon coercitive avec les meilleures intentions du monde' (147) (Not only does [humanism] enter into the particular, but it makes this particular (some cultural or human ideal) into a universal model. In extreme cases it is tempted to impose this model coercively on everyone with the best intentions in the world).
38 Žižek, *Looking Awry*, 140.
39 Žižek, makes the same point in relation to anti-Semitism and social harmony in *Enjoy your Symptom!*, 90.

Chapter 7

1 Duras, *L'Amante anglaise*, 35–6.
2 Duras, *Dix heures et demie du soir en été*, 23–4.
3 Duras, *L'Amante anglaise*, 82; further references are given in the text.
4 Throughout this chapter I distinguish between *La Douleur* (the text as a whole) and 'La Douleur' (the first and largest part of the work); references are given in the text.
5 References to Antelme's *L'Espèce humaine* are given in the text.
6 M... could refer either to Marguerite Duras, or possibly to Antelme's sister, Marie-Louise, to whom *L'Espèce humaine* is dedicated, and who died during the war as a result of deportation; the D. of *La Douleur* is generally taken to be Dionys Mascolo, with whom Duras had a child in 1947.
7 In this chapter I do not deal with the problem of when *La Douleur* was composed. In the liminary text to 'La Douleur' the narrator claims to have no memory of writing the journal. Fragments of the text were published in the seventies, though there are numerous variants between these fragments and the edition of 1985; see Hill, *Marguerite Duras: Apocalyptic Desires*, 174–5. My working assumption is that, although the text may have existed in some form in the forties, it was edited and rewritten much more recently, and with knowledge of Antelme's *L'Espèce humaine*.
8 On connections between the texts, see for example Plottel, 'Memory, Fiction and History', 55; Kritzman, in 'Duras' War', 73, observes rather noncommittally: 'It is interesting to note that the real witness to the horrors of the Nazi concentration camps, Duras's husband, Robert Antelme, published his own account of this history in *L'Espèce humaine* (1947).' Hill makes more substantial comments about the relationship between the texts in *Marguerite Duras*, 129–32. Since the original draft of this chapter was written, I have been able to consult two important articles which analyse the relations between the texts of Duras and Antelme more closely: see Crowley, '"Il n'y a qu'une espèce humaine": Between Duras and Antelme' (which explicitly takes issue with the views expressed in this chapter), and Gorrara, 'Bearing Witness in Robert Antelme's *L'Espèce humaine* and Marguerite Duras's *La Douleur*'. My understanding of the place of the ethical in Duras's work has been immensely

enriched by Martin Crowley's unpublished doctoral thesis, 'Writing and the Ethical in the Works of Marguerite Duras'.
9 More generally, Hill argues that *La Douleur* questions 'the terms on which testimony in general is possible' and that it is 'a work that bears witness to the sheer impossibility of bearing witness' (*Marguerite Duras*, 128–9). See also Wilson, '*La Douleur*: Duras, Amnesia and Desire', which anticipates my own conclusions: '[*La Douleur*] not only testifies to the impossibility of bearing witness but... it also questions the notion that the act of narration can itself be redemptive' (144). However, it should also be stressed that the problem of testimony is one of the topoi of concentration-camp literature, and Antelme's text deals with it in numerous passages from the 'Avant-propos' to the closing pages; see for example *L'Espèce humaine*, 9, 302.
10 Blanchot, *L'Entretien infini*, 191. For discussion of Blanchot and Antelme, see Kofman, *Paroles suffoquées*.
11 Blanchot refers to Levinas in the chapter immediately preceding his discussion of Antelme (189), and goes on to use a series of words and terms with strong Levinassian connections in his account of *L'Espèce humaine*: 'Autrui' (191) (Others), 'l'Autre' (195) (the Other), 'rapport sans rapport' (194) (relationship without relationship), 'face à face' (195) (face to face), 'l'infini' (195) (the infinite).
12 Blanchot, *L'Entretien infini*, 193–5.
13 Blanchot, *L'Entretien infini*, 198.
14 Blanchot, *L'Entretien infini*, 198.
15 Blanchot, *L'Entretien infini*, 199.
16 This phrase is used in the title to Levinas's *L'Humanisme de l'autre homme*.
17 Blanchot, *L'Entretien infini*, 192.
18 For a different reading of Antelme's humanism, see Kofman, *Paroles suffoquées*, 79–82.
19 See Rousset, *L'Univers concentrationnaire*, for example 118.
20 Hill, *Marguerite Duras*, 129–30.
21 Martin Crowley, '"Il n'y a qu'une espèce humaine": Between Duras and Antelme', 16. Crowley convincingly points out that the darker implications of Antelme's views on the indivisibility of the human species are already acknowledged in Antelme's own writing (see 12–13). Even so, the argument of the present chapter is that Duras develops those implications in ways which Antelme could not envisage within the generally humanist frame of his writing.
22 See Hill, *Marguerite Duras*, 128. The *Milice* was an organization established in 1943 to help the occupying German forces in the struggle against the French Resistance. It seems to me to be less clear than is normally assumed that Thérèse in 'Ter le milicien' is sexually attracted to Ter; in the liminary text it is stated that she 'a envie de faire l'amour avec Ter' (134), but this is not explicitly supported in the text itself.
23 Hill, *Marguerite Duras*, 131–2.
24 Hill, *Marguerite Duras*, 132.
25 See Hill, *Marguerite Duras*, 129; Kritzman, 'Duras' War', 72.
26 In '"Il n'y a qu'une espèce humaine": Between Duras and Antelme', Crowley concludes that 'at no point do the implications of Duras's

texts in fact exceed what is already implied – and occasionally highlighted – in *L'Espèce humaine*' (16). Earlier in the paper, Crowley quotes – but does not directly comment upon – Duras's reference to the Nazi horrors as 'un crime de tous' (7, quoting Duras, 61) (everyone's crime). The crux of the difference between Crowley's argument and mine lies in my belief that this reference constitutes one of the key points where Duras does exceed the views expressed in Antelme's book.

27 Compare *La Douleur*, 10 ('Je me suis trouvée devant un désordre phénoménal de la pensée et du sentiment auquel je n'ai pas osé toucher et au regard de quoi la littérature m'a fait honte') (I found myself faced with a phenomenal disorder of thought and feeling which I didn't dare touch and regarding which literature made me ashamed), with *L'Espèce humaine*, 279: 'Moi aussi j'ai mal au ventre. C'est venu brusquement. Je ne peux plus me retenir, attendre le jour. Je déchire un morceau de couverture, je baisse mon pantalon. Jo et Marcel ne disent rien. La honte' (I also have stomach pains. It came quickly. I can't hold back any longer, I can't wait for daylight. I tear off a piece of the blanket, I lower my trousers. Jo and Marcel say nothing. Shame).

28 See Kristeva, 'La Maladie de la douleur: Duras', in *Soleil noir*, 235.

29 See Duras, *Les Yeux verts*, 179: 'C'est parce que les nazis n'ont pas *reconnu* cette horreur en eux qu'ils l'ont commise' (It is because the Nazis didn't *recognize* this horror within themselves that they committed it); quoted Crowley, 8.

Chapter 8

1 Genet, *Notre-Dame-des-Fleurs*, 10; subsequent references to Genet's works are given in the text.

2 For a more complete list of the real and fictional murderers in Genet's novels, see Child Bickel, *Jean Genet: Criminalité et transcendance*, 130–3. The current chapter requires two comments. First, it discusses principally Genet's prose texts up until *Journal du voleur*, so excluding his plays and the late text *Un captif amoureux*. Second, I refer to 'the narrator' of the prose works as if each has the same narrator; whilst this is clearly a questionable assumption, it seems justified in the present context by the relative unity of tone and technique in those works.

3 See Chapter 1.

4 See Bataille, 'Genet' (essay first published in 1952), in *La Littérature et le mal*, 153. On the lack of unambiguous commitment even in Genet's late text *Un captif amoureux*, see my '*Un captif amoureux* and the Commitment of Jean Genet'.

5 Booth, *The Company We Keep*, 8.

6 See for example Nussbaum, *Love's Knowledge*, 282–3, 390.

7 Johnstone, 'Wayne Booth and the Ethics of Fiction', 68.

8 Millett, *Sexual Politics*, 346.

9 Thody, *Jean Genet*, 105, 117.

10 Bersani, *Homos*, 166.

11 This is especially the case with the early criticism of Genet; see Child

Bickel, *Jean Genet: Criminalité et transcendance*, 6. According to Child Bickel, Derrida's *Glas* (1974) marks a break with the moral preoccupations of Genet's earlier readers. Bougon also describes *Glas* as introducing a decisive new perspective into Genet criticism, after Sartre in the 1950s and the interest in Genet's theatre in the 1960s and 1970s; see Bougon, 'Editor's Introduction', in *Jean Genet: Littérature et Politique (Literature and Politics)*, 3.

12 References to Sartre's *Saint Genet, comédien en martyr* are given in the text.
13 See Thody, *Jean Genet*, 29–30, 44.
14 See Thody, *Jean Genet*, 109: 'Once again, Genet destroys with one hand the cult of evil which he is apparently trying to establish with the other, so that in his attitude to politics, as in his glorification of crime, common sense will keep breaking through.'
15 See Bersani, *Homos*, 151–81.
16 Bersani, *Homos*, 160–1.
17 Robinson, *Scandal in the Ink*, 59.
18 On Cixous's view of Genet as a practitioner of *écriture féminine*, see Sellers, *Language and Sexual Difference*, 142. The title of Cixous and Clément's *La Jeune Née* can be read as, amongst other things, an allusion to Genet's name.
19 Millett, *Sexual Politics*, 356.
20 Child Bickel, *Jean Genet: Criminalité et transcendance*, 2.
21 See Child Bickel, *Jean Genet: Criminalité et transcendance*, 15.
22 See, for example, Derrida, *Glas*, 285–6; further references to *Glas* are given in the text.
23 For a fuller discussion of the relationship between Hegel and Genet in *Glas*, see Howells, 'Derrida and Sartre: Hegel's Death Knell'.
24 See for example *Glas*, 50: 'C'est la premiére fois que j'ai peur, en écrivant, comme on dit, "sur" quelqu'un, d'être lu par lui' (It is the first time that I am afraid, when writing, as one says, 'about' someone, of being read by him); see also 210.
25 Elsewhere, however, Sartre is more sensitive to this aspect of Genet's writing; see for example *Saint Genet*, 646, where Sartre refers to Genet as 'l'unique destinataire de son message' (the sole addressee of his message).
26 For discussion of the dynamics of misreading, see Johnson, 'The Frame of Reference: Poe, Lacan, Derrida', in *The Critical Difference*, 110–46.
27 See Meitinger, 'L'Irréel de jouissance dans le *Journal du voleur* de Genet', 71.
28 Genet, *L'Ennemi déclaré*, 214.
29 This aspect of *Journal du voleur* has been thoroughly analysed in Sheringham, 'Narration and Experience in Genet's *Journal du voleur*', 289–306.
30 Genet, *Oeuvres complètes*, volume 4, 26; the incident is also recounted in 'L'Atelier d'Alberto Giacometti', in volume 5 of the *Oeuvres complètes*.
31 On eating Jean, see *Pompes funèbres*, 14, 24; for discussion see Bersani, *Homos*, 156–9.
32 Sartre reports that Genet wrote the phrase in a copy of *Pompes funèbres*; see *Saint Genet, comédien et martyr*, 139.
33 See especially Dobrez, *The Existential and its Exits*, 213–20.

34 See *Miracle de la rose*, 150: 'Il m'en coûterait de dire que les hommes sont mes frères. Ce mot m'écoeure parce qu'il me rattache aux hommes par un cordon ombilical, il me replonge à l'intérieur d'un ventre' (It would be hard for me to say that men are my brothers. That word disgusts me because it attaches me to men by an umbilical cord, it plunges me back inside a womb).
35 See Freud, *Civilization and its Discontents*, in *Civilization, Society and Religion*, 305.
36 For reference to the tradition according to which Cain and Abel were born on the same day, see Wiesel, *Célébration biblique*, 45.
37 Wiesel, *Célébration biblique*, 41–65; see also Banon, *La Lecture infinie*, 207–10.
38 Wiesel, *Célébration biblique*, 58.
39 Levinas, *Entre nous*, 128–9.
40 See also *Querelle de Brest*, 405, which alludes to the mark of Cain.
41 See Wiesel, *Célébration biblique*, 54.
42 See also when Erik kills in *Pompes funèbres*, 81: 'Le plus haut moment de liberté était atteint' (The highest moment of liberty was reached).
43 On love as the search for one's lost half, see Plato's *Symposium*, in *The Collected Dialogues*, 542–6.
44 In Genet's texts the penis is presented as the essence of the male; see for example *Querelle*, 285. See also the description of Harcamone as a penis in *Miracle de la rose*, 228.
45 These and other texts on Jackson are collected in *L'Ennemi déclaré*.
46 Genet, 'Le Rouge et le noir', in *L'Ennemi déclaré*, 101.
47 Genet, *L'Ennemi déclaré*, 103. The equation of art and murder is already made in Genet's fiction; see for example *Querelle*, 316, *Miracle*, 212.
48 Genet, *L'Ennemi déclaré*, 156.
49 On the failure of communication in Genet's writing, see Bataille's response to Sartre's views in *La Littérature et le mal*, 199–244.
50 This may be compared to the situation of the audience in Genet's play *Les Nègres*; the performance put on in front of the court turns out to be a cover for the revolutionary action taking place off stage which the audience is not allowed to see.
51 Genet, *L'Ennemi déclaré*, 164.
52 Levinas, *Totalité et infini*, 312–13; subsequent references are given in the text.
53 Levinas, *En découvrant l'existence avec Husserl et Heidegger*, 191.
54 Levinas, *Autrement qu'être ou au-delà de l'essence*, 19; for discussion, see my *Levinas*, especially 74–9.
55 Levinas, *Autrement qu'être ou au-delà de l'essence*, 5.
56 Blanchot, 'Notre compagne clandestine', 86–7.
57 Levinas, *Difficile liberté*, 406.

Conclusion

1 Hegel, *Phenomenology of Spirit*, 19, quoted in Žižek, *Tarrying with the Negative*, epigraph.

2 Žižek, *The Plague of the Fantasies*, 227.
3 Johnstone, 'Wayne Booth and the Ethics of Fiction', 65–6; subsequent references are given in the text.
4 Nussbaum, *Love's Knowledge*, 308–9.
5 See Bersani, *The Culture of Redemption*.
6 Langer, *Admitting the Holocaust*, 6–7.
7 Iser, 'The Reading Process', 67.
8 Wilson, *Sexuality and the Reading Encounter*, 195.
9 Suleiman, *Risking Who One Is*, 195.
10 Wilson, *Sexuality and the Reading Encounter*, viii, 195.
11 Suleiman, *Risking Who One Is*, 6.
12 Žižek, *Tarrying with the Negative*, 203; see also *Looking Awry*, 165. This may be compared with the passage in Duras's *L'Amante anglaise* where Claire describes her dislike for the food cooked by her eventual victim, Marie-Thérèse, and explains: 'Je dis que j'ai un caractère à ne pas supporter que les gens mangent et dorment bien' (148) (I say that I have a character which cannot bear it when people eat and sleep well).
13 Žižek, *Tarrying with the Negative*, 206.
14 Žižek, *Tarrying with the Negative*, 2.
15 Žižek, *Tarrying with the Negative*, 237.
16 The same point is suggested in Robbe-Grillet's *Un régicide* when the king, whom Boris intends to kill, is absent from the place he is due to occupy: 'Il se rendit compte tout de suite qu'il n'y avait pas de roi, ni personne d'autre, dans l'ascenseur' (164) (He realized immediately that there was no king, nor anyone else, in the lift).

Bibliography

Abrams, Marsha Lynne, 'Coping with Loss in the Human Sciences: A Reading at the Intersection of Psychoanalysis and Hermeneutics', *Diacritics* 23:1 (1993), 67–82.
Agacinski, Sylviane, *Critique de l'égocentrisme: L'Evénement de l'autre* (Paris: Galilée, 1996).
Anderson, Thomas, *Sartre's Two Ethics: From Authenticity to Integral Humanity* (Chicago and La Salle, Illinois: Open Court, 1993).
Antelme, Robert, *L'Espèce humaine* (Tel; Paris: Gallimard, 1957; first published 1947).
Atack, Margaret, *Literature and the French Resistance: Cultural Politics and Narrative forms, 1940–1950* (Manchester: Manchester University Press, 1989).
Banon, David, *La Lecture infinie: Les Voies de l'interprétation midrachique* (Paris: Seuil, 1987).
Barbedette, Gilles, *L'Invitation au mensonge: Essai sur le roman* (Paris: Gallimard, 1989).
Barthes, Roland, *Le Bruissement de la langue* (Paris: Seuil, 1984).
Bataille, Georges, *La Littérature et le mal* (Folio; Paris: Gallimard, 1957).
Bauman, Zygmunt, *Postmodern Ethics* (Oxford: Blackwell, 1993).
Beauvoir, Simone de, *L'Invitée* (Folio; Paris: Gallimard, 1943).
Beauvoir, Simone de, *Le Sang des autres* (Folio; Paris: Gallimard, 1945).
Beauvoir, Simone de, *Tous les hommes sont mortels* (Folio; Paris: Gallimard, 1946).
Beauvoir, Simone de, *Pour une morale de l'ambiguïté, suivi de Pyrrhus et Cinéas* (Idées; Paris: Gallimard, 1947 and 1944).
Beauvoir, Simone de, *La Force de l'âge* (Folio; Paris, Gallimard, 1960).
Bell, Linda, *Sartre's Ethics of Authenticity* (Tuscaloosa, Alabama: The University of Alabama Press, 1989).
Benda, Julien, *La Trahison des clercs* (Paris: Grasset and Fasquelle, 1975; first published 1927).
Bersani, Leo, *The Culture of Redemption*, (Cambridge, Mass: Harvard University Press, 1990).
Bersani, Leo, *Homos* (Cambridge, Mass: Harvard University Press, 1995).
Blanchot, Maurice, *La Part du feu* (Paris: Gallimard, 1949).
Blanchot, Maurice, *L'Entretien infini* (Paris: Gallimard, 1969).
Blanchot, Maurice, 'Notre compagne clandestine', in Laruelle, François (ed.), *Textes pour Emmanuel Levinas* (Paris: Editions Jean-Michel Place, 1980).
Blanchot, 'Enigme', in Nouvet, Claire (ed.), *Literature and the Ethical Question* (New Haven, CT: Yale University Press, 1991), 5–7.
Booth, Wayne, *The Company We Keep: An Ethics of Fiction* (Berkeley and London: University of California Press, 1988).
Bougon, Patrice (ed.), *Jean Genet: Littérature et Politique (Literature and Politics), L'Esprit créateur* 35:1 (1995).

Bowie, Malcolm, *Lacan* (London: Fontana, 1991).
Breton, André, *Manifestes du surréalisme* (Idées; Paris: Gallimard, 1979).
Brooks, Peter, *Reading for the Plot: Design and Intention in Narrative Fiction* (Oxford: Oxford University Press, 1984).
Budick, Sanford, and Hartman, Geoffrey, *Midrash and Literature* (New Haven and London: Yale University Press, 1986).
Burrell, Margaret, 'The Problem of Individual Responsibility in *Le Sang des autres*', *New Zealand Journal of French Studies* 16:2 (1995), 19–37.
Camus, Albert, *Le Mythe de Sisyphe* (Idées; Paris: Gallimard, 1942).
Camus, Albert, *L'Homme révolté* (Idées; Paris: Gallimard, 1951).
Camus, Albert, *Théâtre récits, nouvelles*, edited by Roger Quilliot (Paris: Gallimard, 1962; 1967 printing).
Caputo, John, *Against Ethics* (Bloomington: Indiana University Press, 1993).
Caruth, Cynthia, *Unclaimed Experience: Trauma, Narrative, and History* (Baltimore and London: The Johns Hopkins University Press, 1996).
Child Bickel, Gisèle, *Jean Genet: Criminalité et transcendance* (Saratoga: Anma Libri, 1987).
Cixous, Hélène, and Clément, Catherine, *La Jeune Née* (Paris: Union Générale d'Editions, 1975).
Cloonan, William, 'The Workings of Power: Foucault and *L'Etranger*', in Moretti, Monique Streiff, Cappelletti, Mireille Revol, and Martinez, Odile (eds), *Il senso del nonsenso: Scritti in memoria di Lynn Salkin Sbiroli* (Perugia: Edizioni Scientifiche Italiane, 1994), 457–67.
Costes, Alain, *Albert Camus ou la parole manquante: étude psychanalytique* (Paris: Payot, 1973).
Critchley, Simon, *Very Little... Almost Nothing: Death, Philosophy, Literature* (London and New York: Routledge, 1997).
Crowley, Martin, 'Writing and the Ethical in the Works of Marguerite Duras' (unpublished D.Phil. thesis, Oxford 1997).
Crowley, Martin, '"Il n'y a qu'une espèce humaine": Between Duras and Antelme' (unpublished typescript).
Davis, Colin, '*Un captif amoureux* and the Commitment of Jean Genet', *French Studies Bulletin* 23 (1987), 16–18.
Davis, Colin, 'Interpreting *La Peste*', *The Romanic Review* 85 (1994), 125–42.
Davis, Colin, *Elie Wiesel's Secretive Texts* (Gainesville: University Press of Florida, 1994).
Davis, Colin, *Levinas: An Introduction* (Cambridge: Polity Press, 1996).
Derrida, Jacques, *L'Ecriture et la différence* (Points; Paris: Seuil, 1967).
Derrida, Jacques, *Marges de la philosophie* (Paris: Minuit, 1972).
Derrida, Jacques, *Glas: Que reste-t-il du savoir absolu?* (Paris: Denoël/Gonthier, 1981; first published 1974).
Derrida, Jacques, *De l'esprit: Heidegger et la question* (Paris: Galilée, 1987).
Descombes, Vincent, *Le Même et l'autre: Quarante-cinq ans de philosophie française (1933–1978)* (Paris: Minuit, 1979).
Dobrez, L.A.C., *The Existential and its Exits: Literary and Philosophical Perspectives on the Works of Beckett, Ionesco, Genet and Pinter* (London: The Athlone Press, 1986).
Docherty, Thomas, *Alterities: Criticism, History, Representation* (Oxford: Oxford University Press, 1996).

Dostoyevsky, Fyodor, *The Brothers Karamazov*, translated by David McDuff (Harmondsworth: Penguin, 1993; first published 1880).
Duras, Marguerite, *La Vie tranquille* (Folio; Paris: Gallimard, 1944).
Duras, Marguerite, *Moderato cantabile* (Collection 'double'; Paris: Minuit, 1958).
Duras, Marguerite, *Dix heures et demie du soir en été* (Paris: Gallimard, 1960).
Duras, Marguerite, *L'Amante anglaise* (L'Imaginaire; Paris: Gallimard, 1967).
Duras, Marguerite, *La Douleur* (Paris: P.O.L., 1985).
Duras, Marguerite, *Les Yeux verts* (Paris: Cahiers du cinéma, 1987).
Eaglestone, Robert, *Ethical Criticism: Reading After Levinas* (Edinburgh: Edinburgh University Press, 1997).
Fallaize, Elizabeth, *The Novels of Simone de Beauvoir* (London and New York: Routledge, 1988).
Fell, Joseph P., *Heidegger and Sartre: An Essay on Being and Place* (New York: Columbia University Press, 1979).
Felman, Shoshana, *What Does a Woman Want?: Reading and Sexual Difference* (Baltimore and London: The Johns Hopkins University Press, 1993).
Felman, Shoshana, and Laub, Dori, *Testimony: Crises of Witnessing in Literature, Psychoanalysis, and History* (New York and London: Routledge, 1992).
Finkielkraut, Alain, *La Sagesse de l'amour* (Folio; Paris: Gallimard, 1984).
Finkielkraut, Alain, *La Défaite de la pensée* (Paris: Gallimard, 1987).
Fish, Stanley, *Is There a Text in This Class? The Authority of Interpretive Communities* (Cambridge, Mass: Harvard University Press, 1980).
Fitch, Brian, *'L'Etranger' d'Albert Camus: Un texte, ses lecteurs leurs lectures* (Paris: Larousse, 1972).
Fitch, Brian, *The Narcissistic Text: A Reading of Camus' Fiction* (Toronto: University of Toronto Press, 1982).
Foucault, Michel, *Les Mots et les choses: Une archéologie des sciences humaines* (Paris: Gallimard, 1966).
Freud, Sigmund, *The Interpretation of Dreams*, Pelican Freud Library volume 4 (Harmondsworth: Penguin, 1976; first published 1900).
Freud, Sigmund, *Civilization, Society and Religion*, Pelican Freud Library volume 12 (Harmondsworth: Penguin, 1985).
Freud, Sigmund, *Totem and Taboo* (first published 1913), in *The Origins of Religion*, Pelican Freud Library volume 13 (Harmondsworth: Penguin, 1985).
Fullbrook, Edward, and Fullbrook, Kate, *Simone de Beauvoir and Jean-Paul Sartre: The Remaking of a Twentieth-Century Legend* (London: Harvester-Wheatsheaf, 1993).
Gadamer, Hans-Georg, *Hermeneutik I: Wahrheit und Methode, Grundzüge einer philosophishen Hermeneutik* (Tübingen: J.C.B. Mohr (Paul Siebeck), 1986; first published 1960).
Gadamer, Hans-Georg, *The Relevance of the Beautiful and Other Essays*, edited by Robert Bernasconi, translated by Nicholas Walker (Cambridge: Cambridge University Press, 1986).
Gadamer, Hans-Georg, *Hermeneutik II: Wahrheit und Methode, Ergänzungen, Register* (Tübingen: J.C.B. Mohr (Paul Siebeck), 1993).
Gelley, Alexander (ed.), *Unruly Examples: On the Rhetoric of Exemplarity* (Stanford, Cal: Stanford University Press, 1995).
Genet, Jean, *Miracle de la rose* (Folio; Paris: Marc Barbezat-L'Arbalète, 1946).

Genet, Jean, *Notre-Dame-des-Fleurs* (Folio; Paris: Marc Barbezat-L'Arbalète, 1948).
Genet, Jean, *Journal du voleur* (Folio; Paris: Gallimard, 1949).
Genet, Jean, *Pompes funèbres* and *Querelle de Brest*, in *Oeuvres complètes* volume 3 (Paris: Gallimard, 1953).
Genet, Jean, *Les Négres* (Folio; Paris: Marc Barbezat-L'Arbalète, 1958).
Genet, Jean, *Oeuvres complètes* volume 4 (Paris: Gallimard, 1968).
Genet, Jean, *L'Ennemi déclaré: Textes et entretiens* (Paris: Gallimard, 1991).
Gide, André, *Les Faux-Monnayeurs* (Folio; Paris: Gallimard, 1925).
Girard, René, *La Violence et le sacré* (Paris: Grasset, 1972).
Goldberg, S.L., *Agents and Lives: Moral Thinking in Literature* (Cambridge: Cambridge University Press, 1993).
Goldthorpe, Rhiannon, *Sartre: Literature and Theory* (Cambridge: Cambridge University Press, 1984).
Goodheart, Eugene, *The Reign of Ideology* (New York: Columbia University Press, 1997).
Gorrara, Claire, 'Bearing Witness in Robert Antelme's *L'Espèce humaine* and Marguerite Duras's *La Douleur*', *Women in French Studies* (Winter 1997), 243–51.
Green, Mary Jean, 'Writing War in the Feminine: de Beauvoir and Duras', *Journal of European Studies* 23 (1993), 223–37.
Greene, Robert, *Just Words: Moralism and Meta-Language in Twentieth-Century French Fiction* (University Park: The Pennyslvania State University Press, 1993).
Guérin, Jeanyves, *Albert Camus: Portrait de l'artiste en citoyen* (Paris: F. Bourin, 1993).
Haidu, Peter, 'The Semiotics of Alterity: A Comparison with Hermeneutics', *New Literary History* 21 (1990), 671–91.
Hand, Seán (ed.), *Facing the Other: The Ethics of Emmanuel Levinas* (Richmond: Curzon Press, 1996).
Harold Bloom (ed.), *Modern Critical Views: Albert Camus* (New York and Philadelphia: Chelsea House, 1988).
Harris, Nadia, *Marguerite Yourcenar: Vers la rive d'une Ithaque intérieure* (Saratoga: Anma Libri, 1994).
Hartman, Geoffrey, *The Fate of Reading and Other Essays* (Chicago: University of Chicago Press, 1975).
Hayat, Pierre, 'Epreuves de l'histoire, exigence d'une pensée', in Levinas, Emmanuel, *Les Imprévus de l'histoire* (Montpellier: Fata Morgana, 1994), 7–23.
Hegel, G.W.F., *Phenomenology of Spirit*, translated by A.V. Miller (Oxford: Oxford University Press, 1977; first published 1807).
Heidegger, Martin, *Sein und Zeit* (fifth edition; Tübingen: Max Niemeyer Verlag, 1979; first published 1927).
Heidegger, Martin, *Lettre sur l'humanisme*, translated by Roger Munier (Paris: Aubier, 1964; first published 1946).
Heidegger, Martin, *Holzwege* (Frankfurt am Main: Klostermann, 1950).
Heidegger, Martin, *Poetry, Language, Thought*, translated by Albert Hofstadter (New York: Harper Colophon, 1975).
Hill, Leslie, *Marguerite Duras: Apocalyptic Desires* (London and New York: Routledge, 1993).

Hillis Miller, J., *The Ethics of Reading: Kant, de Man, Eliot, Trollope, James, and Benjamin* (New York: Columbia University Press, 1987).
Hirsch, David, *The Deconstruction of Literature: Criticism after Auschwitz* (Hanover and London: Brown University Press, 1991).
Hirsch, Jr, E.D., *Validity in Interpretation* (New Haven and London: Yale University Press, 1967).
Howells, Christina, *Sartre's Theory of Literature* (London: MHRA, 1979).
Howells, Christina, *Sartre: The Necessity of Freedom* (Cambridge: Cambridge University Press, 1988).
Howells, Christina. 'Derrida and Sartre: Hegel's Death Knell', in Silverman, Hugh (ed.), *Derrida and Deconstruction* (New York and London: Routledge, 1989), 169–81.
Hughes, Alex, 'Murdering the Mother: Simone de Beauvoir's *Mémoires d'une jeune fille rangée*', French Studies 48 (1994), 174–83.
Hughes, Alex, *Simone de Beauvoir: 'Le Sang des autres'* (Glasgow: University of Glasgow French and German Publications, 1995).
Iser, Wolfgang, 'The Reading Process: A Phenomenological Approach' in Tompkins, Jane (ed.), *Reader-Response Criticism: From Formalism to Post-Structuralism* (Baltimore: Johns Hopkins University Press, 1980), 50–69.
Jardine, Alice, 'Death Sentences: Writing Couples and Ideology', Poetics Today 6 (1985), 119–31.
Johnson, Barbara, *The Critical Difference: Essays in the Contemporary Rhetoric of Reading* (Baltimore: Johns Hopkins University Press, 1980).
Johnson, Barbara, *A World of Difference* (Baltimore: Johns Hopkins University Press, 1987).
Johnson, Paul, *A History of the Jews* (London: Weidenfeld and Nicolson, 1987).
Johnstone, Monica, 'Wayne Booth and the Ethics of Fiction', in Antczak, Frederick (ed.), *Rhetoric and Pluralism: Legacies of Wayne Booth* (Columbus: Ohio State University Press, 1995), 59–70.
Judt, Tony, *The Burden of Responsibility: Blum, Camus, Aron and the French Twentieth Century* (Chicago and London: The University of Chicago Press, 1998).
Kant, Immanuel, *Grundlegung zur Metaphysik der Sitten* (Hamburg: Felix Meiner Verlag, 1965; first published 1785).
Kant, Immanuel, *Critique of Practical Reason*, translated by Lewis White Beck (New York and London: Macmillan, 1956; first published 1788).
Kant Immanuel, *Kritik der Urteilskraft* (Hamburg: Felix Meiner, 1974; first published 1790).
Kant, Immanuel, 'On a Supposed Right to Tell Lies from Benevolent Motives', in *Kant's Critique of Practical Reason and Other Works on the Theory of Ethics*, translated by Thomas Kingsmill Abbott (London, New York and Bombay: Longmans, Green and Co, 1898), 361–5.
Keefe, Terry, *Simone de Beauvoir: A Study of her Writings* (London: Harrap, 1983).
Keenan, Thomas, *Fables of Responsibility: Aberrations and Predicaments in Ethics and Politics* (Stanford, Cal: Stanford University Press, 1997).
Kermode, Frank, *The Genesis of Secrecy: On the Interpretation of Narrative* (Cambridge, Mass: Harvard University Press, 1979).

King, Adele (editor), *Camus's 'L'Étranger': Fifty Years On* (Basingstoke and London: Macmillan, 1992).
Kofman, Sarah, *Paroles suffoquées* (Paris: Galilée, 1987).
Kojève, Alexandre, *Introduction à la lecture de Hegel* (Paris: Gallimard, 1947).
Kristeva, Julia, *Soleil noir: Dépression et mélancolie* (Paris: Gallimard, 1987).
Kristeva, Julia, *Etrangers à nous-mêmes* (Folio; Paris: Fayard, 1988).
Kritzman, Lawrence, 'Duras' War', *L'Esprit créateur* 33:1 (1993), 63–73.
Kruks, Sonia, *Situation and Human Existence: Freedom, Subjectivity and Society* (London: Unwin, 1990).
Kruks, Sonia, 'Gender and Subjectivity: Simone de Beauvoir and Contemporary Feminism', *Signs* 18:1 (1992), 89–110.
Lacan, Jacques, *Ecrits*, 2 volumes (Points; Paris: Seuil, 1966).
Lacan, Jacques, *Le Séminaire Livre XI: Les Quatre Concepts fondamentaux de la psychanalyse* (Points; Paris: Seuil, 1973).
Lacan, Jacques, *Le Séminaire Livre II: Le Moi dans la théorie de Freud et dans la technique de la psychanalyse* (Paris: Seuil, 1978).
Lacan, Jacques, *Le Séminaire Livre VII: L'Ethique de la psychanalyse* (Paris: Seuil, 1986); translated by Denis Porter as *The Ethics of Psychoanalysis, 1959–1960: The Seminar of Jacques Lacan* (London and New York: Routledge, 1992).
Langer, Lawrence, *Admitting the Holocaust: Collected Essays* (New York: Oxford University Press, 1995).
Levinas, Emmanuel, *Le Temps et l'autre* (Paris: PUF, 1979; first published 1947).
Levinas, Emmanuel, *Totalité et infini: Essai sur l'extériorité* (Livre de Poche; The Hague: Martinus Nijhoff, 1971; first edition 1961).
Levinas, Emmanuel, *Quatre lectures talmudiques* (Paris: Minuit, 1968).
Levinas, Emmanuel, *L'Humanisme de l'autre homme* (Montpellier: Fata Morgana, 1972).
Levinas, Emmanuel, *Autrement qu'être ou au-delà de l'essence* (Livre de Poche; The Hague: Martinus Nijhoff, 1974).
Levinas, Emmanuel, *En découvrant l'existence avec Husserl et Heidegger* (Paris: Vrin, 1974; third edition).
Levinas, Emmanuel, *Difficile liberté: Essais sur le judaïsme* (Livre de Poche; Paris: Albin Michel, 1976; third edition).
Levinas, Emmanuel, *Noms propres* (Livre de Poche; Montpellier: Fata Morgana, 1976).
Levinas, Emmanuel, *Du sacré au saint: Cinq nouvelles lectures talmudiques* (Paris: Minuit, 1977).
Levinas, Emmanuel, *L'Au-delà du verset: Lectures et discours talmudiques* (Paris: Minuit, 1982); translated by Gary Mole as *Beyond the Verse: Talmudic Readings and Lectures* (London: The Athlone Press, 1994).
Levinas, Emmanuel, *Ethique et infini*, with Philippe Nemo (Livre de Poche; Paris: Arthème Fayard and Radio-France, 1982).
Levinas, Emmanuel, *A l'heure des nations* (Paris: Minuit, 1988).
Levinas, Emmanuel, *Entre nous: Essais sur le penser-à-l'autre* (Paris: Grasset et Fasquelle, 1991).
Levinas, Emmanuel, *Les Imprévus de l'histoire* (Montpellier: Fata Morgana, 1994).

Llewelyn, John, *The Middle Voice of Ecological Conscience: A Chiasmic Reading of Responsibility in the Neighbourhood of Levinas, Heidegger and Others* (London: Macmillan, 1991).
Low, Peter, 'Simone de Beauvoir's Wartime Novel *Le Sang des autres* et les yeux de l'auteur', *New Zealand Journal of French Studies* 13:1 (1992), 25-36.
Lyotard, Jean-François, *Le Différend* (Paris: Minuit, 1983).
Malraux, André, *Les Conquérants* (Livre de Poche; Paris: Grasset, 1928).
Malraux, André, *La Condition humaine* (Folio; Paris: Gallimard, 1946; first published 1933).
Marks, Elaine, *Simone de Beauvoir: Encounters with Death* (New Brunswick: Rutgers University Press, 1973).
Marks, Elaine, *Marrano as Metaphor: The Jewish Presence in French Writing* (New York: Columbia University Press, 1996).
Mauriac, François, *Thérèse Desqueyroux* (Livre de Poche; Paris: Grasset, 1927).
McGinn, Colin, *Ethics, Evil, and Fiction* (Oxford: Oxford University Press, 1997).
Meitinger, Serge, 'L'Irréel de jouissance dans le *Journal du voleur* de Genet', *Littérature*, 62 (1986), 65-74.
Millett, Kate, *Sexual Politics* (London: Virago, 1977; first published 1969).
Moi, Toril, *Simone de Beauvoir: The Making of an Intellectual Woman* (Oxford: Blackwell, 1994).
Newton, Adam Zachary, *Narrative Ethics* (Cambridge, Mass, and London: Harvard University Press, 1995).
Norris, Christopher, *Truth and the Ethics of Criticism* (Manchester and New York: Manchester University Press, 1994).
Nouvet, Claire (ed.), *Literature and the Ethical Question* (New Haven: Yale University Press, 1991).
Nussbaum, Martha, *Love's Knowledge: Essays on Philosophy and Literature* (New York and Oxford: Oxford University Press, 1990).
Parker, David, *Ethics, Theory and the Novel* (Cambridge: Cambridge University Press, 1994).
Plato, *The Collected Dialogues*, edited by Hamilton, Edith, and Cairns, Huntingdon (Princeton, NJ: Princeton University Press, 1961).
Plottel, Jeanine Parisier, 'Memory, Fiction and History', *L'Esprit créateur* 30:1 (1990), 47-55.
Radiguet, Raymond, *Le Diable au corps* (Folio; Paris: Gallimard, 1982; first published 1923).
Reader, Keith, 'The Self and Others', in Forbes, Jill, and Kelly, Michael, (eds), *French Cultural Studies: An Introduction* (Oxford: Oxford University Press, 1995), 213-31.
Renaut, Alain, *Sartre, le dernier philosophe* (Paris: Grasset and Fasquelle, 1993).
Richards, I.A., *Science and Poetry* (London: Kegan Paul, Trench, Trubner and Co., 1935).
Ricoeur, Paul, *De l'interprétation: Essai sur Freud* (Paris: Seuil, 1965).
Robbe-Grillet, Alain, *Un régicide* (Paris: Minuit, 1978).
Robbins, Jill, 'Aesthetic Totality and Ethical Infinity: Levinas on Art', *L'Esprit créateur* 35:3 (1995), 66-79.
Robinson, Christopher, *Scandal in the Ink: Male and Female Homosexuality in Twentieth-Century French Literature* (London: Cassell, 1995).

Rockmore, Tom, *Heidegger and French Philosophy: Humanism, Antihumanism and Being* (London and New York: Routledge, 1995).
Rorty, Richard, *Contingency, Irony, and Solidarity* (Cambridge: Cambridge University Press, 1989).
Rousset, David, *L'Univers concentrationnaire* (Paris: Minuit, 1965; first published 1946).
Sartre, Jean-Paul, *La Nausée*, (Folio; Paris, Gallimard, 1938).
Sartre, Jean-Paul, *Le Mur* (Folio; Paris: Gallimard, 1939).
Sartre, Jean-Paul, *L'Etre et le néant: Essai d'ontologie phénoménologique* (Tel; Paris: Gallimard, 1943).
Sartre, Jean-Paul, *L'Existentialisme est un humanisme* (Paris: Nagel, 1970; first published 1946).
Sartre, Jean-Paul, *Situations II* (Paris: Gallimard, 1948).
Sartre, Jean-Paul, *La Mort dans l'âme* (Folio; Paris: Gallimard, 1949).
Sartre, Jean-Paul, *Saint Genet, comédien et martyr* (Paris: Gallimard, 1952).
Sartre, Jean-Paul, *Situations IV* (Paris: Gallimard, 1964).
Sartre, Jean-Paul, *Oeuvres romanesques*, edited by Michel Contat and Michel Rybalka (Paris: Gallimard, 1981).
Sartre, Jean-Paul, *Cahiers pour une morale* (Paris: Gallimard, 1983).
Sellers, Susan, *Language and Sexual Difference: Feminist Writing in France* (London: Macmillan, 1991).
Sheringham, Michael, 'Narration and Experience in Genet's *Journal du voleur'*, in Gibson, Robert (ed.), *Studies in French Fiction in Honour of Vivienne Mylne* (London: Grant and Cutler, 1988), 289–306.
Showalter, Jr., English, *'The Stranger': Humanity and the Absurd* (Boston: Twayne, 1989).
Siebers, Tobin, *The Ethics of Criticism* (Ithaca, NY: Cornell University Press, 1988).
Siebers, Tobin, *Morals and Stories* (1992).
Silverman, Hugh (ed.), *Gadamer and Hermeneutics* (New York and London: Routledge, 1991).
Simons, Margaret, 'Beauvoir and Sartre: The Philosophical Relationship', *Yale French Studies* 72 (1986), 165–79.
Soper, Kate, *Humanism and Anti-Humanism* (London: Hutchinson, 1986).
Suleiman, Susan Rubin, *Authoritarian Fictions: The Ideological Novel as a Literary Genre* (New York: Columbia University Press, 1983).
Suleiman, Susan Rubin, *Risking Who One Is: Encounters with Contemporary Art and Literature* (Cambridge, Mass: Harvard University Press, 1994).
Sweeney, Kevin, 'Lying to the Murderer: Sartre's Use of Kant in "The Wall"', *Mosaic* 18:2 (1985), 1–16.
Szondi, Peter, *Introduction to Literary Hermeneutics*, translated by Martha Woodmansee (Cambridge: Cambridge University Press, 1995).
Thody, Philip, *Jean Genet: A Study of his Novels and Plays* (New York: Stein and Day, 1968).
Todorov, Tzvetan, *Nous et les autres: La Réflexion française sur la diversité humaine* (Points; Paris: Seuil, 1989).
Tournier, Michel, *Le Vent Paraclet* (Paris: Gallimard, 1977).
Wiesel, Elie, *Célébration biblique: Portraits et légendes* (Paris: Seuil, 1975).
Wilson, Emma, *Sexuality and the Reading Encounter: Identity and Desire in*

Proust, Duras, Tournier and Cixous (Oxford: Oxford University Press, 1996).

Wilson, Emma, '*La Douleur*: Duras, Amnesia and Desire' un Peitsch, Helmut, Burdett, Charles and Gorrara, Claire (eds), *European Memories of the Second World War* (New York and Oxford: Berghahn Books, 1999), 141–8.

Yourcenar, Marguerite, *Alexis ou le traité du vain combat suivi de Le Coup de grâce* (Folio; Paris: Gallimard, 1971; first published 1929 and 1939).

Yourcenar, Marguerite, *Mémoires d'Hadrien* (Folio; Paris: Gallimard, 1974; first published 1951).

Yourcenar, Marguerite, *L'Oeuvre au noir* (Folio; Paris: Gallimard, 1968).

Žižek, Slavoj, *For they know not what they do: Enjoyment as a Political Factor* (London and New York: Verso, 1991).

Žižek, Slavoj, *Looking Awry: An Introduction to Jacques Lacan through Popular Culture* (Cambridge (Mass.) and London: The MIT Press, 1991).

Žižek, Slavoj, *Enjoy your Symptom! Jacques Lacan in Hollywood and out* (New York and London: Routledge, 1992).

Žižek, Slavoj, *Tarrying with the Negative: Kant, Hegel, and the Critique of Ideology* (Durham, NC: Duke University Press, 1993).

Žižek, Slavoj, *The Metastases of Enjoyment Six Essays on Woman and Causality* (London and New York: Verso, 1994).

Žižek, Slavoj, *The Plague of the Fantasies* (London and New York: Verso, 1997).

Index

Abrams, Marsha, 199
Agacinski, Sylviane, 207, 209–10
altericide, 1–2, 14–15, 25, 26–9, 46, 57–8, 61, 63, 64, 65, 66, 70, 71, 72–3, 75, 78, 84–5, 86, 98, 102, 135, 176, 188, 192, 194–5
Anderson, Thomas, 197
Antelme, Robert, 135–42, 143, 144, 145, 146, 147, 148, 149–50, 210, 211, 212
Aristotle, 5, 6, 7, 47
Ast, Friedrich, 33–4, 199
Atack, Margaret, 87, 104, 205, 206
Austen, Jane, 9
Aylesworth, Gary, 33, 199

Balzac, Honoré de, 59
Banon, David, 214
Barbedette, Gilles, 202
Barthes, Roland, 60–1, 202
Bataille, Georges, 9, 13, 159, 212, 214
Baudelaire, Charles, 13
Bauman, Zygmunt, 206
Beaufret, Jean, 108, 113
Beauvoir, Simone de, 86–107, 130, 207
 La Cérémonie des adieux, 86
 Le Deuxième Sexe, 28
 La Force de l'âge, 204, 205, 207
 L'Invitée, 14, 26, 86, 87, 90, 91–2, 98, 102, 206
 Pour une morale de l'ambiguïté, 92–6
 Pyrrhus et Cinéas, 92–6
 Le Sang des autres, 86–90, 96–107
 Tous les hommes sont mortels, 86
 Une mort très douce, 86
Beckett, Samuel, 6, 190
Bell, Linda, 197
Benda, Julien, 13, 108–9, 197, 207

Bersani, Leo, 157, 191, 212, 213, 215
Blake, William, 13
Blanchot, Maurice, 13, 87, 138–41, 187, 197, 205, 211, 214
Bloom, Harold, 202
Booth, Wayne, 2, 3–4, 5, 8, 56, 155, 196, 202, 212
Bougon, Patrice, 213
Bowie, Malcolm, 15, 197
Breton, André, 201
Brontë, Emily, 13
Brooks, Peter, 22, 198
Brosman, Catherine Savage, 203
Burrell, Margaret, 89, 205

Camus, Albert, 64–85, 130, 173
 La Chute, 64–5, 66, 74–82, 84, 85
 L'Etranger, 26, 61, 64, 65–72, 74, 77, 78, 79–80, 82–5, 194
 L'Homme révolté, 65, 72–4, 75, 78, 203
 Les Justes, 132
 Le Mythe de Sisyphe, 72, 203
 La Peste, 74, 75, 79, 204
Caputo, John, 42, 200
Caruth, Cynthia, 10, 196
categorical imperative, 51–2, 53, 54, 58, 59, 111–12
Child Bickel, Gisèle, 158, 212, 213
Cixous, Hélène, 157, 213
Clément, Catherine, 213
Cloonan, William, 203
Cocteau, Jean, 60
Constant, Benjamin, 52
Corbin, Henri, 110
Costes, Alain, 203
Critchley, Simon, 198
Crowley, Martin, 143, 210, 211, 212

Derrida, Jacques, 110, 158–60, 162–3, 196, 200, 208, 213

226 Index

Descombes, Vincent, 196, 197, 208
Dobrez, L.A.C., 170, 213
Docherty, Thomas, 12, 13, 196
Dostoyevsky, Fyodor, 87, 90, 92, 165, 205, 206
Duras, Marguerite, 130, 131–8, 142–51
   L'Amante anglaise, 61, 131, 133, 134–5, 210, 215
   Dix heures et demie du soir en été, 132, 134, 210
   La Douleur, 135–8, 140, 142–50, 210, 211, 212
   Moderato cantabile, 26, 61, 131–2, 133
   La Vie tranquille, 131
   Les Yeux verts, 212

Eaglestone, Robert, 196
ethical criticism, 1–11, 12–14, 56, 155–9, 190–2, 196
existentialism, existentialist ethics, 90, 91–5, 110–13, 116, 117, 173

Fallaize, Elizabeth, 89, 98, 205, 206, 207
Fell, Joseph, 207
Felman, Shoshana, 10, 64–5, 78–81, 82, 196, 203, 204
Finkielkraut, Alain, 200, 208
Fish, Stanley, 43, 200
Fitch, Brian, 84, 203, 204
Foucault, Michel, 109, 207
Freud, Sigmund, 20–5, 57, 171, 194, 198, 201, 206, 214
Fullbrook, Edward, *and* Fullbrook, Kate, 206

Gadamer, Hans-Georg, 30, 31, 32–8, 43, 46, 199
Gay-Crosier, Raymond, 72, 203
Gelley, Alexander, 200
Genet, Jean, 13, 130, 151, 152–88, 190, 213
   Journal du voleur, 160–8, 177–8, 179, 187, 212
   Miracle de la rose, 152–3, 154, 169, 179, 180, 214

   Notre-Dame-des-Fleurs, 152, 159, 180, 212
   Les Nègres, 214
   Pompes funèbres, 153–4, 155, 159, 167, 169, 178, 179, 214
   Querelle de Brest, 26, 154, 170–6, 179, 183, 185–6, 190, 214
   'Le Rouge et le noir', 176–7, 214
   Un captif amoureux, 212
Gide, André, 32, 43–6, 54, 200
Girard, René, 23–5, 198
Goldberg, S.L., 7, 196
Goldthorpe, Rhiannon, 197
Goodheart, Eugene, 9, 196
Gorrara, Claire, 210
Green, Mary Jean, 206, 207
Greene, Robert, 196, 198
Grimaud, Michel, 203
Guérin, Jeanyves, 202

Habermas, Jürgen, 37
Haidu, Peter, 37, 199
Hand, Seán, 41, 200
Hargreaves, Alec, 202, 203
Harris, Nadia, 208
Hartman, Geoffrey, 44, 61, 200, 202
Hayat, Pierre, 200
Hegel, Georg Wilhelm Friedrich, 14, 86, 87, 94, 95, 109–10, 158, 189, 192, 193, 197, 213, 214
Heidegger, Martin, 15, 31–2, 37, 40, 43, 108, 109–10, 111, 113–17, 119, 123, 198, 199, 200, 208
Hill, Leslie, 142–3, 145–7, 149, 210, 211
Hillis Miller, J., 51, 61, 196, 201, 202
Hirsch, David, 3, 196
Hirsch, Jr, E.D., 34, 37, 38, 199
Howells, Christina, 197, 201, 213
Hughes, Alex, 86, 88–9, 205, 207
humanism, 9, 64, 108–17, 119, 123, 128–30, 135, 140, 141, 147, 155, 173, 208, 211
Husserl, Edmund, 109–10

Iser, Wolfgang, 191, 215

Jackson, George, 176–7
James, Henry, 6, 9, 190
Jardine, Alice, 86, 204
Johnson, Barbara, 10, 56, 196, 201, 202, 213
Johnson, Paul, 209
Johnstone, Monica, 190, 212, 215
Judt, Tony, 202

Kafka, Franz, 13
Kant, Immanuel, 5–6, 46, 48–52, 53, 54, 55, 56, 57, 58, 59, 93, 94, 95, 111–12, 200, 206, 208
Keefe, Terry, 88, 205, 206
Keenan, Thomas, 10, 196
Kermode, Frank, 51, 201
King, Adele, 84, 204
Kofman, Sarah, 211
Kojève, Alexandre, 14, 109, 197
Kréa, Henri, 202
Kristeva, Julia, 150, 208, 209, 212
Kritzman, Lawrence, 210
Kruks, Sonia, 206

Lacan, Jacques, 14, 15–17, 20, 26, 49–50, 134, 192, 193, 197, 198, 200–1
Lang, Fritz, 26
Langer, Lawrence, 191, 215
Laub, Dori, 10, 196, 204
Lawrence, D.H., 5
Levinas, Emmanuel, 1, 9, 10–11, 14, 17–20, 26, 28, 30, 31, 32, 38–43, 46, 73, 122–3, 134, 138, 140, 160, 171–2, 181–8, 190, 196, 197, 198–9, 200, 203, 205, 208, 211, 214
Llewelyn, John, 41, 200
Lloyd, David, 200
Low, Peter 207
Lyons, John, 200
Lyotard, Jean-François, 209

Malraux, André, 22, 27–9, 98, 198
Marks, Elaine, 118, 204, 208
Mascolo, Dionys, 210
Mauriac, François, 6, 61, 202

McGinn, Colin, 2, 3, 4, 5, 7, 196
Meitinger, Serge, 213
Michelet, Jules, 13
Millett, Kate, 157–8, 212, 213
Misgeld, Dieter, 199
Moi, Toril, 86, 91, 204, 206
Montaigne, Michel de, 200
Mörike, Eduard, 37
murder, 18–19, 20–1, 23–4, 27, 61, 62, 65–6, 84, 86, 131–4, 152–5, 160, 170–2, 176, 180, 181, 185–7, 194, 195

Nabokov, Vladimir, 2, 5
Newton, Adam Zachary, 10, 196
Nicholson, Graeme, 199
Norris, Christopher, 196
Nouvet, Claire, 196
Nussbaum, Martha, 2, 4, 5–7, 8, 56, 155, 190, 196, 212, 215

Orwell, George, 5, 193

Parker, David, 3, 7, 196
Plato, 32, 47, 113, 174, 198, 214
Plottel, Jeanine Parisier, 210
poststructuralism, 3, 8, 9, 10, 11, 115, 117, 146, 197
Proust, Marcel, 6, 13

Radiguet, Raymond, 206
Reader, Keith, 196–7
readers, reading, 12, 13, 39, 56–63, 64, 65, 78–85, 104–7, 150–1, 155, 160, 164–5, 176–80, 181, 189–90, 191–2
Renaut, Alain, 197
Resistance, Resistants, 87, 89, 96, 100, 101, 102, 104, 107, 136, 138, 145, 146, 147, 148, 149, 150
revolt, 65, 72, 73
Richards, I.A., 1, 196
Ricoeur, Paul, 200
Rigaud, Jan, 203
Robbe-Grillet, Alain, 26, 61, 62, 202, 215
Robbins, Jill, 41, 199, 200
Robinson, Christopher, 157, 213

Rochmore, Tom, 207, 208
Rorty, Richard, 2, 5, 196
Rousset, David, 141, 211

Sade, Marquis de, 5, 9, 13
Sartre, Jean-Paul, 14–15, 18, 20, 40, 52, 64, 86, 94, 95, 110, 119, 130, 170, 173
  Cahiers pour une morale, 17, 197
  'Erostrate', 58, 201
  L'Etre et le néant, 15, 16, 29, 59, 92, 197, 206
  L'Existentialisme est un humanisme, 108, 111–13, 116, 118, 121, 201
  Huis clos, 58
  L'Idiot de la famille, 13
  Les Mains sales, 58
  La Mort dans l'âme, 58, 202
  Les Mouches, 26, 58, 132
  'Le Mur', 46, 48, 51, 53–8, 59–60, 62, 63, 201
  La Nausée, 109, 111, 208
  Qu'est-ce que la littérature?, 13, 60, 202
  Saint Genet, comédien et martyr, 13, 155–6, 158, 159, 160, 162, 163–4, 182–3, 213, 214
Schofer, Peter, 203
Sellers, Susan, 213
Sheringham, Michael, 213

Showalter, Jr., English, 84, 202, 204
Siebers, Tobin, 7–8, 196
Simons, Margaret, 206
solidarity, 65, 73, 74, 75
Soper, Kate, 208
Staiger, Emil, 37
Suleiman, Susan Rubin, 47–8, 87–8, 104, 105, 106, 107, 191–2, 200, 205, 206, 207, 215
Sweeney, Kevin, 54, 201
Szondi, Peter, 199, 209

Thody, Philip, 157, 212, 213
Todorov, Tzvetan, 208
Tournier, Michel, 202, 207

Weinsheimer, Joel, 199
Wiesel, Elie, 202, 214
Wilde, Oscar, 5, 202
Wilson, Emma, 191–2, 211, 215
Woolf, Virginia, 190

Yourcenar, Marguerite, 117–30
  Le Coup de grâce, 118, 119, 208–9
  Mémoires d'Hadrien, 110, 117–30, 209
  L'Oeuvre au noir, 117, 118, 208

Žižek, Slavoj, 16, 25–6, 62, 129–30, 189, 192–3, 194, 197, 198, 200–1, 202, 210, 214, 215